Campaign Finance and Political Polarization

Campaign Finance and Political Polarization

When Purists Prevail

Raymond J. La Raja and Brian F. Schaffner

University of Michigan Press
Ann Arbor

Published in the United States of America by the
University of Michigan Press
Manufactured in the United States of America
⊚ Printed on acid-free paper

2018   2017   2016   2015   4   3   2   1

A CIP catalog record for this book is available from the British Library.

Library of Congress Cataloging-in-Publication Data
Library of Congress Cataloging-in-Publication data has been applied for.

ISBN 978-0-472-07299-6 (hardcover : alk. paper)
ISBN 978-0-472-05299-8 (paper : alk. paper)
ISBN 978-0-472-12160-1 (e-book)

Support provided by The William and Flora Hewlett Foundation.
The opinions expressed in this report are those of the authors and do not
necessarily reflect the views of The William and Flora Hewlett Foundation.

To my children, Alex, Luca, and Téa, whose zest for life, hopefulness, and humor brighten my days

Raymond La Raja

To my parents, who instilled in me a thirst for knowledge and a love of politics

Brian Schaffner

Contents

List of Figures and Tables

Figures

Tables

Preface

The public intensely dislikes how campaigns are financed in the United States. We can understand why. The system of private financing seems rigged to favor special interests and wealthy donors. Much of the reform community has responded by calling for tighter restrictions on private financing of elections to push the system toward "small donor democracy" and various forms of public financing. These strategies seem to make sense and, in principle, we are not opposed to them.

But our research and professional experience as political scientists have led us to speculate that these populist approaches to curtailing money in politics might not be alleviating, but contributing to, contemporary problems in the political system, including the bitter partisan stand-offs and apparent insensitivity of elected officials to the concerns of ordinary Americans that appear to characterize the current state of U.S. politics. Indeed, we began to sense that the populist approach to campaign finance reform may reflect a larger pattern of populist assumptions about how democracy works that have in fact led to ill-conceived reforms in other areas, as Bruce Cain argues in *Democracy More or Less* (2014). We wondered if anticorruption rules, which purportedly make the wealthy less influential, were in fact doing the opposite: making the system even less responsive to broad constituencies and rendering political discourse even more acerbic than it would otherwise be.

Our hunch was that prevailing approaches to reform may reinforce the influence of a small fraction of citizens and groups that already dominate the financing of politics. How could this be? One plausible reason is that such donors already have the means and motive to contrive ways to get around the most stringent elements of campaign finance laws. But there may be more to the story. We have observed that there is an essential element missing from most campaign finance reform strategies: the realization that restrictions on money in politics actually enfeeble political parties.

Our growing conviction that most contemporary campaign reform initiatives have undervalued the roles that political parties play in U.S. politics led us to undertake the research project that culminated in this book. In fact, a vast body of research on democratic politics indicates that parties play several vital roles, including aggregating interests, guiding voter choices, and holding politicians accountable with meaningful partisan labels. Yet this research seems to have been ignored in the design of post-Watergate reforms.

The consequence, as we show in this book, is the continuation of a shift begun in the early 20th century from party-centered politics to candidate-centered politics. The counterintuitive result has been a system in which interest groups and intensely ideological—and wealthy—citizens play a disproportionately large role in financing candidates for public office. This dynamic has direct implications for many of the problems facing American government today, including ideological polarization and political gridlock. The campaign finance system is certainly not the only source of polarization and gridlock, but we think it is an important part of the story. In this book, we tell this story by considering the rich variation in campaign finance laws in the 50 American states and comparing their effects on political discourse and elections.

Our motivation to write this book reflects both our scholarly interests and our concerns as citizens. We take seriously the urging of the leadership in our profession, particularly reflected in the American Political Science Association (APSA), to make political science relevant for broader societal concerns. In the past decade APSA presidential addresses have called for greater attention to problems associated with inequality, partisan polarization, and the dysfunction of the American political system. This book addresses some of these issues. We embarked on the project not simply to solve a "puzzle" in the scholarship about financing in the party system, but to understand how campaign finance laws affect elections and governance, with an eye toward making useful policy recommendations.

Our work developed from emergent research about the dynamics of partisan polarization and new conceptions of American political parties, particularly those formulated by a group we call the UCLA school. The ideas for this book advanced from ongoing conversations and blog exchanges (via the Monkey Cage and Election Law Blog) with our colleagues who study and/or practice election law, including Steve Ansolabehere, Bob Bauer, Bob Biersack, Rob Boatright, Adam Bonica, Bruce Cain, Guy-Uriel Charles, Tony Corrado, Diana Dwyre, John Fortier, Michael Franz, Erika Fowler,

Ben Ginsberg, Keith Hamm, Rick Hasen, Paul Herrnson, Eitan Hersh, Ruth Jones, Dave Karpf, Robin Kolodny, Michael Malbin, Tom Mann, Seth Masket, Ken Mayer, Eric McGhee, Sid Milkis, Jeff Milyo, Nate Persily, Rick Pildes, Trevor Potter, Lynda Powell, John Samples, and John Sides.

We also benefited significantly from the leadership of forward-thinking foundations and policy centers that have been trying to address emergent problems of governance in the United States. Together the leaders in these organizations created a forum for robust dialogue on political reform. This group includes Joe Goldman of the Democracy Fund, who initiated a round of discussions that convened academics, practitioners, and reformers. These excellent forums were led by John Fortier of the Bipartisan Policy Center and Nate Persily of Stanford University Law School. Above all, we would like to thank Daniel Stid and Larry Kramer of the Hewlett Foundation for providing the support that made this project feasible, as well as program officers Jean Parvin Bordewich and Kelly Born.

The timing for conducting this research was fortunate. We benefited from an extraordinary amount of new data recently made available at the state level. We greatly appreciate the dedication of the people who gathered these data and their generosity in sharing them with us. The National Institute on Money in State Politics, through Ed Bender and Denise Roth Barber, provided abundant campaign finance data; Keith Hamm and Jeff Milyo both shared their data on campaign finance laws, as did Jennie Drage Bowser at the National Conference of State Legislatures; Boris Shor and Nolan McCarty provided an immensely useful dataset on the ideological scores of state legislators. Carl Klarner offers an invaluable resource to scholars by posting his historical data on election outcomes in state legislatures. We thank Neil Reiff for arranging interviews with leaders of state party committees.

We appreciate the enthusiasm for this project from our editor Melody Herr at the University of Michigan Press. She has built up an impressive library of books on campaign finance and elections, and we are honored to have our work included among this select group of publications. We would also like to thank our colleagues at the University of Massachusetts–Amherst who are part of the American Politics Research Group and who read significant portions of this work, including Maryann Barakso, Bruce Desmarais, Seth Goldman, Rahsaan Maxwell, Tatishe Nteta, Jesse Rhodes, and Libby Sharrow. Bruce Cain at Stanford also read the entire manuscript, provided valuable comments, and gave us a chance to present our work to a wide-ranging group of scholars and practitioners at Stanford's Program on American Democracy in Comparative Perspective. Finally, we thank our graduate student Wouter Van Erve for keeping up with our unending requests for data, Ed Murphy for his wise copyediting, production editors Kevin Rennells and Nicholle Lutz, and political science department staff Trish Bachand and Michelle Gonçalves for their support in helping to bring this book to fruition.

All of the data and program files necessary to replicate the results from this book are available at https://dataverse.harvard.edu/dataverse/laraja_schaffner.

Raymond J. La Raja
Brian F. Schaffner
Amherst, Massachusetts, October 2015

CHAPTER 1

Campaign Finance Laws, Purists, and Pragmatists: Who Benefits?

Politics in Washington appears hopelessly polarized. The widening ideological gap in the U.S. Congress has received most of the attention (McCarty, Poole, and Rosenthal 2006; Rohde 1991), but similar dynamics have been playing out in many state legislatures (Shor and McCarty 2011). While the consequences of such polarization are not always clear, there seems little doubt of one effect: partisan rancor in legislatures has increased dramatically. In recent decades we have observed an unusual degree of policy gridlock and the deterioration of Congress as a deliberative body (Mann and Ornstein 2012). A complete lack of compromise appears to block government from acting on pressing issues such as immigration or tax reform, which are widely acknowledged in both parties as ripe for policy transformation.

The problems do not stop there. A strong case has been made that policy gridlock exacerbates wealth inequality through a basic failure to adjust policies to new economic and demographic realities (Hacker and Pierson 2010; McCarty, Poole, and Rosenthal 2006). Perhaps most worrisome for the long-term health of American democracy is the possibility that our institutions do not adequately represent citizens, with parties standing for highly ideological policies that are at odds with the preferences of the vast majority of voters (Fiorina, Abrams, and Pope 2005).

Why We Write

As close observers of American politics, we worry about polarization and its potential impact on the democratic process. That is why we are writing this book. We see no magic remedy for this problem, but we can help identify underlying causes, which might lead to fruitful reforms. Our experience in analyzing elections and governing suggests to us that a link might exist between the ideological distancing of the parties and the weakened state of party organizations in the United States. In an era when money is an essential electoral resource, party organizations have often struggled to finance politics because campaign finance laws and court jurisprudence constrain political parties more tightly than they limit interest groups or individual donors.

Party-Centered versus Candidate-Centered Financing

Given our concerns, the question posed in this book is a practical one, although it is informed by theory and research about political parties. Would a party-centered campaign finance system improve our politics? In other words, we ask whether rules giving political parties more freedom to raise and spend money on candidates would attenuate the excesses of ideological polarization between the major political parties.

We present our detailed response to this question in the remaining chapters of this book. Our argument is that financially strong party organizations should reduce party polarization. It may seem odd that making parties stronger organizationally would abate their programmatic intensity, but we will present evidence that this is so. As we explain in the following chapters, party organizations behave somewhat differently from other political actors in the campaign finance system. Specifically, parties are the sole political organizations whose primary goal is to win elections. We will argue that this unique characteristic forces parties to exercise a moderating effect on those who win office. One of the main thrusts of our argument will be that the introduction of party-friendly campaign finance laws would moderate the distancing of the major political parties in Congress and the states.

Aside from seeming paradoxical, our position may not be popular. Political parties are not the most admired institutions in American life. According to a recent poll by Rassmussen, 53 percent of U.S. voters think that neither party in Congress is the party of the American people.[1] The disdain for political parties is an American tradition dating to the Founding and expressed anxiously by George Washington in his Farewell Address; Washington admonished his compatriots to shun the "incongruous projects of faction," which often serve "a small but artful and enterprising minority of the community."[2]

Despite Washington's urgent call to avoid organizing by faction, political parties soon became mainstays of American democracy. However, their place in the political culture took a decidedly negative turn during the Progressive era of the early 20th century when political reformers recast political parties as institutions that damaged democracy and governance (Milkis 2009; Milkis and Mileur 1999; Rosenblum 2008). To this day, the image of the corrupt party machine lives on, even during an era when machines and party bosses are rarities. Many citizens continue to visualize these quasi-public organizations as doing business behind closed doors and interposing themselves between voters and candidates in ways that thwart the will of the people. The idea of empowering these organizations, which have been the object of distrust during the past 100 years or so, may seem uncomfortable to many readers.

Our position may also be unpopular because our findings suggest that increasing or entirely removing limits on how much money party organizations can raise and spend would be a step toward reducing polarization. As we will see in chapter 6, this is quite at odds with the opinion of a significant segment of the public, which supports the imposition of low contribution limits on groups such as political parties—or even the prohibition of contributions by such groups entirely. This opinion reflects the understandable fear that allowing parties to raise a lot of money will increase the potential for corruption, or at least afford moneyed interests an undue influence contrary to the public interest. There is the perception that allowing parties to take large donations increases the risk that wealthy individuals and special interests will have their way in statehouses across the nation. This very concern was at the heart of arguments for Congress to pass the Bipartisan Campaign Reform Act (BCRA) of 2002, better known as the McCain-Feingold Act, which banned so-called party "soft money."[3]

We are sympathetic to such concerns and we acknowledge that our book cannot completely address the problem of corruption and undue influence.[4] However, we will make the argument that the intense focus of campaign finance policy on preventing corruption has blinded policymakers to the broader effects of these policies on the political system. We will argue that a zealous anticorruption approach can lead to unintended negative consequences. We will make the case that this approach reflects an overly romanticized view that democracy is solely about individual citizens having a direct and equal voice in public affairs (Pildes 2015). A less naïve view is that democracy functions primarily through intermediary organizations—like parties, interest groups, and the media—that help inform, mobilize, and channel citizen preferences (Cain 2014). We make the point that the anticorruption strategy, which seeks to "level down" contributions through low limits, has had the ironic effect of pushing political money toward obscurely named groups, sometimes called "super PACs," that now pervade federal and state campaigns. We are concerned because such groups lack transparency and accountability. But we have another major concern.

Campaign Finance Reforms and Polarization

A major hypothesis in this book is that laws that push money away from party organizations to partisan interest groups have accentuated the highly polarized political environment in many American states. We expect too that our findings can legitimately be generalized beyond the states to the U.S. Congress, where many of the same polarizing forces are clearly at work. Through our discussion of the research and observations supporting this hypothesis, we hope to broaden the policy debate beyond a narrow focus on preventing corruption, without repudiating longstanding efforts to maintain integrity and equality in the political system through campaign finance reform.

Our study depends on a system-level approach that is attentive to the broader flows of political money rather than the one-to-one exchanges that occupy most research on the political influence of donors. Instead of studying the dyadic relationship between donors and officeholders (e.g., to see if money buys votes or effort), we propose a holistic framework that applies itself to what is referred to as the "hydraulics" of campaign finance rules. In our view, regulations do not tend to keep money out of politics but mostly redirect its currents through different channels. We have mentioned the super PACs that raise and spend millions of dollars outside the formal structure of campaign finance laws.[5] These groups arose, in part, because the limits on contributions to candidates and parties were tightened with the BCRA of 2002. Money constrained from flowing directly to candidates and parties was squeezed in another direction.

Historical data also suggest that the relationship between campaign finance laws and campaign spending in U.S. elections is surprisingly inelastic. One study shows a roughly linear relationship over time between GDP and election-related spending, suggesting in economic terms that campaign spending is akin to a consumption activity (Ansolabehere, deFigueiredo, and Snyder 2003). In other words, spending is relatively immune to laws that attempt to restrain it. Campaign finance laws may change the paths that money takes, but the total amount in the system appears to depend on other factors, such as the availability of money, the electoral stakes, and political competition (Hogan 2000).

The crux of our argument is that, although laws fail to stop the flow of money into politics, they do affect the channels through which it flows. By constraining one set of players—namely party committees—campaign finance laws force candidates to rely more heavily on other sources of funds. These funds may come from individuals, interest groups, and a variety of "party-like" organizations that emerge to replace the formal parties. These nonparty actors may all be partisans in the broader coalition, but their priorities differ from those of the party organization. And as we will see, by making candidates more reliant on nonparty supporters than on party committees, the rules have broad effects on the electoral system and governing. We will demonstrate that one of these effects is to push candidates away from the center and toward the ideological poles.

In our view, the architecture of campaign finance laws in most American states is not party-friendly. The laws have institutionalized a "candidate-centered" system of financing, which encourages candidates to reach out to nonparty sources for funds. At the same time, the role of party organizations has been circumscribed; they are permitted to give only relatively small amounts of money to candidates precisely because reformers fear that party organizations might be used as conduits to funnel large contributions to them. As we have noted, the unintended consequence of imposing lower limits on parties is that candidates seek a greater share of donations directly from highly ideological individual and group donors.

Perhaps more consequentially, under this system "the center cannot hold": the party coalition unbundles organizationally. That is, partisan factions that compose the party, including party-aligned issue groups (e.g., environmental groups, gun rights advocates, etc.), choose to engage directly and independently in elections rather than work through the umbrella of the formal party organization. In this way, constraints on parties enable partisan interest groups to assume a larger and less constrained role in elections. The dynamic is especially acute in states where control of the legislature hangs in the balance and where partisan organizing is imperative. The outcome is to tilt the playing field toward ideological candidates favored by "policy demanders," and to put pressure on moderate officeholders to defend highly ideological policy positions or risk loss of financial support.

To be clear, we are not arguing that the candidate-centered campaign finance system *caused* partisan polarization. There has been much else going on, and scholars continue to unravel the dynamic that spurred the distancing of the parties. In the category of "causes" one might include changes in demography and technology, or any range of institutional transformations, including how candidates are nominated by an increasingly ideological partisan electorate.[6] We also recognize that the nationalization of policy issues may have allowed ideological debates to seep into the politics of statehouses where such debates were muted before.

Our theoretical argument about partisan polarization builds on an emerging scholarly view of political parties as an extended network of partisan activists who care deeply about some contentious issues (Bawn et al. 2012). These activists have worked through interest groups and party-affiliated organizations to press their cause with candidates and officeholders. They are influential because they volunteer for campaigns, attend conventions, provide expertise, make endorsements, mobilize their constituencies in primary elections, and raise money. Many of them run for office too. The financing of campaigns is but one element in their drive to shape the direction of party politics and policies. But we think it is an important one, given how critical money is in financing modern campaigns.

For this reason, we think campaign finance laws matter greatly.

Political Parties and Democracy

We start with the premise that political parties are key institutions in a democracy because they help mediate between citizens and governing elites. In theory and practice, parties help link government to citizens by recruiting candidates, waging campaigns that inform and mobilize voters, and ultimately organizing the government to implement broadly supported policies. Voters generally comprehend what the major American parties stand for with respect to principles about the role of government, and they have the opportunity during elections to hold party candidates accountable for campaign promises and policy outputs. Because the party wants to control government, it is motivated to tailor policies that will attract votes and win elections. Moreover, parties typically serve as interest aggregators that pull together various factions into a coalition that pursues broader public purposes than any single faction. In this way, parties help to overcome the inherent fragmentation of interests in a diverse country by forging alliances among constituent groups; this gives the parties legitimacy in claiming to govern for the common good.

To be sure, political parties have a controversial history, rife with examples of monumental corruption and "back-room deals" that serve narrow interests rather than the wider public. But, on the whole, the major American political parties have tended to be broad-based entities with mechanisms strong enough to hold political elites accountable. Despite shortcomings, their enduring party "brand" and institutionalized roles across all levels of government have promoted stability, collective action, and responsiveness in the American political system.

Many contemporary observers seem to blame the parties themselves for pushing politics to the extremes. A common (if inaccurate) argument is that parties have insulated themselves through redistricting so they do not have to be responsive to the broader electorate.[7] Two noted economists specifically indict the so-called party duopoly on campaign money for the current climate of hyperpartisanship in American politics and the failure of government to tackle problems (Hubbard and Kane 2013). They claim that the FECA reforms of 1974 enriched the parties and cut money off from individual candidates and groups that might have challenged party orthodoxy. For them, the decision in *Citizens United v. FEC* allowing corporations and unions to spend without limits ended a "four decade period of repression of independent voices" (133).

We believe that such thinking reflects a one-dimensional understanding of political parties. In particular, critics who fear financially well-off political parties fail to understand that "the party" is made up of many factions and is hardly monolithic in its pursuit of political goals. Some factions focus intensely on influencing specific policies while others tend to engage in the game of winning elections. We think parties behave differently based, in part, on which factions control resources within the party. In our view, parties (like any organization) survive and thrive based on the availability of resources, and the factions that provide those resources have more power over the direction of the broader party.[8] Importantly, for our argument, the *rules* on how people control and use resources affect the leverage of various factions within the party.

Two Conceptions of Political Parties

Our theory of resource dependency is informed by two different conceptions of political parties. One view sees parties primarily as unitary actors, controlled by "insiders" who seek electoral gains that will give them power and its perquisites. The other view sees parties controlled mostly by "outsiders" who work through issue coalitions to advance policy objectives. At this point, it would be helpful for us to explain more clearly what we mean by "parties" and how these two conceptions of parties inform our analysis.

PARTIES CONTROLLED BY INSIDERS

There is a lengthy scholarly tradition that views political parties as controlled largely by leaders inside the party organization (Michels 1949; Ostrogorski and Clarke 1902). These party leaders might emerge in the legislature, as is common in the United States today, or they might be unelected party bureaucrats, as in much of Europe. Historically, 19th-century party committees in the United States, like those in Europe, were controlled by non-elected officials. These were the local party "bosses" of the machine era. With the weakening of local organizations during the Progressive era, party leaders in legislatures have assumed more responsibility for recruiting candidates and supporting them in elections.

The primary vehicle for partisan activity remains the party organization, although the contemporary party is less oriented than in earlier years toward providing patronage to campaign workers in exchange for their support. Moreover, the modern party organization is chiefly a technical operation for waging political campaigns rather than a broader source of social activity, as it was in the past.[9] To be sure, the party continues to hold meetings and conventions to rally activists around party platforms and (in some states) preprimary nominations; but day-to-day activities are carried out by experienced campaign professionals, called "executive directors," appointed by a party chair. The party chair, in turn, is accountable to an executive party committee that includes elected officials, donors, and activists.

The main objective of insiders is typically to use the party committee to win elections. Only by winning elections and pursuing majorities can insiders hope to gain the power and wherewithal to reward supporters. For this reason, insiders have a deep interest in seeing the party organization survive as a means of securing control of government. Certainly insiders can create nonparty entities to help advance their electoral goals (and they often do), but they generally prefer the vehicle of the formal party organization to deploy electoral resources. The organizational label conveys a sense of public legitimacy among voters and gives its leaders legal status to place candidates on the election ballot. Moreover, the organization can exploit the historical loyalties of donors and activists from all factions who identify strongly with the party.

Insiders often contend with other factions for control of the party organization. It is typical of modern parties to allow for elections in which activists can run for positions on the executive committee. However, when insiders control the party apparatus completely (as they did in the 19th century), the organization is dedicated almost exclusively to serving the goals of insiders, which means winning elections. Elections are the path to securing power and status. And by controlling government, leaders can reward followers with material benefits such as jobs, high-level appointments, contracts, and other forms of favoritism. These rewards, in turn, enable leaders to foster the commitment of followers who sustain the organization with their contributions of labor, money, or knowledge.

We consider the insiders to be the *pragmatist* faction of the party with a decidedly Hobbesian view of the world in their quest for instrumental power. The pragmatists are materialists and assume that individuals have a basic animal nature, which compels self-interested behavior. For this reason, the insider creates mutually beneficial arrangements to satisfy those willing to join the party coalition against rivals who might take benefits away. The rampant bargaining and horse-trading that inevitably ensue may appear unprincipled, but the byproduct tends to satisfy large constituencies that help the party to win elections. This dynamic is captured nicely in the words of famed 19th-century Tammany Hall boss, George Washington Plunkitt:

> When the voters elect a man leader, they make a sort of contract with him. They say, although it ain't written out: "We've put you here to look out for our Interests. You want to see that this district gets all the jobs that's comm' to it. Be faithful to us, and we'll be faithful to you."[10]

The party-as-insider approach offers several different models that vary by the degree to which the party focuses exclusively on electoral goals at the expense of policy goals. The classic model, for example, understands parties as "unitary teams" that are overwhelmingly concerned with winning elections. This approach is best reflected in Anthony Downs's economic theory of democracy in which party teams move toward the median voter to maximize electoral opportunities, assuming that the ideological distribution of voters is single-peaked (Downs 1957). In the Downsian perspective, the party is simply a collection of people who seek office solely in order to "enjoy the income, prestige and power that goes with running the governing apparatus." Downs's theory has motivated a significant body of empirical research on party behavior. His approach, however, has been weak in explaining the puzzle of why parties diverge from the median voter. While Downs acknowledges the role of core activists in shaping a distinctive party brand, he fails to convincingly explain why the parties would move considerably away from the center.[11] This weakness has become more glaring today as we observe two highly distinctive and distant U.S. parties.

A second insider model also sees parties as unitary actors but with distinctive policy preferences. The teams are not exclusively seeking to win, but want to implement policies they strongly prefer. This is emblematic of the conception of party proposed by Edmund Burke in the 18th century, that parties are "a body of men united for promoting by their joint endeavors the national interest upon some particular principle in which they are agreed."[12] In Burke's view, members mostly agree about the governing or policy direction of the party. Given solidarity on principles and the electoral resources of the party organization, the insider party has significant bargaining advantages over narrowly backed interest groups. The party can avoid the "drift" in governing that occurs when officeholders are incessantly picked off by special interests or seized by local prejudices. At the same time the party is inured from being pulled too far to the extremes by issue factions whose policies could undermine the insiders' broad governing philosophy in pursuit of the common good.

This model of a "responsible party" is exactly the one extolled by the American Political Science Association (APSA) in its 1950 report on strengthening American political parties.[13] At the time, scholars feared the parties were too loosely organized and decentralized to address major challenges facing the nation. The authors would be pleased to learn that the party system has strengthened since the report was issued, but its responsible model of political parties at the national level is not necessarily what we have today. We argue instead that contemporary national parties have been controlled increasingly by narrow interest factions—the ones that George Washington may have feared—that do not necessarily sustain the Burkean goal of putting forth a coherent governing philosophy in the national interest.

A third model of the insider approach sees parties as more heterogeneous than the other two models. This is the party-in-service model theorized by John Aldrich (1995), which argues that the party comprises ambitious officeholders who campaign on their own individualistic terms. The institutional party helps to solve collective action and social choice problems by managing the coordination of members on legislation and political campaigns. It is not necessary, however, for party officeholders to agree on all policies; only that they agree to stick together as a long-term coalition to help pass their different policies. Moreover, officeholders do not necessarily have to champion the same causes when they campaign—they can pursue their own set of home style issues in getting reelected (Cain, Ferejohn, and Fiorina 1987; Fenno 1978). At the same time, however, they can use the campaign services offered by the party organization (voter files, consulting, etc.) to help mobilize electorates. In this fashion, the party sticks together for activities that require collective action, but allows considerable discretion to insider officeholders to use the party apparatus to the degree they need it to advance personal goals.

The strength of the party and its leadership varies depending on agreement over policy preferences. As members become increasingly similar on policy preferences they will give power to leaders in the legislature to enforce party discipline that aids in passing legislation overwhelmingly favored by party members (Rohde 1991). Conversely, greater heterogeneity of preferences leads to a decentralized power structure in the legislature, which typically results in shifting legislative coalitions, including bipartisan lawmaking. The important distinction in Aldrich's approach is that the party primarily serves the goals of the personal ambitions of individual legislators rather than the goals of a unified party leadership.

In each of the three models the party organization serves the pragmatic insiders who want to stay in power or acquire more power. Elections have high stakes because the insiders have something tangible to lose: an incumbent legislator might fail in a bid for reelection, or a party boss might lose access to patronage and other spoils. For this reason, insiders have strong incentives to avoid extremism that might jeopardize seats in the legislature. In general, when insiders control a significant share of electoral resources, they will use them in ways that keep the party close to the median voter, thereby precluding high variance in ideology that might hurt the party brand. While the parties are "big tents," keeping low variance on party positions is essential for conveying clear information to voters (Snyder and Ting 2002). Consequently, when the political environment favors strong party organizations (e.g., depending on rules, culture, etc.), the pragmatist insiders will use their control of the party to screen out extremist candidates and convey a slightly off-center partisan message to attract persuadable voters. The clear implication of the insider conception of parties is that they will use party organizations in ways that attenuate partisan polarization. Moderation is a byproduct of their pursuit of power.

PARTIES CONTROLLED BY OUTSIDERS

A second theoretical approach views parties as entities controlled by groups and activists outside the formal party structure. This emergent view, which is attributable primarily to scholars associated with UCLA's political science department, provides an important challenge to traditional models of parties.[14] The proponents of the UCLA approach argue that theories based on Downsian electoral incentives fail to explain the strong ideological divergence of parties. Even a watered-down version of Downs's theory that makes room for policy-motivated activists is not a convincing explanation for why political parties take strong—indeed risky—policy positions that are often at odds with the preferences of most voters.

The group-centric approach gives greater attention to the role of interest groups and activists in parties. Indeed, theorists espousing this view argue that groups and activists *constitute* the party. Such partisans do not merely provide shades of color for the party brand (as Downs or Aldrich would have it), but forge its very principles and governing agenda. The party, then, is not a big-tent coalition reflecting blocs of voters, but a dense core of committed issue activists and networked groups with relatively narrow policy goals. By helping to elect candidates who bear the party label, these policy demanders seek to capture and use government to achieve their distinctive policy goals.

The goals are typically ideological, although they do not have to be. They range from high-minded idealism, such as a commitment to protecting the environment or the unborn, to material self-interest, such as pushing for progrowth policies that serve particular business interests. Not surprisingly, the goals often reflect a mix of idealism and self-interest. Thus, a conservative group like the Club for Growth, which favors limited government and low taxes as a means to achieving national prosperity and freedom, attracts business elites who would benefit materially from such policies. More typically, however, the dominant issues form the basis of the so-called "Culture War," which pits political elites—social liberals and social conservatives—against each other on a range of issues (Hunter 1991; Lindaman and Haider-Markel 2002).

The standoff between activists on the pro and con sides of these issues shapes the contours of partisan strife in the political system. For example, narrowly focused abortion rights groups such as NARAL in the Democratic coalition oppose conservative Christians in the pro-life movement who constitute a faction in the Republican Party. Similarly, the organization Defenders of Wildlife, which seeks to protect gray wolves and other endangered species, faces off against hunters and ranchers who oppose government intervention. Critically, the groups do not typically represent broad segments of the population, but small, cohesive memberships or constituencies focusing intensely on narrow policy issues.

The glue that holds the groups together as partisans is not mutual admiration but necessity. The issues they embrace are often disparate, seemingly disconnected. Ironically, this disconnection helps activist coalitions stick together because factions focusing on different issues can avoid internal battles over broader policy.[15] Since no single group could achieve the task of taking over government alone, they form "long coalitions" that stay unified under a party label. Through the umbrella of the party they are able to coordinate an agenda of mutually acceptable policies. These policies are not at the top of the list of concerns for the broader public, but politicians give them disproportionate attention because the political system rewards groups that are highly organized, provide electoral resources (members, money, expertise), and lobby intensely over the long haul (Grossmann 2012).

Importantly, these groups and activists do more than simply lobby like a special interest; rather, they behave collectively like a party coordinating their actions in recruiting, nominating, and electing candidates who favor their policy positions. Groups do this because a traditional lobbying strategy on their core issues would not yield the same results. As with any lobbying effort, groups would encounter the principal–agent problem whereby freestanding politicians might shirk or cut side deals that would undermine the groups' goals. At the same time, incumbents might be reluctant to take electoral risks on issues that could jeopardize their standing among core constituencies in the district.

The surest strategy for groups is to help elect people who agree with them. By serving as gatekeepers for those who enter office, the policy demanders in the coalition largely shape the priorities of legislators. The key strategy of the long coalition is to coordinate on candidate vetting and support. If a challenger or open-seat candidate meets its approval, the coalition converges to support the candidate and markedly improves her prospects of winning the seat (Desmarais, La Raja, and Kowal 2014).[16] To the casual outsider, the "party" is nowhere to be seen because the action—endorsements, fundraisers, voter mobilization, and so on—takes place outside the formal party organization (Masket 2009).

The group-centric approach offers a powerful explanation for why parties are polarizing ideologically. Adherents of this approach can point to highly influential groups of citizens who constitute the party and who are disproportionately ideological relative to American voters. They are emblematic of what Fiorina and Abrams (2009) call the "the purists," a term they borrow from Wildavsky (1965) and one that we will use in this book. These two classes of party activists were first conceptualized by James Q. Wilson more than a half-century ago in his prescient book, *The Amateur Democrat*. Wilson termed those concerned primarily with the outcomes of winning and losing the "professionals," and those who care intrinsically about ideas and principles the "amateurs" (Wilson 1962). Essentially, the amateurs—whom we call purists—have come to dominate public life because of the decline of material incentives that once attracted poorer Americans to participate in electoral politics (Fiorina and Abrams 2009). Civil service reforms at the turn of the 20th century winnowed the patronage that attracted material-oriented followers to the party. The consequence is that the party includes fewer activists drawn from the ranks of people having a personal stake in political participation relative to those who have lifestyle or moral concerns. For this reason, the group-centered party has been more willing to take electoral risks by staking out extreme positions.

If party insiders are materialists, then party outsiders might be considered idealists. Rather than focus on the world as it is, they prioritize principles and values over concrete realities. Kant, not Hobbes, is their lodestar. To be sure, we are oversimplifying our distinction between insider pragmatists and outsider purists; we concede that motives often overlap. But we tend to agree with Fiorina that the purists now have more clout in party affairs. And this explains some of the gridlock in Congress. While Hobbesian pragmatists concerned with material gains are more likely to compromise when necessary to get half a loaf, Kantian purists are less likely to do so. Compromise devalues the moral underpinnings of their commitments and dissipates the passion of followers. Better to lose a standoff and use that fear-inducing loss to raise more money from membership, than to allow politicians to compromise far short of the policy goals sought by activists.

Let us be clear that we are not arguing that polarization is simply the consequence of changing the reward system for partisans. Demographics and changing technology play a role as well. For example, because of government programs and a larger middle class, fewer citizens today need the material rewards or social services that party organizations once offered. Additionally, contemporary campaigns require capital more than labor, which makes donations from wealthier segments of the population more important than previously. On the left, donor activists are concerned with promoting social issues like abortion and the environment, which are not necessarily top priorities for low-income voters. On the right, in contrast, donors appear concerned with promoting limited government and championing economic policies that are not necessarily desired by the middle-class constituencies that Republicans claim to represent (Bartels 2008; Gilens 2005; McCarty, Poole, and Rosenthal 2006).

An important part of the argument in the group-centric approach is that activists are able to pull parties to the extremes because of an inattentive public. While passionate partisans follow politics closely, the mass public remains barely aware of campaigns and policies being debated in statehouses. Lack of sophisticated media coverage of politics widens the gap in knowledge between activists and the typical American voter. In this way the parties find the public "blind spot" that allows them to embrace policies that their broader electorates would not necessarily agree with, much less consider a policy priority. For this reason, the outsider model implies an unsettling disconnect between party activists and the American electorate. The party loyalists that constitute the Democratic and Republican brands reflect a bimodal ideological distribution with peaks on the right and left. In contrast, the ideological preferences of American voters tend to look more like a normal distribution, with most citizens near the median voter.[17]

Our Theoretical Approach: Parties as Competing Factions

Both the insider and outsider perspectives are ideal conceptual models and have much to commend them in explaining party behavior. At the same time, we see critical weaknesses in each approach. We start by observing that these party models largely reflect the facts on the ground at the time. The insider models were developed during a postwar period in which candidates seemed to have lots of individual discretion in campaigning and legislating. Some prominent scholars, in observing the seeming "wishy-washiness" of American parties, believed that the party system was ill-equipped to address the pressing social and economic needs of citizens. Not without reason, they feared democracy in a large, industrialized nation could not function well without cohesive Westminster-style political parties. Such parties could provide distinctive governing philosophies that offered voters real choices and the organizational strength to implement the party platform. Given this set of assumptions, theorists in the 1940s and 1950s buttressed their normative views of party with proposals to fortify party organizations, including allowing them greater access to finance (both private and public money) and mechanisms to give additional power to party leadership, as means of ensuring discipline and accountability among rank-and-file party members and candidates (American Political Science Association 1950).

Paradoxically, contemporary parties are now viewed as *too* ideologically rigid, and current scholarship reflects the new dynamics of the party system. The emergent "group-centered" approach has taken root during a period in which the two major parties display the kind of ideological distinctiveness that many leading political scientists appeared to desire back in 1950. In contrast to previous efforts to explain why the major parties displayed all the distinctiveness of Tweedledum and Tweedledee, scholars today seek to explain party divergence and the formidable obstacles to effective governance that American democracy faces. While the parties of the 1940s and 1950s seemed adrift, we now have parties that appear perhaps too highly disciplined, with members of Congress voting almost exclusively with their party (McCarty, Poole, and Rosenthal 2006). Indeed, party members appear so distinctive that congressional and White House leadership look hapless in trying to forge bipartisan compromises to pass laws. The value of the group-centric model is that it explains persuasively why parties find it difficult to cooperate and converge on policies that appear to be in the national interest, even when a majority of voters support compromise.

In our view, neither model does a good job of explicating the periods outside the immediate era in which they were constructed. The insider models developed by Downs, Schattschneider, or Aldrich come up short in the contemporary era of highly partisan politics. And the more recent group-centric model proposed by the UCLA school does not adequately explain the extended periods of limited ideological warfare during the postwar era. The outsider model does not take seriously the possibility that parties were previously dominated not so much by issue factions as by politicians, including the party bosses and officeholders accountable to blocs of voters rather than to narrow policy demanders.[18] Indeed, the rise of ideological activists as party gatekeepers might be an anomaly in American history. Given the relatively high levels of education and affluence in American society, politics is no longer a matter of survival for access to jobs and opportunities, but an arena for intensely political citizens to push for principled social and economic commitments.

Factional Struggle: Pragmatists versus Purists

We think the theoretical insights contained in both perspectives help to explain party dynamics through time, if we assume a broader view of the party coalition than either set of models warrants. Both perspectives see parties too narrowly. At times parties can be issue interests in pursuit of narrow policy objectives, but not always. They can also be Downs/Aldrich teams of politicians, or bureaucratically sustained formal organizations like the machines, or the professionalized staff envisioned by Schattschneider (1942). These two perspectives are subsets of the whole picture.[19]

We are not merely splitting the difference between the two perspectives. We tend to side closely with those who view parties as broader than the legal and formal definition portrays them. Like the UCLA school, we see parties in the United States as large, factional coalitions. They are mostly a decentralized group of actors who are bound by both formal and informal ties to other partisans. These factions work together to help each other gain power and status, and to implement preferred policies of important factions.

Our difference with the pure outsider perspective is this: factions might have overlapping political goals, but the coalition is fraught with tension.[20] We argue that the push-and-pull of factional strains shapes the direction of the party. The UCLA school assumes that partisans unite by offending no one in the party coalition. Yet keeping the peace in a large coalition is no easy task. The group-centered approach appears to neglect the bitter internal politics of major parties. We contend that factions are *ceaselessly* trying to gain the upper hand in party affairs. While the overarching goal of partisans is to beat the rival party, each faction has its own set of priorities. And the clashing of priorities is exactly what drives the dynamics of the major parties (DiSalvo 2012; Frymer 1999). Partisans fight internally to put their goals above others, and they do this by supporting the ambitions of politicians who give priority to their issues. This includes helping them advance to leadership positions in Congress and nurturing presidential aspirations. We can observe such fights today between conservative Tea Party activists and establishment Republicans. A recent victim of this particular factional strife is Republican Eric Cantor, the former House majority leader, who was defeated by an extremist faction of Republican voters in the 2014 primary when a small primary electorate, dominated by the most conservative voters, selected David Brat, a political newcomer and economics professor espousing hard-right policies.[21] Such tensions also exist in the Democratic Party between progressives who favor a strong regulatory state, such as Massachusetts senator Elizabeth Warren, and business-friendly centrists such as Hillary Clinton or Mark Warner.

We acknowledge that parties comprise more than two factions, but for analytical purposes we organize them into broader conceptual categories consisting of pragmatist insiders and the purist outsiders. As noted, pragmatists are concerned primarily with staying in power, while purists pursue policies. Not surprisingly, the purists have the moral high ground because they endow the party with the backbone of principles and legitimacy. The pragmatists, however, help make the American system of separate government work through daily betrayals of principle in pursuit of power. Such betrayals often lead to bipartisan compromise. At any given point in historical time, the degree of power controlled by these two archetypes of factions can stimulate or suppress ideological polarization in the party system. Today, the political environment—its media, its demographics, and its electoral rules—favors the purists. And for this reason we are living with highly polarized politics.

Resources and Factional Power

We contend that factions gain leverage in party affairs by having control over valuable political resources. Politicians need these resources to get elected, to get their message out, and to implement policies. Some equate resources with money, but that view is too narrow. Other types of resources are valuable to politicians. In politics, affiliation with membership organizations, especially those that are distributed broadly throughout the nation, is valuable because it provides direct access to voters. Having access to information, knowledge, and expertise is also prized. Politicians, for example, need expert testimony and the lobbying muscle of interest groups to help pass legislation. Politicians also value endorsements from groups that are viewed positively by many voters (e.g., firefighters, nurses). And, of course, politicians value campaign money, which helps them to get their message out, set governing agendas, and win elections.

The relative value of different kinds of resources may vary over time, which is one reason why some factions emerge more powerfully with changes in technology or shifting demographics. To provide one example, the value of labor relative to capital has changed considerably over the last century. Gains in productivity from emerging technologies allow all kinds of organizations, including political groups, to reach voters and keep track of them, without having to rely on armies of partisan workers walking the precincts. This is not to say that walking the precincts is unimportant, but only that the need for such people has diminished and that other means of communication have emerged—TV advertising, social media—to identify and mobilize key voters.

In this book we focus on campaign funds as a source of factional influence. While we emphasize that influence in the party is not solely a product of the resource environment, we admit that the availability of such resources is especially important during an era when money matters so much for reaching voters. The ability to finance political campaigns shapes whether pragmatists or purists have more influence in pushing the direction of the party coalition.

The Importance of Campaign Finance Laws in Shaping Factional Power

Access to resources is shaped, in part, by the electoral rules. In the realm of campaign finance, rules that allow unlimited contributions from partisan interest groups allow purist outsiders to play a large role in financing candidate elections. This gives issue groups additional leverage in deciding who runs for office and who wins. In contrast, rules that restrict issue groups but do not similarly constrain party organizations tend to give the Hobbesian insiders greater influence on candidate selection and support. Today's rules at the national level and in most states favor the purist outsiders in the party.

The creation of rules, of course, is not exogenous; that is, rules are not only imposed from without. This makes our analysis rather challenging. We acknowledge that factions fight over the nature of these electoral rules precisely because they confer access to resources and influence. Given the coalitional nature of American parties, scholarship has not only focused on the battles over political rules *between* the parties, but on fights *within* the large and unwieldy party coalitions.

Historically we know that pragmatists and purists have fought for domination. In the modern era, the policy-demanding purists have pursued a variety of rules and regulations to weaken the influence of party pragmatists. California politics provides a good example with regard to rules governing its party nominating process. According to Masket (2009), California party activists pushed to eliminate the cross-filing of candidates, a practice that allows candidates to run in the primary election of more than one party. Cross-filing (also called a "fusion ballot" in some states) can enable a candidate in the primary to win the general election by emerging from the primary as the first choice among multiple parties, thereby eliminating or reducing the strength of other competitors. Importantly, cross-filing helps candidates get a slot on the general election ballot without the vetting of party purists in the primaries. If the candidate, for instance, cross-files with both the Democratic and Liberal parties, she could get on the general election ballot as a Liberal Party candidate even if she loses the Democratic primary vote. In short, with cross-filing, candidates have a multiparty path to get on the ballot. Without cross-filing, they would have to earn their place on the ballot by going through just *one* party nominating process. The abolition of cross-filing in California in 1959 made candidates more attentive to the policy preferences of activists in the major parties and, as Masket argues, encouraged the kind of ideological politics for which the state is known today.

Moderate factions fight back too. Once again California provides a telling example. In 1996, a centrist faction in the Republican Party introduced Proposition 198, which called for a "blanket primary" in which voters could select one candidate for each office, regardless of party affiliation, in an attempt to weaken the grip of the conservative wing that routinely nominated extremist candidates who lost in the general election. The proposition was ultimately declared unconstitutional by the U.S. Supreme Court, but that did not stop pragmatists like Governor Arnold Schwarzenegger from introducing in 2010 a "top-two" primary reform, by which voters could pick any candidate for an office, regardless of party affiliation, and the two candidates receiving the most votes would engage in a runoff vote in the general election. This measure, like the blanket primary, had the purpose of moderating the parties.[22] This law, now in place, appears to have withstood constitutional scrutiny.

With respect to campaign finance regulations, we know from studies of European parties that such rules tend to alter the nature of power within parties. Specifically, the introduction of generous public financing of political parties appears to make party organizations less attentive to the concerns of issue activists. Political parties in Europe that rely heavily on state funding rather than membership dues appear to lose their ideological edge. Activists complain that their parties become more concerned with staying in power than pursuing the parties' historical agenda (Katz and Mair 1995). We argue that U.S. campaign finance laws have also affected the balance of power within parties. In contrast to Europe, however, the parties have not become more tame, but more ideological, precisely because of the heavy reliance of candidates on ideological sources of support. That is, compared with the past, candidates now rely more profoundly on issue activists (rather than the party organization), which is counter the trend in Europe.

Party Organizations and Insiders

Party organizations are the natural home of pragmatists (insiders), and not purists (outsiders). This is so for three reasons. First, the party organization is not a venue for the development and deliberation of policy issues. In the United States that activity has been outsourced to partisan think tanks and interest groups, while the party organization has traditionally been focused on the electoral machinery of campaigns. To be sure, purists bring issues to formal discussions of the party platform during conventions hosted by the party organization. But the party organization itself is a rather inhospitable place to incubate policy issues and energize issue activists. The instrumental role of the party organization as a campaign operation makes it more attractive to pragmatists.

Second, the party organization is the broadest representation of the party, which perforce requires the balancing of multiple interests. While narrow-issue activists might have a significant voice in the affairs of the party committee, their clout is muted in Madisonian fashion by the multiplicity of interests affiliated with the organization. The governance structures—which involve elections to the executive committee and the appointment of party chairs—compel party officials to be accountable to a broad constituency. The leadership of party organizations typically includes elected officials, campaign consultants, issue activists, and longtime partisans whose dedication to the party exceeds their loyalty to any particular issue group. The fact that these partisans are under "one roof" of the formal party organization allows for the kind of bargaining that naturally mutes the ideological shrillness of any particular faction within the coalition.

Third, the party is a legally distinctive entity with a strong history attached to its label. Pragmatists, particularly elected officials, are most covetous of controlling this label so that the party brand does not become electorally poisonous to their careers. Since the party organization coordinates elections up and down the ticket it cannot stake out extreme or narrow positions, which might hurt individual candidates in particular districts at the federal or state level. To be sure, there are abundant fights over the control of party committees in many states. But purists typically find working solely through the party organization to be overly constraining and compromising to their ultimate goals. For this reason, they remain committed to the organizations outside the formal party structure, while pragmatists invest their energies within the formal organization. The party label is vital to the careers of pragmatists, while purist issue activists, in contrast, may regard the label mostly as a convenient vehicle to push their policies. Thus, purists have weaker loyalties to the party label and even weaker loyalties to the party organization.

A recent example illustrates the point. The 2014 primary for the U.S. Senate in Mississippi pitted six-term incumbent Thad Cochran against Tea Party–backed Chris McDaniel. Party insiders wanted Cochran to be reelected and took the unusual step in a primary of throwing the financial weight of the National Republican Senate Committee (NRSC) behind him. McDaniel and his purist supporters cried foul; among these supporters was the newly minted senator from Texas (and champion of the Tea Party), Ted Cruz.

The Senate Republican leadership had appointed Senator Cruz as vice-chair of the NRSC, hoping to tame him of his bomb-throwing efforts to radicalize the GOP. But despite his status as a member of the party's inner circle, Cruz has been a relatively inactive NRSC fundraiser. His lethargy on behalf of the NRSC contrasts with his energetic fundraising for the Senate Conservatives Fund, a nonparty organization that seeks to make the party more conservative by supporting hard-right candidates. Cruz clearly felt that the NRSC should have stayed out of the primaries (presumably to help the conservative candidate win). In contrast, the pragmatists in both the state and national party spoke publicly about their fears that candidates like McDaniel would shrink the party with their narrow appeal to highly conservative voters.[23]

The distinctions between pragmatists and purists are not impermeable. Individuals representing the purist faction may at times work for the formal party organization. However, organizational location shapes behavior: where you sit changes your incentives. Purists who work for party organizations become more pragmatic, because even a former issue activist who consents to be adopted, however temporarily, by the party is more likely to view objectives from the electoral perspective of the party. This may well be why the GOP leadership wanted to bring Senator Cruz into the NRSC leadership. An ideologue who becomes a party leader will be pulled in new directions that diverge at times from former factional loyalties. Again, the case of Republican majority leader Eric Cantor comes to mind. At the time he lost in the primary to an obscure and inexperienced candidate in Virginia's conservative Seventh District, he was almost as conservative as the insurgent who beat him. However, in his role as a party leader, he had taken on the responsibility of raising money from broader party constituencies, such as corporate and Wall Street elites, who were intensely disliked by his own constituents. He was also amenable, on occasion, to making compromises with the opposition when it suited the broader strategies of the party. This pragmatic work as a party leader put him in jeopardy electorally because he could no longer satisfy the purist activists in his district.

We want to make one more point about party organizations and insiders. Legislative parties (such as the DCCC and NRCC) are more likely to provide a natural home for insiders than executive-centered parties (such as the DNC and RNC).[24] Legislative parties—sometimes called "caucus" committees—are controlled by leadership in the legislature, with minimal direct influence of activists. These leaders embody the hard-headed realism of insiders who want to control majorities in the legislature by winning elections. In contrast, executive-centered committees—sometimes called "state central committees"—have governing boards in which factions vie to get their members into positions of influence. State central committees are usually umbrella organizations that provide formal representation for county-based committees, which nurture some of the most ideological activists in the party. Indeed, activist insurgents from local parties often try to take over the central party apparatus to create party platforms and recruit statewide (and sometimes legislative) candidates who conform to their ideological preferences (Conger 2010; Green, Rozell, and Wilcox 2003). A strong local party with highly mobilized and well-resourced membership, such as the Republican Party of Orange County, California, can have disproportionate influence in shaping the state party platform and vetting statewide candidates. This is one reason why the California Republican Party has seemed well to the right on issues, compared to rank-and-file GOP voters and members of the state legislature who belong to the GOP caucus.

The national parties are better insulated against purist capture because there are so many factions contending for influence that no single one can dominate. (In this way, the Madisonian argument in *Federalist* 10 about how an extended republic attenuates tyrannical factionalism applies to the party system as well.) Additionally, by tradition the DNC and RNC are largely controlled by the president or presidential candidate who assigns his loyalists and experienced campaign advisors to control the party apparatus in pursuit of the instrumental goal of winning the upcoming election.

In our analysis, we do not distinguish between state legislative and central party committees because of the limits of the data. But we point to the distinction because our findings may be attenuated or even somewhat biased against our contention that stronger party organizations help to moderate politics. In many states, such as Florida and Minnesota, the state central committees are highly active not only in statewide races but in legislative contests as well. And since state central committees can be more easily captured by purists from local parties, these committees may not always support moderate candidates.

The Moderating Influence of Party Organizations

There are two main ways in which strong party organizations moderate politics. The first is through financial support: because party insiders are chiefly interested in winning elections, their priority is to invest in candidates who will be most competitive in a general election—candidates whose views are closest to those of the median voter. This means that party insiders prefer to support moderate candidates. This contrasts with the riskier investment strategy of outsiders, who prefer to support candidates with positions as similar to their own as possible. The hope of outsiders is that voter inattention to issues will enable the election of candidates whose views are at odds with the preferences of the median voter.

The second way party committees moderate politics is in their role as financial mediators. The party can receive money from ideological donors—who would otherwise give most of their contributions to ideological candidates—and reinvest it in moderate candidates. However, we want to be clear that party organizations are not interested in moderation as a goal; they are simply interested in winning. They give to candidates based on their likelihood of winning—in other words, they support candidates who take more moderate positions. This mediation role helps to insulate candidates from ideologically driven donors who might pull candidates in their direction, either by threatening to withhold funding or by financing other candidates who agree with them. When the party organization mediates the funding, the candidate is less concerned with ideological purity. Indeed, studies show that formal party organizations do not typically punish candidates financially for taking positions that stray from the party line (Bianco 1999; Damore and Hansford 1999; Herrnson 1989; Leyden and Borrelli 1990; Nokken 2003).

A purely "party-centered" campaign finance system would allow parties unlimited access to funds (no source or size restrictions) and permit parties to finance their candidates without limits. We will argue in this book that a party-centered system is most likely to attenuate ideological polarization between the major parties because (1) more money flows to moderate candidates, and (2) money is rinsed of its ideological origins. On this latter point we acknowledge that the party can only go so far in ignoring the kind of ideological candidates preferred by outsiders. We will elaborate on this point in chapter 2 when we examine the giving patterns of activist donors, especially conservatives, who view parties as too moderate. On the other hand, party organizations benefit from attracting resources from multiple constituencies, which makes them less dependent on a narrow faction of the party.

The Polarizing Influence of Candidate-Centered Politics

Candidate-centered systems, which restrict party financing, tend to incite ideological polarization. As we will see in chapter 2, when party organizations face financing constraints, candidates rely more heavily on direct support from interest groups and activist donors, who are the purist outsiders with strong policy preferences. In this way, candidates' positions are pulled toward the ideological poles, especially in the early stages of an election when money is particularly important in elevating the name recognition and electoral viability of new candidates. This is the point in a campaign when interest groups already have a built-in advantage: party organizations typically cannot become directly involved in primaries because of laws or norms preventing them from supporting a favored candidate.

Some argue that laws constraining parties do not matter because the larger party (the coalition, not the organization) will adapt amoeba-like to new constraints.[25] We agree about the tendency to adapt, but we are not sanguine about the form the adaptations take. Party adaptations are not equal in style or substance to those undertaken by pragmatist factions through the formal party organization. When much of the coalition campaigning takes place outside the party organization, purist factions benefit as candidates are forced to rely more heavily on issue-based interest groups. And while "shadow parties" might emerge, they are no replacement for actual party committees. These nonparty campaign organizations, typically run by former party operatives (i.e., pragmatists), focus their efforts primarily on running TV ads in a few targeted races. They do not contribute to long-term party building, and they cannot work closely with local parties at the grassroots level. According to an experienced election lawyer, the "outside shadow parties are not accountable at all for the messaging. And the consultants want to spend it all on media. Field programs and canvassing are too labor intensive. The consultants want to get paid, get in and get out."[26]

A related problem is that constraints on the formal party organization will encourage partners in the party coalition to pursue campaign finance strategies through nontransparent organizational forms.[27] As we will argue later in this book, this dynamic imposes a heavy social cost on the political system. But here we attend to the ways in which political reforms can affect the balance of power within parties by giving advantages to some factions over others. We argue that laws that constrain the party organizations give the purists in the party greater influence than the pragmatists to shape the direction of the party coalition. The outcome is a party system that is decidedly more polarized than it would otherwise be. And such a party system engenders political fragmentation among factional interests because party leaders cannot impose sufficient discipline on coalition members to advance broad interests. This proclivity toward fragmentation leads to problems of governance (Pildes 2015).

Our contention that campaign finance laws strengthen one faction of the party over another challenges the conventional wisdom of party scholars about what makes a party "strong." In theory, parties can be strong programmatically (they offer distinctive policies) and organizationally (they have significant control over the political process, including nominations, organizing campaigns, and governing). The classic scholarship on political parties, as embodied in the 1950 report on political parties by the American Political Science Association, implies that strong party organizations are tightly linked to strong programmatic parties. In other words, when organizational leaders have significant control over rank-and-file members, they can discipline them to follow a coherent party program. Our suggestion is that the two aspects of party strength are not necessarily linked and may even be inversely related. A strong party organization may serve as a buffer against ideological programmatic parties because the pragmatists who dominate the party organization would have the power to challenge policy-demanding purists, based within partisan interest groups, who favor uncompromising positions on policies.[28] In this way, strong party organizations may lead, paradoxically, to party coalitions with softer policy edges.

A State-Based Empirical Approach

In this book we examine the effects of campaign finance laws on ideological polarization. While polarization has been most commonly studied in national politics—particularly in the U.S. Congress—it has also been occurring across the 50 state legislatures. Shor and McCarty have recently provided an excellent data source to scholars of state politics by compiling the roll call votes from state legislatures over nearly two decades and using those roll call votes to derive estimates of the ideology of each state legislator (Shor and McCarty 2011). This exercise has allowed Shor to document increasing polarization in state legislatures. He reports that from 1996 to 2010, 59 of the 99 state legislative chambers experienced increased polarization.[29] In only 16 of those chambers was polarization decreasing, and in the remaining 24 chambers polarization remained steady. Thus, a majority of state legislative chambers were polarizing, but polarization was not by any means universal.

It is on the state legislatures that we focus our study for one important reason: while there is only a single set of campaign finance laws in place at any given point of time at the national level, different states have implemented very different types of campaign finance laws for state legislative elections over the past several decades. This fact provides us with a way of assessing the impact of different campaign finance laws. Specifically, we can compare states that empower parties to raise and spend unlimited amounts of money on legislative candidates with states that impose strict limits on what parties can spend in elections.

For this book we collected information on campaign finance laws in the 50 American states for the years 1990 through 2010. For each election year in each state we determined whether the state placed limits on how much money parties could raise from various sources and whether the state placed limits on what parties could contribute to candidates. We used several sources

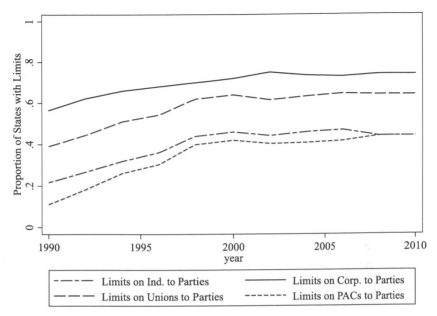

Figure 1.1. Limits on Contributions to Parties from Various Sources. (*Note:* Lines show proportion of states with laws for each type of limit for state legislative elections in a particular election year.)

to construct this information, including data from the National Council of State Legislatures and various secretary of state or election agency offices.[30] We also wanted to account for whether the state placed limits on the other types of political actors we have discussed so far—individuals and interest group organizations. Fortunately, we were able to draw on (and supplement) data collected by Jeff Milyo for those entities.[31]

Figure 1.1 shows the proportion of states that placed limits on how much money parties could raise from four different sources across the two decades for which we have data. Several points are worth making from this figure. First, states have been consistently more likely to limit what corporations and unions can contribute to parties compared to PACs and individuals. Second, states have been increasingly likely to implement limits on what parties can raise from all sources over time. This is especially true for PACs and individuals. In 1990, only about one state in five limited how much individuals could contribute to a political party and only about one in ten placed such limits on PACs. However, by 2010 the proportion of states placing such limits on individuals and PACs had more than doubled. This reflects an increasing tendency of states to limit the role that parties can play in financing candidates.

A third point from this figure, however, is that throughout the time period, there has always been significant variation in how states regulate parties. Even in the more recent election years, a significant number of states have allowed corporations, unions, PACs, and individuals to contribute unlimited sums to party organizations, while other states have limited what all of these organizations can give. Such variation in state laws provides leverage in evaluating the impact of campaign finance laws on who donates, who gets money, and how these arrangements affect partisan polarization. These factors will be the subject of detailed analysis in the later chapters of this book.

Figure 1.2 shows the proportion of states that limited what parties, individuals, and interest group organizations could contribute *to candidates* in each of the election years between 1990 and 2010. The pattern in this graphic is similar to that in figure 1.1. Specifically, the proportion of states limiting what parties can contribute to candidates started relatively small (about one in five states had such limits in 1990), but has increased significantly during the past two decades. Indeed, in 2010, just under half of the states placed limits on party contributions to candidates. While limits on contributions from individuals and organizations have always been more common than limits on parties, the prevalence of such limits has not increased as much during the period. Indeed, in 1990, 26 states placed no limits whatsoever on what parties could raise from individuals or contribute to state legislative candidates. By 2010, only 15 states had no limits on party fundraising from individuals and spending on candidates.

The patterns in figures 1.1 and 1.2 have not been good for party organizations, which are now much more constrained than they were two decades ago in what they can raise and spend in many states. But the changes in those figures provide us with additional variance to aid in our investigation. Indeed, we are able not only to examine the consequences of differences in campaign finance laws across states in a given year, but also to consider the effects of different campaign finance laws within several states that changed their laws over time.

Of course, it is important to confirm that these limits actually have an effect on how much of a role parties play in state legislative campaigns. Figure 1.3 shows the amount of money raised, per capita, by state political parties in 2012. These figures come from the National Institute on Money in State Politics, a data source we use extensively in our book and which we describe in more detail in chapter 3. The light bars in figure 1.3 represent states that do not limit what individuals can contribute to parties and the dark bars are for states that do have such limits. The horizontal lines identify the means for each group of states. There are two important points to draw

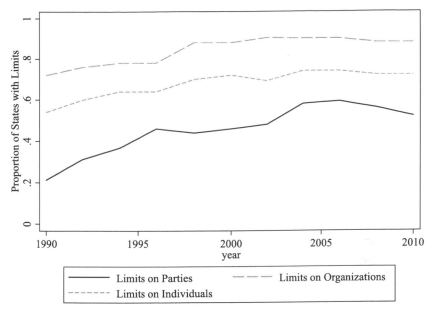

Figure 1.2. Limits on Contributions to Candidates from Various Sources. (*Note:* Lines show proportion of states with laws for each type of limit for state legislative elections in a particular election year.)

from this figure. First, the type of campaign finance laws a state has in place clearly matters. Indeed, parties in states with no limits on what can be raised collect, on average, more than twice as much money as those in states where such limits do exist. It is quite simply the case that when parties are limited in what they can raise from any given individual, they are less likely to be able to raise large sums overall.

The second point from this figure, however, is that there is significant variance in how much parties raise in a given state, even beyond what can be explained by the types of laws a particular state has in place. Indeed, campaign finance laws are only one of many factors that are likely to influence how much of a role parties play in financing campaigns in a particular state. In some states parties are simply more powerful and active than in others, for reasons that may have more to do with historical factors than the current legal regime. Thus, it is important to recognize that while campaign finance laws are influential, they are not determinant.

In the next few chapters, we will use the significant variance in campaign finance laws and actual party financing that the states exhibit during the period we study to draw strong inferences about the role of campaign

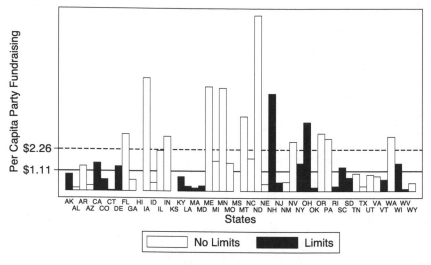

Figure 1.3. Per Capita Fundraising by State Parties, 2012 Elections. (*Note:* Data from authors' analysis of data from the National Institute on Money in State Politics and Federal Election Commission. Bars show the amount of money raised by party committees in each state per capita.)

finance in affecting polarization in the states. We will examine, for example, (a) whether parties are more active when they are not limited by campaign finance laws; (b) whether parties tend to contribute to more moderate candidates compared to other actors; and (c) whether legislative polarization is lessened when parties are more active in state legislative elections. In short, the varied experiences of the states over the past two decades will provide us with significant insight about how campaign finance laws matter for parties and for legislative polarization. We also expect that the insights we gather regarding the individual states will generalize to the U.S. Congress, where polarization and gridlock are likewise apparent. Congress, no less than the states, feels the effects of campaign finance laws and policies; it is reasonable to expect that findings drawn from, and recommendations applied to, state legislatures will be roughly applicable at the federal legislative levels.

A Note About Determining Whether Campaign Finance Laws Matter

Testing whether campaign finance laws matter is not simple. For example, elected officials tend to select the types of campaign finance laws that a state enacts, and they undoubtedly make these decisions based at least partly on strategic considerations.

As a basic example, consider the results we present in figure 1.3. In that figure, we show that political parties in states that limit what individuals can contribute raise significantly less money per capita than parties in states without such limits. This finding makes sense, but can we be sure that it results from the laws? Perhaps it is the case that states where people contributed less money to parties in the first place were more likely to adopt restrictions on what individuals could donate. After all, passing such a restriction may have been easier if the state's population was not that interested in donating to parties anyway.

In this book, we take care to support with the data the causal claims we make about the impact of laws. For example, whenever possible, we use temporal data to consider how changes in laws may have created changes in the behaviors of donors, politicians, and other political elites.

As a first step, let's examine here whether states that adopted restrictions on political parties and states that did not do so are systematically different in ways that might affect the conclusions we draw. For example, let's ask whether states that restrict what individuals can give to parties have populations that are less supportive of parties generally. One way to investigate this question is to compare the donation behavior of state residents to the *federal* party committees. Because the laws limiting donations to national party committees are consistent across all states, if we find that individuals in some states donate more money to the national party committees than individuals in other states, we cannot attribute this difference to campaign finance laws, but rather to the underlying preferences of those populations.

Using Federal Election Commission data from the same election cycle (2011–2012) to make this comparison, we find no support for the notion that the state electorates in these two groups had different preferences in contributing to parties. Table 1.1 compares the per capita giving to state and national parties based on whether the state has limits on what individuals can give to state parties. The results from the table show that states that limit contributions to state parties contribute $1.15 less per eligible voter to those parties than states with no limits (the same result shown in figure 1.3). However, those same states actually give about 28 cents more per capita to the national party organizations than states without limits (though this difference is not statistically significant). Thus, the results in table 1.1 provide us with additional support for the notion that it is the laws that matter in reducing what individuals contribute to the state parties, not some other unaccounted-for difference in the state populations.

TABLE 1.1.   Comparing Per Capita Contributions to Parties (2011–2012 Election Cycle)

Measure	States with Limits on Giving to State Parties	States with No Limits on Giving to State Parties	Difference
Per capita contributions to state parties	$1.11	$2.26	–$1.15*
Per capita contributions to national parties	$1.26	$0.98	$0.28

*$p < .01$, difference of means test.

Many of the outcomes we will focus on in this book have to do with the involvement of parties in state elections and the amount of polarization observed among elected officials as a result. If we are to attribute to the campaign finance laws some responsibility for these effects, then we will be on stronger footing if the states that did and did not enact restrictions on parties are similar on other variables that might account for party activity and polarization. That is, our argument is stronger if these states are as similar as possible aside from the fact that some enacted restrictions on parties and others did not.

Table 1.2 shows how states that limit the ability of parties to either raise or spend money compare to those who have no such limits on four variables related to party activity and polarization. The 1912 vote for Taft is a measure of the state's progressive tradition, as those states voting more heavily for Taft were much less supportive of the progressive movement, which tended to be hostile to political parties. The second measure is David Mayhew's Traditional Party Organization index, which is a measure of the extent to which a state had a history of strong party organizations (Mayhew 1986). The measure ranges from 1 (no history of strong party organizations) to 5 (for states with a history of strong party organizations). The folded Ranney Index is a measure of the amount of competition between the two major parties in each state.[32] And the mass polarization measure is the difference between issue positions of the average Republican in a state and the average Democrat based on data from the Cooperative Congressional Election Study (described in more detail in chapter 2).

Each of the measures in table 1.2 shows only small and statistically indistinguishable differences between states that enacted limits on parties and those that did not. Remarkably, whether a state placed limits on party fundraising or spending appears to be unrelated to the progressive tradition in the state, the extent to which party organizations have a history of being strong and active in the state, the extent to which there is competition between the

TABLE 1.2.   Comparing States With and Without Limits on Political Parties

Measure	States Limiting Party Fundraising/Spending	States Not Limiting Party Fundraising/Spending	Difference
Vote for Taft (1912)	21.73	21.98	−.24
TPO Index	2.20	2.06	.14
Folded Ranney Index	.87	.86	.01
Mass polarization	12.56	12.38	.18

Note: None of the differences in this table approach conventional levels of statistical significance.

parties in the state, and the extent to which the electorate is polarized. This is crucial for the analyses that follow in this book, because it means that we can rule out the above characteristics as potential alternative explanations for why we might find differences between states that have limits on parties, and those that do not.

Plan of This Book

To this point, we have discussed the history and nature of political parties, noting that, contrary to popular belief, parties perform positive functions in practical politics by aggregating disparate interests, reducing fragmentation of interests and policies, moderating extreme advocacy positions, and diminishing partisan polarization. We have drawn a distinction between insider, party-centered politics and outsider, candidate-centered politics, which will serve us well as we develop our argument and analysis in the next chapters. We have stated our contention that, to the extent that campaign finance laws limit the level of funding flowing to and from the organized (insider) parties, they have the unintended consequence of exacerbating (outsider) factional polarization. We have argued that such laws affect not only campaigns, but also governance, by empowering highly ideological positions and helping to elect candidates whose views are distant from those of the majority of voters. By tracing the effects of campaign laws on parties, we have begun to establish our case for enacting campaign finance policies that loosen or even annihilate restrictions on the financial participation of political parties in electoral politics at the state and federal levels.

In the next chapters we expand and develop our argument through an analysis of data relating to campaign financing. Our analysis unfolds in three parts as we look, in essence, at the effect of campaign finance laws on who gives money, who gets it, and how it affects polarization in the legislature.

In chapter 2, we begin by examining the link between donors and campaign finance laws. We first illustrate the unique characteristics, motivations, and behaviors of political contributors in state legislative elections. Not surprisingly, we find that those who contribute are unique compared to most Americans. Our results at the state level confirm prior research on federal elections, showing that political donors tend to be highly polarized and partisan compared to the rest of the population. A key part of our analysis is to examine how donors make choices about where to give money. Using a rich collection of surveys, voter files, and campaign finance data we reveal intriguing patterns of political contributions based specifically on donor ideology. Our analysis will shed light on the direction that both major parties have taken in recent years. In doing so, we will take notice of a surprising asymmetry that emerged from our data. For while both parties have strayed from the center, it appears that the Republican Party has made a particularly hard turn to the right. We will suggest in our analysis some reasons why this phenomenon has occurred.

In chapter 3, we turn our focus to the candidates. Specifically, we look at how campaign finance laws affect which candidates get political funds. Our theory of parties suggests that, compared to interest groups and activist donors, they will choose to invest in moderates and challengers precisely because parties uniquely want to maximize opportunities to win legislative seats. Using data from the National Institute on Money in State Politics we observe the flow of money to different types of candidates across American states with different campaign finance laws. Our system-level approach shows how the source of funds to candidates varies depending on the ideology of the incumbent and her incumbency status.

In chapter 4, we examine the consequences of campaign finance laws on the ideological extremism of officeholders and the polarization of the parties. Our main hypothesis is that money that flows outside party channels tends to promote ideological polarization between partisan officeholders. Conversely, we propose that money that is controlled by the party will tend to moderate politics. We test our hypotheses by comparing the polarization of legislators in states with party-centered versus non-party-centered laws. The last two chapters pull together our findings and address their implications. In chapter 5 we summarize the findings from the analytical chapters and extend the analysis to the impact of antiparty laws on the emergence of independent spending, including spending by PACs, which has drawn concern especially at the federal level. Importantly, we connect independent spending to our broader argument about how laws constraining the political parties tend to increase ideological polarization.

Finally, in chapter 6 we offer policy recommendations for reforming the campaign finance system. Some of our recommendations may be controversial, either because they challenge the conventional wisdom about campaign finance reform, or because they appear to lack broad public support. Still, we feel obliged to suggest potential strategies that might attenuate the kind of polarization that makes governing so challenging in a system of separated powers. At the very least, we hope our study establishes that the prevailing reform strategy of putting limits on party financing has potentially adverse consequences on our political system. These effects should be considered against other goals of reform, such as preventing corruption. A more balanced approach to campaign finance might gain public legitimacy, improve political representation, and promote better governance (Cain 2014).

CHAPTER 2

The Ideological Wellsprings of Campaign Money

There is understandable concern among American voters that political donors use money to bend politicians to their favored policies. Voters may worry that shiftless politicians are easily bought and sold by wealthy contributors. Borrowing loosely from Groucho Marx, they hear politicians saying: "These are my principles. If you don't like them, I have others . . . if you'll contribute generously to my campaign." Even if politicians are not necessarily on the take, the whole business of raising money *looks bad* and plausibly undermines faith in the democratic process. In the past century, reform advocates have commonly responded to these anxieties by limiting the size of contributions that donors are permitted to make to candidates and political parties. In Colorado, for example, the limit is just $200 per election, the lowest in the nation.[1] This reform strategy seems intuitively appealing because its intent is to restrain candidates from courting contributions from big donors, whose gifts may seem unsavory—too much like bribes.

The Effects of Limits on Contributors

We suggest, however, that this approach fails to appreciate the larger system-wide effects of contribution limits on the flow of political money in the electoral system. Indeed, this reform strategy focuses only on the one-to-one relationship between the donor and candidate, while ignoring the fact that such rules incentivize behaviors that ripple out to touch the broader aspects of the political system. In subtle ways, campaign finance rules allocate power among the partisan factions that we have grouped into the competing categories of pragmatists and purists.

In our view, rules that excessively constrain political parties enhance the influence of the most ideological factions of the party coalition—the "purist" outsiders whose primary focus is to push policies in government. The purists gain leverage because contribution limits on political parties encourage politicians, blocked from gaining financial support from parties, to turn more intensively to alternative sources of support. And these alternative sources tend to be more extreme in outlook than are most Americans. Among such sources are the narrow issue groups that have the means and motive to run independent campaigns, as well as the highly ideological donors who readily give money to politicians who espouse their views. Others have made a similar argument with respect to constraints on political action committees (PACs), which are largely nonideological, pragmatic business interests (Barber 2013).

The underlying point is that constraints on pragmatist groups, such as political parties and traditional PACs, make politicians more reliant on the purist factions. This pro-purist slant appears benign when viewed through the traditional lens employed by political reformers. Purist ideological groups do not appear to be guilty of corrupting the political system in the conventional sense, and their influence does not fit the corruption narrative of old-fashioned party machines and rent-seeking special interests. Nonetheless, highly constrained campaign finance rules shift the resource terrain in favor of the most ideological elements of the polity and away from materially oriented interests. To some, that is good news. Better that government decisions be motivated by ideals than by material incentives. On the other hand, as we pointed out in the previous chapter, governing in a separated system of powers often requires the lubricant of impure material interests to forge deals and bipartisan compromises.

A Look at Individual Donors

But we are getting ahead of ourselves. Our purpose in this chapter is to focus on the behavior of *individual donors* who make up the vast bulk of contributions to candidates. According to data from the National Institute on Money in Politics, candidates in state legislatures receive nearly half of their campaign money *directly* from individuals. We will examine the ideological leanings of these donors; whom they choose to give money to; and how campaign finance laws affect their decisions.

This chapter will focus on three questions. First we will look at who tends to contribute money in politics. We will look at donors' ideological leanings and intensity, focusing not only on big donors but also on so-called "small donors." We expect larger donors to be much more ideological than the typical American voter, a finding that has been shown to be true in federal elections (Bafumi and Herron 2010; Francia et al. 2003). Here we ask whether the same kinds of activist donors who operate nationally are also heavily engaged in legislative elections in the American states. We will then be in a position to consider whether ideological extremism characterizes smaller donors as well as larger ones.

Second, we examine to whom these ideological donors give their money. Our hypothesis is that donors tend to prefer giving directly to candidates who think like them instead of giving to political parties, which they may see as too *moderate*. If this is proven, the implication is that candidates reap contributions to the degree that they are highly ideological (Ensley 2009; Moon 2004). While this kind of donor–candidate relationship does not constitute traditional corruption, it can distort the electoral system by inducing politicians to rely heavily for campaign money on a subset of Americans with relatively extreme views. In this way, resource dependency constitutes an electoral bias.

Finally, we address the question of whether campaign finance laws can alter decisions about where donors will give their money. The purpose is to see whether changing the laws might diminish the direct flow of money from ideological donors to candidates. We will consider whether laws favoring contributions to parties instead of candidates would encourage all donors—even the most ideological donors—to contribute money to the political parties.

Together these questions address the feasibility of introducing an alternative approach to regulating the campaign finance system based on the concern that the political parties have grown too far apart ideologically. Paradoxically, we are exploring whether party committees should play a bigger role in mediating the transfer of funds to candidates as a way to make "the party" (i.e., the broader coalition) programmatically weaker and less rigid. As we argued in the previous chapter, party committees tend to be broad-based entities that coordinate and build consensus around the preferences of various partisan factions. We have noted that party committees tend to moderate extreme views and follow pragmatic principles and practices, including compromise, geared to ensuring electoral success. This means they are likely to use resources in the most efficient manner possible, supporting candidates in close races regardless of their ideology (Herrnson 1989; Kolodny 1998).

A party-centered campaign finance system would privilege the pragmatist insiders by allowing large or unlimited donations to parties while limiting individual donations to candidates. In this way more donors—even ideological donors—might feel compelled to give money to the party, which in turn would choose where to allocate campaign funds. In these circumstances, moderate candidates might do better under a party-centered system.

The Hydraulics of the Campaign Finance System

We begin our assessment of campaign finance dynamics by examining the incentives of individual donors. We reason that, in a world without any contribution limits, the more ideological donors would prefer to give money directly to favored candidates rather than making contributions through political parties or interest groups. A free market in contributions would allow them to pick and choose favorites, and subsequently reap the gratitude of candidates. In a system in which limits on giving to candidates were imposed, however, we contend that donors would turn to parties and interest groups as alternative options for contributing.

The thinking behind imposing contribution limits through a candidate-centered framework necessarily entails making efforts to prevent donors from finding a "back door" to finance candidates. For this reason, many states impose relatively low contribution limits on political parties because of the unique relationship that parties have with candidates. The concern is that without limits the party might serve as a conduit to funnel money from donors to candidates who face limited contributions. Thus, campaign finance systems frequently contain anticircumvention statutes, including rules against earmarking contributions to the parties for particular candidates. In states with laws of this type, the political parties tend to become highly constrained under a candidate-centered framework for regulating money in politics.

The candidate-centered system of campaign finance rules is built on at least two assumptions that, to our knowledge, appear to lack empirical support. The first assumption is that it is possible through regulatory restrictions to prevent wealthy citizens from financing elections. In any free society this would be a challenging goal, but in the United States it is particularly problematic. The First Amendment of the U.S. Constitution places powerful constraints on the ability of the government to prevent people from spending money on politics. Even when the Supreme Court upholds rules that limit the size of contributions, they do this on the very narrow grounds that government has a compelling interest in thwarting quid pro quo corruption (see *Buckley v. Valeo*, 424 U.S. 1 (1976)). The Supreme Court has ruled, however, that the government cannot intervene with restrictions on independent political *spending* that attempt to level the playing field.[2]

Recent Supreme Court decisions have made it even easier for wealthy donors to make unlimited contributions to a variety of "independent" political committees that attempt to elect candidates.[3] Based on the anticorruption logic of *Buckley*, the quid pro quo between donor and candidate is attenuated significantly when candidates do not receive direct contributions or coordinate with groups supported by donors. For this reason, "super PACs" emerged in 2012 as a venue for very wealthy donors. Super PACs can spend unlimited amounts by independently supporting favored candidates. In short, the rich have ready alternatives when they face constraints on contributing money to candidates or party committees. This was true even before *Citizens United,* since donors could always give to a variety of PACs that supported their causes (not to mention giving money to think tanks and lobbyists that provide influential information to officeholders). In short, wealthy ideological donors have a multitude of choices, and their passion for politics will encourage them to figure out ways to help favored politicians with their money.

A second questionable assumption is that limiting contributions will democratize the pool of people who contribute money to politicians. The main argument is that limits should compel politicians to broaden fundraising efforts to include donors who are less wealthy than traditional donors (Migally and Liss 2010). On the face of it, this dynamic seems unlikely because making a donation to a candidate is a rare form of political participation that emerges from having discretionary income and a very strong interest in politics (Verba, Schlozman, and Brady 1995). In fact, few Americans actually contribute money. One study estimates that less than 10 percent of the population donate money to a political campaign (Verba, Schlozman, and Brady 1995). Data gathered by the Federal Election Commission indicate that just .06 percent of Americans give $200 or more in federal elections, and that these donors provide at least 65 percent of the disclosed contributions to candidates, parties, and PACs.[4]

In reality, contribution limits make politicians spend additional time raising money from more of the same kinds of ideological donors. To be sure, the Internet provides greater opportunities for politicians to solicit donations from people with modest incomes. But as we show in this chapter, this expanded pool of donors remains remarkably dissimilar to most Americans in terms of wealth, ideology, and other demographic characteristics.

Given such faulty and unsubstantiated assumptions about the impact of contribution limits, we are skeptical that a candidate-centered framework that relies on a strategy of limiting contributions will change the representational bias of the campaign finance system. For this reason, we explore a system-level approach, which considers the hydraulics of regulatory rules. It assumes that donors will find alternative ways to help support favored politicians, and that candidates too will intensify efforts to expand their fundraising from the same pool of ideological donors. Thus, our analysis focuses on the *flow of money* into campaigns rather than the total amount that comes from particular types of donors.

We hypothesize that the flow of money affects the ideological bias of the political system, even when the money comes from the same unrepresentative pool of donors. The significance of contribution rules is not so much that they restrain the wealthy from giving money, but that such rules generate incentives for donors to channel money to committees they would otherwise not choose. Where that money ends up is vitally important for both elections and governing.

The Systemic Impact of Campaign Finance Laws

We start with the proposition that individual donors seek to finance candidates who embrace their highly ideological positions. Research shows that individual donors are extreme, and that they are not typically concerned with a strategic assessment of a candidate's proximity to the views of the median voter of the district (Ensley 2009; Stone and Simas 2010). These ideologically driven donors are conceivably contributing as a consumption activity rather than a strategic investment (Barber 2013; Snyder 1990). Some people enjoy politics and, if they are sufficiently wealthy, it might please them to express support through donations for particular candidates and ideals that appeal to them. Regardless of the underlying motive, we believe that many individual donors have few inhibitions about supporting candidates who are far from the mainstream of voters in the district. The overall effect of their contributions is to pull the party in their extreme direction. Even if their favored candidate loses, they potentially help to advance a policy agenda or mobilize extreme factions of the party for future contests. And by promoting an extremist challenger in primaries, they may compel the relatively moderate incumbent politician to adopt more extremist positions (Boatright 2013).

To demonstrate our theory about the system-level impact of campaign finance laws, we focus in this chapter on the motivations and behaviors of political donors. First, we identify *who contributes money* in the political system, demonstrating that contributors tend to be ideological extremists. Next, we show *to whom these ideological donors tend to contribute money,* hypothesizing that, without constraints of rules, extremist donors tend to prefer giving to candidates and groups rather than to political parties. We then assess *whether laws might affect who contributes money* in the political system, suspecting that even strict regulatory laws do little to change the profile of political contributors. The last part of our analysis focuses on our finding that *laws can indeed affect the flow of money into politics.* It should be quite possible to channel money to broad-based political parties by constraining the amount that contributors can give directly to candidates and allowing parties greater freedom in raising money. The impact, of course, would be to push ideological donors into the political parties where they are less likely to help elect the kind of ideologically polarizing politicians they prefer (we examine this dynamic further in chapter 3).

Sources of Evidence

To test our hypotheses, we draw on two primary sources of data that have not previously been used to study political donors in the United States. These data sources provide us with unique and important leverage for studying donors because they are much larger and richer than the much more limited surveys that have been used to study donors in the past.

The first data source is a very large, nationally representative survey of American adults called the Cooperative Congressional Election Study (CCES). The CCES is a survey venture involving more than 50 universities that has been conducted every year since 2006. The CCES asks respondents a variety of questions about themselves, about their views on political issues, and their evaluations of candidates and politicians. Most important for our purposes, the CCES also asks each respondent if he or she has donated to a candidate, campaign, or political organization during the previous year. In 2010, 15,025 of the 46,684 respondents to the CCES indicated that they had made at least one political donation during the previous year. While this may seem like a large number of political donors, it is important to keep in mind that this would include anyone who made any kind of political donation at any level of politics. Indeed, most of these donors are what we would think of as "small donors." Half of those who identified themselves as donors reported giving a total of just $100 or less during the previous year and three in four gave $300 or less. Only 1,187 of the self-identified donors reported giving $1,000 or more to politics during the previous year; this amounts to just 2.5 percent of the CCES sample.

The CCES, therefore, provides us with a rich source of survey data that allows us to compare donors to nondonors and small donors to large donors. Of course, even in a very large survey such as this one, the total number of "large donors" is limited. Furthermore, the nature of the CCES data makes it impossible for us to determine which candidates, parties, or groups the donors contributed to. Fortunately, we are able to consult a second source of data that allows us to address these issues.

Catalist is one of the nation's premier voter file firms. The company maintains a database of nearly every American adult, including voter registration and turnout data as well as appended demographic and marketing information. The company primarily sells access to its database to political campaigns and groups, but it has also recently allowed academic teams to purchase access. The database is ideal for our purposes for two reasons. First, because the database includes a record for nearly every American adult, it provides us with the ability to gain precise information on even very small groups (such as large donors) who would otherwise be too small to study with traditional survey data. Second, Catalist allows users to match their own lists to its database in order to identify subgroups of interest. This means that we can match publicly available lists of political donors to the database so that we can separate donors from nondonors. We did this to the data from the Federal Election Commission to identify individuals who contributed to congressional campaigns, and we did the same to lists from the National Institute on Money in State Politics to identify donors to state legislative campaigns and state parties. Our use of these combined resources yielded interesting results.

Who Gives Money?

As mentioned above, contributing to political committees constitutes a relatively rare form of political participation in the United States, and political contributors are atypical of the broader electorate. The most salient characteristic of donors is their relative affluence. Additionally, research shows that active campaign donors in congressional elections tend to hold ideologically extreme views (Bafumi and Herron 2010; Francia et al. 2003), or at the very least have worldviews different from those of other citizens (Bramlett, Gimpel, and Lee 2010). In these circumstances, it literally pays for candidates to tout their extreme views. Studies show that ideological candidates

TABLE 2.1.   Campaign Donors versus American Adults

Characteristic	Congressional Donors	State Donors	American Adults
Average age	61	60	49
% Men	67%	61%	45%
% Married	64%	66%	41%
% with children	33%	32%	28%
% White	91%	90%	73%
% Homeowners	67%	68%	45%
Average ideology	47	45	46
Median wealth	300k to 1 mil	300k to 1mil	100k to 300k
Median income	above 100k	above 100k	60k to 100k

Note: Based on the authors' analysis of data obtained from Catalist. Congressional and state donors are those who donated to campaigns in 2010 in an amount that required public disclosure.

in congressional elections are more successful at raising money from constituencies outside the district (Gimpel, Lee, and Pearson-Merkowitz 2008; Johnson 2010); given this finding, it is natural for candidates to position themselves ideologically to attract additional donations (Ensley 2009; Moon 2004; Stone and Simas 2010).

Our research on political donors in state legislative elections confirms the participatory bias in congressional elections that has been found by others. Quite clearly, *citizens who make political contributions are unrepresentative of the American electorate.* Table 2.1 uses the Catalist database described above to compare the characteristics of donors to congressional campaigns, donors to state legislative campaigns, and all American adults. Compared to the general population of American adults, donors are disproportionately more old, male, white, and wealthy. State-level and congressional donors are very similar. Both groups of donors tend to be much older than most Americans (with an average age around 60, compared to 49 for most Americans). They are also overwhelmingly white (around 90 percent versus 73 percent), predominantly male (61 percent or more versus 45 percent), and married (64 percent or more versus 41 percent). Our data are limited with respect to reporting wealth, but based on the broad wealth categories used by Catalist, we find that donors have a median range of household wealth somewhere between $300,000 to $1 million compared to most American adults, whose median household wealth ranges from $100,000 to $300,000.

On one critical dimension—average ideology—donors do not appear to diverge from other voters. Catalist uses demographic, political, and marketing data to generate a prediction on how conservative or liberal each individual is. The ideology predictions take on values ranging from 0 (most conservative) to 100 (most liberal). Table 2.1 shows the average ideology for each group and, notably, the average donor and average voter have roughly the same ideology score. Given that these two subpopulations differ on so many other characteristics, this finding might seem reassuring from the perspective of democratic theory because ideology reflects underlying policy preferences. Despite differences in race, age, gender, and wealth, these data suggest that policy outcomes might not be biased since donors share the same ideological preferences as the rest of the population. However, this statistical average obscures at least one large difference across these subpopulations. *Donors tend to be more extremist than the rest of the American electorate.*

Figure 2.1 reveals this dynamic by showing how voters and donors are arrayed across Catalist's ideological scale. The first panel shows the distribution of registered voters, who are largely centered around the midpoint of the scale. This distribution provides some support for the argument that most Americans are not polarized—at least when one measures ideology in this way (Fiorina, Abrams, and Pope 2005). The second panel in figure 2.1 shows the ideological distribution among individuals who donated to state legislative campaigns in 2010, while the third panel shows the distribution of donors to congressional campaigns in that same year. Note that these two distributions take on a much different shape from the distribution of registered voters. In both cases, the distribution is bimodal, demonstrating significant polarization. One group of donors is centered on the conservative end of the scale while a second group of donors is centered on the liberal side. These distributions show clearly that even though the average ideology among each of these groups is nearly equal, the donors tend to be much more ideologically extreme than registered voters. In this way, the figure shows in stark terms why candidates from either party might be unlikely to converge to the median voter because of a counterforce in the electoral process. The vast majority of the campaign financing comes from citizens whose views are at the ideological extremes of the electorate.

As noted above, Catalist relies on a model to produce its ideology scores; it does not know precisely the ideological leanings of each individual. Furthermore, we were able to match only donors who gave enough money to campaigns in 2010 to trigger the requirement that they disclose their names and addresses. Thus, in many cases, these figures exclude "small donors." Perhaps if we had a more precise measure of ideology or if we were able to include small donors in our analysis, we might not have found such dramatic differences.

To address this possibility we turn to CCES data, which allows us to identify all self-reported political donors, big and small, and their positions

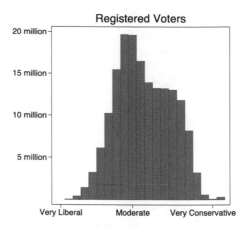

Registered Voters

20 million

15 million

10 million

5 million

Very Liberal　　Moderate　　Very Conservative

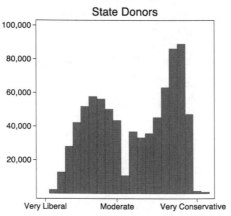

State Donors

100,000

80,000

60,000

40,000

20,000

Very Liberal　　Moderate　　Very Conservative

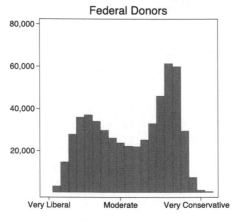

Federal Donors

80,000

60,000

40,000

20,000

Very Liberal　　Moderate　　Very Conservative

Figure 2.1. Ideology of Registered Voters, State Donors, Federal Donors. (*Note:* Data from authors' analysis of 2010 donors matched to Catalist database.)

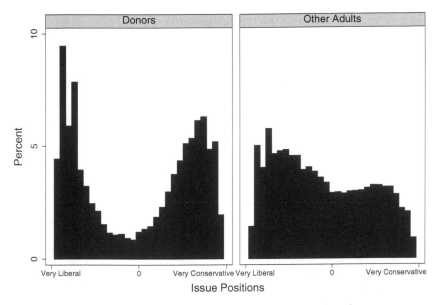

Figure 2.2. Issue Positions of Donors and Other Adults. (*Note:* Data from authors' analysis of 2010 CCES data. Donors are defined as individuals reporting a contribution to a political candidate or group. Other adults are individuals in the sample who were not donors.)

on 15 policy issues. For each individual in the CCES survey, we created a score based on how many liberal or conservative positions the respondent took on each of the 15 issue questions. If a respondent gave a liberal response on each of the 15 issues, he was coded as a –15, and if she took a conservative position each time, she was coded as a +15. Individuals coded at 0 took an equal number of liberal and conservative positions on the 15 issues. Figure 2.2 compares how donors and nondonors were distributed across this issue scale. The findings are much like those we found in figure 2.1. Donors are highly polarized: very few fall near the center of the scale and most are distributed near the extremes. Nondonor adults, on the other hand, are distributed more evenly across the issue scale. Thus, the CCES data confirm that all donors are unrepresentative in their high degree of polarization compared to nondonor adults.

To Whom Do Donors Give?

Next, we turn to the choices that donors make with their money. Our theory about party factions suggests that purists would rather give money directly to candidates (presumably those who share their views) than to political parties, which include the moderating elements of a broad coalition. We would expect that these donors, with their strong policy preferences, would be less strategic with their support, not always giving to candidates with the greatest odds of winning. In short, for purists, principles should trump practical considerations when choosing to give money. A clear example of this is the wealthy casino magnate Sheldon Adelson. Adelson gave millions to a super PAC to promote Newt Gingrich in the 2012 Republican presidential primaries even though most polls showed Gingrich was a long shot to win the nomination. Instead of focusing on winning, Adelson undoubtedly wanted to advertise his strong preference for policies that limited government regulations and supported Israel. Gingrich vigorously promoted these positions in his campaign.

Now consider contributors to political parties. In contrast to donors who give directly to candidates, we expect party donors to reflect more moderate ideologies. In theory, their underlying motives are to win elections because they are driven by partisan loyalty as much as ideology (although the two are increasingly intertwined). Party donors are strategic in the electoral sense. They give to the party because they believe party-based resources will advance the collective position of party candidates. By giving to the party, they are also expressing a willingness to defer to party leaders on where funds are most effectively invested.

To explore these hypothetical distinctions, we used the Catalist measure of ideology to compare the ideological distributions of donors to state legislative *candidates*, on the one hand, with those of donors who give to state *parties*. Rather unexpectedly, we found that these two types of donors did not appear to differ ideologically. Figure 2.3 shows a strong bimodalism in ideological scores for both types of donors. However, it is worth noting again that the liberal donors exhibit greater moderation compared to the conservative donors. The right side of the charts shows a significant peak for those who are considered "very conservative."

Of course, the first panel of figure 2.3 simply shows the number of donors at each point along the ideological scale; it does not reveal how much money each of these donors is contributing. Because candidates think first and foremost in terms of dollars, rather than in terms of numbers of donors, they will undoubtedly be most affected by where most of their money comes from. To portray this information, the second panel in figure 2.3 shows the distribution of total dollars to candidates and parties based on the ideology of the donors giving that money. For the most part, these distributions are similar to those in the first panel (although note the different scales on the

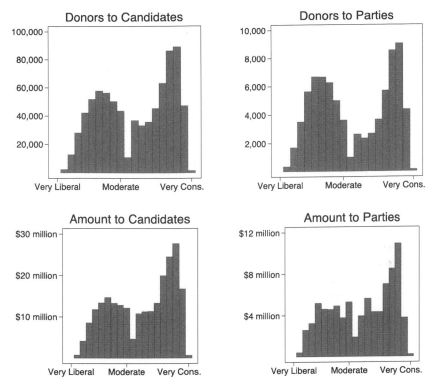

Figure 2.3. Donor Ideology Based on Giving to Candidates versus Parties. (*Note:* Data from authors' analysis of 2010 state legislative and state party donors matched to Catalist database.)

y-axis showing that candidates receive much more money than parties from individual donors across the ideological spectrum). This indicates, again, that if candidates or parties wish to chase money, they must stray from the middle of the ideological spectrum to do so.

The findings against our expectation that party donors and candidate donors would differ significantly force us to reconsider our understanding of donor motivations. Additional analysis suggests why distinctions between the two kinds of donors appear initially to be weak or nonexistent. Many donors tend to give to *both* candidates and parties. According to our CCES data, one-fourth of all donors reported donating to both a party and a candidate. This considerable overlap in candidate and party donors means that differences are likely to be muted. A more fine-grained analysis, however, shows that sharp distinctions can be observed at the extremes of the

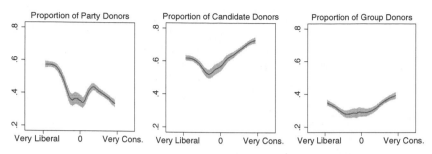

Figure 2.4. Proportion of Donors Who Give to Parties, Candidates, or Groups, Based on Their Ideology. (*Note:* Data from authors' analysis of 2010 CCES data. *X*-axis indicates respondents' position on the issue scale and *y*-axis is the proportion of donors giving to a particular target.)

ideological scale if we look at how donors allocate their contributions across different recipients.

Figure 2.4 uses the CCES data to show where donors choose to target their donations based on their own ideological dispositions. The figure uses our issue scale on the *x*-axis and traces the proportion of individuals at each point on the scale who donate to parties, candidates, and other political groups. Overall, donors typically give money to candidates rather than to parties. But the figure shows that the proportion of donors making contributions to different recipients changes depending on the ideology of the donor. Ideology clearly matters in determining where to send money, and does so in ways that are asymmetrical across the liberal-conservative spectrum. On the liberal side, we observe that, compared to moderately liberal donors, a high proportion of very liberal donors choose to contribute to the party. Then, as we continue to move to the center-right of the ideological scale, the propensity of giving to the parties increases at first, and then declines among the most conservative donors. Overall, the most liberal donors tend to contribute to the party more frequently than any other group, while the most conservative donors give to the party less than moderate conservatives. We will discuss the potential implications of this dynamic momentarily.

The second panel in figure 2.4 generally shows that the observed pattern for giving to candidates matches the pattern we expected. A high proportion of ideological donors on either end of the issue scale give to candidates, which suggests to us that extremist donors like to support candidates who reflect their ideologies (we examine this relationship in the next chapter). The association is particularly pronounced on the right sides of the ideological spectrum among conservatives. Once again, there appears to be an asymmetrical dynamic among liberal and conservative donors.

The third panel shows the proportion of donors making contributions to interest groups at each point on the ideological spectrum. Interest groups are often focused on a single issue or advocate a particular ideological stance. For this reason, we expect extremists on either side to be more likely to give to interest groups. This is exactly what we observe. As donors become more ideologically extreme, they tend to prefer giving directly to candidates and groups that reflect their ideological preferences.

A Fearful Asymmetry?

Without getting too far ahead of our analysis, we suggest that the asymmetries we observe in figure 2.4 might explain some of the polarizing dynamics of the contemporary party system, with the Republican Party in the U.S. Congress moving much further to the right over the past decade than the Democratic Party moved to the left (McCarty, Poole, and Rosenthal 2006). Our intuition is that very conservative donors are pulling the Republican Party further to the right by focusing their largesse on like-minded candidates and groups, while ignoring the party organization, which tends to invest in more moderate candidates. We examine this dynamic in the subsequent chapter. At this point in the analysis, however, we are focused on accounting for the ideological asymmetries that we have observed in patterns of giving to candidates versus parties.

To do this, we will bring ideological perceptions into the analysis. Specifically, we will seek to understand how decisions about political contributions are affected by donor perceptions of where political parties—as distinct from candidates—stand on matters related to ideology. The CCES asks respondents to indicate where they think each political party is located on a 7-point ideological scale; respondents are also asked to place the congressional candidates running in their districts on that same scale. Figure 2.5 shows where Democratic and Republican donors place their parties and their congressional candidates as a function of their own ideology. We find that *donor perceptions of the party and candidates vary depending on their own ideology.* Interestingly, Democratic and Republican donor behaviors are not symmetric. Democratic donors largely view the party (the broken line) and their own candidates (the solid line) as indistinguishable in terms of their ideologies. This can help to explain why the most liberal Democratic donors are just as willing to donate to the party as they are to a candidate—they see each as reflecting relatively similar views.

Notably, the dynamic is entirely different for Republican partisans. GOP donors see the party and candidates quite differently, depending on their ideological extremism. The extremist donors—who provide most of the political contributions—tend to see the party as much more moderate than candidates, who are viewed as more conservative (and thus closer to their own views). Republican moderates, on the other hand, tend to see both the party and its candidates as "very conservative." This finding may account for why highly conservative GOP donors give a greater proportion of their money to candidates compared to moderate GOP donors (as shown in figure 2.4). Conservative Republicans may not trust the party organization to accurately represent their views when choosing which candidates to support.

Overall, the findings in figures 2.4 and 2.5 paint a relatively simple view of donor behavior. Donors appear to give to entities that are more likely to reflect their political viewpoints. On the left, candidates and parties are seen as equally likely to do this, and thus liberal donors give to both at roughly equal rates. Donors on the right, however, perceive large differences between the Republican Party and Republican candidates for Congress, with the latter coming much closer to their viewpoints than the former. Thus, it is not surprising to find that conservative donors prefer to send their donations directly to candidates by a margin of almost 3 to 1.

The patterns we illustrate might help to explain some of the dynamics in the Republican Party over the past decade. While GOP moderates contribute to partisan causes, the vast majority of campaign money comes from more conservative elements. And among the most conservative donors there is a strong preference for giving to candidates, because highly conservative donors do not think the party is sufficiently conservative. Thus, conservative donors target funds to conservative candidates, who consequently pull party officeholders further to the right. In an exchange among prominent activists at *Redstate.com*, the conservative website, most commentators urged activists to give directly to candidates over the party committees if they wanted to steer the Republican Party in their direction. One commentator summed up the general sentiment this way:

> It's up to the individual conservative. The [party] money is used to support the Republican brand, not per se conservatism, so it's a nice spot to put your donations if you want to see your money go toward defeating Dems. If you want to donate to a candidate who agrees with your conservatism, give to the candidate.[5]

On the Democratic side, there appears to be full-throated support for party committees even among the most liberal elements in the party. The proportion of "very liberal donors" giving to the party and to candidates is

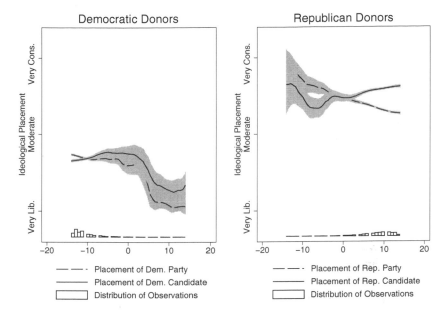

Figure 2.5. Donor Perceptions of Party and Candidates, Based on Donor Ideological Self-Placement. (*Note:* Data from authors' analysis of 2010 CCES data. X-axis is respondent's placement on the issue scale, *y*-axis is respondent's placement of party and candidate on the 7-point ideological scale. Democratic donors are defined as donors who identify as Democrats and Republican donors are defined similarly. The shaded areas represent 95% confidence intervals.)

the same. Bear in mind that these very liberal donors view both the parties and candidates as "moderate." Thus, there is no apparent difference in their perception, which might have pushed them toward candidates rather than party committees (which is the dynamic in the Republican Party). To be sure, these very liberal donors give to kindred-minded interest groups, much as very conservative donors do. And these interest groups, through *their* contributions and electioneering, work to pull the party toward the extremes.

How Laws Affect Who Gives Money

In this section, we begin exploring whether campaign finance laws have consequences for the behavior of donors. In this first cut, we simply look at whether laws affect the demographics of giving (i.e., who gives money and who does not). Our claim is that we do not expect laws to make a significant difference in shaping the demographic profile of donors. In this we challenge a common assumption of conventional political reformers that contribution limits stimulate participation at the "grassroots." Given the motives of donors, the plethora of choices they have, and the very limited potential pool of citizens who might contribute money in politics, we do not think limits will reduce participatory bias in the system by expanding the demographic variance of donors. An analysis of donors in states with very different laws confirms our expectations.

Table 2.2 compares the demographics of donors across different extremes of campaign finance systems in the American states. We selected two large states in which donors may give unlimited sums to candidates and parties (Texas and Virginia), and two large states in which there are low contribution limits on both candidates and parties (Massachusetts and Maryland). For each of these states, we collected and analyzed the same data on donor characteristics that we used in table 2.1. Our analysis suggests that, regardless of whether a state has low limits on contributions or no limits, donors tend to be quite unrepresentative of the state's population.

These findings about the impact of contribution limits (or lack thereof) have important implications for policies designed to democratize political donations. Contribution limits do not necessarily broaden grassroots participation in making donations. Instead, the policy increases the number of citizens giving money, but it does not necessarily expand the socioeconomic base of donors. From our perspective, increasing the pool of donors seems like good public policy because it plausibly renders candidates less reliant on a small group of very wealthy donors to pay for campaigns. That said, even in states where contributions are unlimited, candidates are unlikely to rely on a handful of wealthy contributors. Successful candidates are strategic, and raising money from many donors is a signal of candidate quality. These signals matter among influential elites who eventually choose to endorse and work on behalf of candidates (beyond fundraising). Candidates likely benefit from the handshaking and conversations with acquaintances of donors who hold house parties for the candidate. Spending time with more people at campaign fundraisers boosts their positive name recognition among opinion makers in the district through social networking.

How Laws Affect to Whom Donors Give Money

If laws do not necessarily change *who* gives money, it remains plausible that they can change patterns of *where* donors send their donations. For

TABLE 2.2. Characteristics of Donors in States with Low Contribution Limits versus No Limits

Texas (No limits)

Characteristic	Congressional Donors	State Donors	Texas Adults
Average age	59	61	48
% Men	66%	59%	45%
% Married	67%	62%	40%
% with children	35%	30%	30%
% White	86%	88%	60%
% Homeowners	72%	68%	50%
Average ideology	36	32	44
Median wealth	300k to 1 mil	300k to 1mil	100k to 300k
Median income	above 100k	above 100k	60k to 100k

Massachusetts (Limits)

Characteristic	Congressional Donors	State Donors	Mass. Adults
Average age	58	59	49
% Men	65%	60%	45%
% Married	69%	70%	43%
% with children	38%	37%	29%
% White	94%	94%	79%
% Homeowners	71%	73%	48%
Average ideology	58	56	54
Median wealth	300k to 1 mil	300k to 1mil	100k to 300k
Median income	above 100k	above 100k	60k to 100k

Virginia (No limits)

Characteristic	Congressional Donors	State Donors	Virginia Adults
Average age	57	53	48
% Men	65%	62%	46%
% Married	67%	57%	41%
% with children	37%	32%	29%
% White	89%	82%	70%
% Homeowners	73%	64%	45%
Average ideology	46	49	45
Median wealth	300k to 1 mil	300k to 1mil	100k to 300k
Median income	above 100k	above 100k	60k to 100k

Maryland (Limits)

Characteristic	Congressional Donors	State Donors	Maryland Adults
Average age	59	61	48
% Men	63%	59%	44%
% Married	67%	65%	38%
% with children	39%	35%	30%
% White	83%	81%	59%
% Homeowners	78%	79%	53%
Average ideology	57	49	50
Median wealth	300k to 1 mil	300k to 1mil	100k to 300k
Median income	above 100k	above 100k	60k to 100k

Note: Values based on estimates from Catalist after matching donors to database.

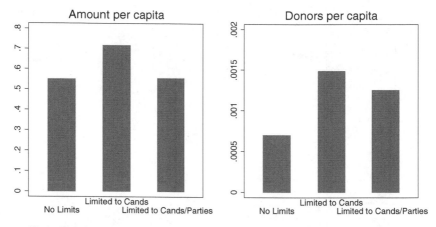

Figure 2.6. Contributions to Parties Based on State Contribution Laws (2010). (*Note:* Data from authors' analysis of data from the National Institute on Money in State Politics. Left panel shows the amount of money contributed to state political parties per capita and right panel shows the number of donors giving to state political parties per capita. In 2010, 14 states had no limits, 13 had limits on giving to candidates, and 23 had limits on giving to candidates and parties.)

our purposes, we are interested in knowing whether laws might encourage donors to give to parties instead of candidates. The hydraulic theory of campaign finance reform suggests this is so. While contributions to the party are not perfect substitutes for donations to candidates, we expect many donors to contribute more substantially to the parties when they are constrained in giving money to candidates. This is precisely what we find. States with party-centered laws alter donation patterns and boost party finances.

The first panel in figure 2.6 shows the amount per capita donated to parties in 2010 under different campaign finance systems—those where there are no limits on giving to candidates or parties (14 states); those where there are only limits on giving to candidates (13 states); and those with limits on donations to both candidates and parties (23 states). The figure shows that in states where there are limits on contributions to candidates and no limits on contributions to the parties, the amount of money going to the party increases. In other words, contributions that might go to the candidates get channeled to the party. When both parties and candidates face limits, the party gets no more per capita than if there were no limits at all on candidates or parties. This analysis suggests that the party needs a relative advantage in rules for money to flow to the party rather than to candidates.

The panel on the right side of figure 2.6 also shows that the number of donors to parties per capita increases when limits are imposed on candidates. The mechanism is straightforward. The threshold of a contribution to a candidate may be well below what donors desire to contribute. Some may choose to give additional amounts to the party. Under a regime with no limits on candidates or parties, the parties do not get many donors per capita because donors can give exclusively to candidates if they want (note, however, that even with fewer donors per capita, the parties end up with the same amount per capita as in the situation with limits on both parties and candidates). The optimal situation for parties, of course, is to have no limits on contributions to the parties but limits on contributions to candidates. This situation maximizes the amount per capita that is given to parties and the number of party donors who give.

This analysis suggests that rules can channel additional money to the party. But it is just as important to know whether it is the ideologically polarized donors who are pushed toward donating to parties when states put limits on donations to candidates. In other words, it is important to know if these rules attract highly ideological donors who might otherwise donate directly to candidates. If party-centered laws do indeed steer ideological donors to the party, in theory this would temper the ability of such donors to support ideologically extreme candidates (as in a candidate-centered system).

To see whether the imposition of limits on donations to candidates does, in fact, push ideologues into giving to the party, figure 2.7 uses our data from Catalist to show the amount of polarization among donors to the party organization in states with and without limits on contributions to candidates. Polarization is measured as the interquartile range in ideology among donors. A higher interquartile range indicates more polarization and a lower interquartile range indicates lower levels of polarization. To control for overall polarization among voters in the state, we separate our analysis into states that have low, medium, and high polarization in the population.

We find that party-centered laws tend to increase polarization among donors to the party organization. In low-polarization states, the configuration of laws does not appear to have any effect on party donor polarization simply because there is not much polarization in the state. When there is medium polarization in the state and when there are no limits on candidate donations, the effect is to make party donors less polarized precisely because the most ideological money can go directly to the candidates. In high-polarization states, we observe the most significant changes in polarization associated with changes in the law. Without limits on candidate giving, the most ideological donors focus their donations on the candidates (so party

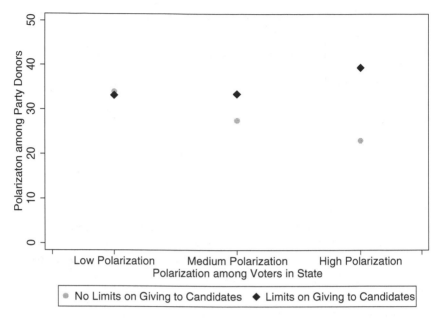

Figure 2.7. Limits on Candidate Donations and Polarization among Party Donors (2010). (*Note:* Authors' analysis of data from Catalist. Y-axis is the interquartile range in ideology among donors to state political parties. X-axis divides states into thirds based on levels of polarization among the general public in those states.)

donors are not polarized). However, when candidate donations are limited, many ideological donors appear compelled to give to the party. Thus, the overall group of donors to the party appears more polarized because there are more ideological donors among them.

In the next chapter, we will examine our hypothesis that parties will not necessarily feel beholden to ideological donors in choosing where to invest the money they receive from them. Our prediction has been that parties will take this "ideological" money and use it strategically to support candidates in closely contested races, where candidates tend to be moderates. In this way, we expect that the parties will have a potentially "cleansing" effect on the polarization that might have resulted from highly ideological money going directly to highly ideological candidates.

Summary of Findings

In this chapter we showed that individual donors in state elections are unrepresentative of the broader electorate. Specifically, we demonstrated that donors are highly polarized ideologically compared to other Americans. We also illustrated that the most ideological donors have a strong propensity to contribute to candidates directly rather than to the political parties. This dynamic is abetted by the candidate-centered campaign finance system that exists in most American states. The inclination to give to candidates over parties is especially true of conservative donors.

Upon further analysis we showed that this pattern of giving was associated with donor perceptions of the political parties. Conservatives viewed the party as moderate compared to candidates. Liberals, in contrast, viewed both the party and its candidates as relatively moderate. These perceptions may explain the asymmetric pattern of political giving across the ideological spectrum. Liberals, not seeing many differences between the party and candidates, are as likely to give to one as to the other. Conservatives, meanwhile, appear to prefer focusing contributions on candidates who reflect their views rather than on the more moderate party. This partisan asymmetry in donor perceptions might be important in explaining why the Republican Party has shifted to the right more dramatically than the Democratic Party has moved to the left. Our theory suggests that Republican Party organizations have not been mediating the flow of money to candidates from ideological sources as much as the Democratic Party.

Given these dynamics, we believe that campaign finance laws have an important impact on money in politics—but not necessarily in the way that most observers think. In contrast to the conventional wisdom, we show that contribution limits do little to alter the basic demographic profile of donors, who are a rarefied group even among small donors. Instead, limits alter the flow of money to candidates, parties, and groups. With ideological donors strongly desirous of financing ideological candidates, we hypothesized and demonstrated that laws limiting money to candidates but leaving party contributions unlimited would channel more money and donations to parties. We also showed that the most ideological donors can be "pushed" into supporting the parties when they face constraints against giving to candidates but not to parties (i.e., under a "party-centered" campaign finance system). This finding is salient in highly polarized states. We believe this dynamic has the potential to dampen the tendency to elect highly ideological candidates who will not necessarily receive financial support from the political party.

In the next chapter we will build on this finding about individual donors by examining the characteristics of candidates who are the beneficiaries of donations from different sources of campaign money. Parties have the potential to serve a mediating role in the use of ideological money if, as we hypothesize, parties tend to focus their contributions on moderates as opposed to individuals and issue groups that support ideological politicians.

CHAPTER 3

Who Gets Campaign Money and Why Rules Matter

In American legislative elections candidates in all but a few states must raise their campaign funds from private contributors.[1] These funds are a vital resource for informing and mobilizing voters, especially in an environment with limited news media coverage of elections. The pool of donors from whom candidates must seek campaign money is of course limited. As the previous chapter illustrated, individual donors who provide the vast majority of contributions are rather unrepresentative of most Americans, in that they tend to be located at the ideological extremes. While candidates in states in which campaigning is relatively inexpensive can rely on friends and neighbors for their funds, candidates in other states need to reach out to a larger network of activist donors—those both within and outside a district who care deeply enough about particular issues to contribute to candidates they might not even know personally.

We are not the first to point out that relatively few citizens have the wealth to participate as donors in any significant way (Verba, Schlozman, and Brady 1995). If wealthy contributors had the exact same political preferences as the rest of the American electorate, this situation would be less problematic. But they often do not. One potential consequence of having immoderate partisan donors is gridlock in government on issues where most Americans might want compromise (Bonica et al. 2013). More critically, some scholars have speculated that the ideological bias of donors leads to the adoption of important policies that do not reflect the preferences of most voters, particularly lower-income voters (Gilens 2012). As Larry Bartels (2008) has demonstrated, the real driver of many important policy choices is elite ideology—not the interest group lobbyists ("rent-seekers") that are typically feared as corrupting the system. We would argue, like Bartels and Gilens, that the influence of such ideology-driven elites comes in part from their overrepresentation as donors in American politics.

It is natural that donors will exercise their influence by giving their money to candidates and policy-demanding groups who hold views like their own. Their influence is not so much in buying votes in the legislature as in shaping the policy agenda and influencing the choice of who gets into office. We expect donors to gravitate toward candidates with similar ideological perspectives. Given two experienced and qualified candidates for office, the one who shares an ideological affinity with the donors should be able to raise more money from them (Moon 2004). This is a form of candidate vetting on policies that takes place in an extended party network (i.e., party coalition) that includes partisan activists and interest groups (Bawn et al. 2012). Candidates, therefore, are more likely to succeed in winning office to the degree they earn the collective financial support of a dense core of partisan supporters in the partisan network (Desmarais, La Raja, and Kowal 2014).

This sort of ideological vetting of candidates is not the kind of corrupt behavior that most Americans fear. Instead, the primary concern of most Americans is the potential for a quid pro quo where officeholders receive campaign contributions in exchange for legislating in favor of narrow economic interests rather than for the public welfare. And yet, the influence of ideological donors is a strong form of resource dependency that biases political outcomes. Indeed, legislators may fear defying ideological donors more than economic interests because ideological activists are likely to mobilize in campaigns for or against candidates who betray them, whereas economic interests, particularly public corporations, tend to avoid public partisan battles that might roil relationships with their constituencies and customers.

We are not opposed normatively to this kind of activist influence within the parties. As we explained at the outset, the partisan purists are the backbone of political parties and make them stand for principles. Without the purist activists, the Hobbesian pragmatists who typically run the party organization might allow the party to shift its stance from position to position just to win elections. This situation would make it more difficult for less knowledgeable voters to know what the parties stand for and undermine electoral accountability. Nonetheless, we argue that a candidate-centered (as opposed to party-centered) finance regime has the potential to give too much power to the purists over the pragmatists if party organizations are overly constrained in efforts to support moderates and are unable to mediate the flow of ideological money to candidates.

This is the argument we will make in this chapter. Focusing at the *system level* on "who gets money" in politics, we show how the source of money varies depending on candidate ideology. Specifically, centrist politicians tend to receive more money from parties, while the more ideological elected officials tend to raise more money from individuals and ideologically oriented groups. We will also lay out the argument for our contention that campaign finance laws make a difference to election outcomes by privileging the flow of money to candidates who are ideologues versus moderates. We will show that such laws also affect the balance of funds going to incumbents versus challengers since the same incentive to win elections that causes party organizations to support moderates also induces them to support challengers. For this reason, campaign finance laws that privilege party organizations would not only have the potential to decrease polarization, but would also provide additional financing to challengers. And we argue that by financing challengers, parties would indirectly help to diminish polarization, because research indicates that greater competition causes candidates from opposing parties to move closer to the median voter (Burden 2004).

We begin by providing some background on why many American states have laws that confine political parties to a minimal financing role. We examine why this arrangement causes money to flow disproportionately to ideologues and incumbents, and we explain why a party-centered system might improve the situation by examining the unique ways in which political parties mediate the flow of campaign money. Finally, we provide a comparative analysis of the flow of contributions to moderates and challengers (as opposed to incumbents) in states that have no limits on party financing of candidates versus those that constrain parties. These findings suggest that party-centered laws might attenuate two major problems with the candidate-centered campaign finance system: that incumbents control most of the money and that ideological candidates benefit disproportionately from a system in which politically passionate donors give money directly to candidates.

The Emergence of the Candidate-Centered System in American Politics

The United States is unusual in its emphasis on making legislative candidates chiefly responsible for raising money for their own campaigns. Most democratic nations give the dominant role of financing elections directly to the political parties. Parties assemble the bulk of the money, often supplemented by government grants, and choose how to allocate it. Indeed, most nations refer to money in politics as "party finance" rather than campaign finance because it is assumed that the money flows through the political parties.

The financing of politics in the United States started to devolve to candidates and away from political parties in the 1880s. Mugwump and Progressive reforms, such as the secret ballot and the direct primary, weakened the role of party organizations and gave candidates more autonomy to manage their own campaigns (McGerr 1986). Throughout the 20th century, the gradual demise of patronage made parties less attractive to partisan campaign workers (Wilson 1962) and opened opportunities for candidates to attract personal followings among different factions of voters (Cain, Ferejohn, and Fiorina 1987; Polsby 1983). Changes in technology also abetted decentralization by decreasing the importance of labor-intensive campaign strategies championed by parties and elevating the use of polling and mass media techniques made available through political consultants. These consultants could be hired to support individual candidates instead of the party organization. The 1970s and 1980s probably reflected the high-water mark of candidate-centered politics, which led some observers to claim that the "party was over" (Broder 1972; Wattenberg 1984).

Given the dynamics of party decline over the course of the century, it was not surprising that Congress crafted a set of campaign finance laws in 1974 that advanced the institutionalization of candidate-centered electoral politics. To avoid repeating the excesses of the Watergate scandal, reformers at the federal level made candidates chiefly responsible for raising and spending money (Sorauf 1992). Under the Federal Election Campaign Act (FECA), the party committees were treated hardly better than political action committees (PACs) in that they could contribute no more than $5,000 per election to their candidates. However, unlike PACs, parties could "coordinate" additional party spending with candidates, but even these coordinated expenditures were limited because of fears that candidates would use the parties to circumvent the contribution limits.

Many states copied the candidate-centered model codified by the FECA. For this reason, among others, most state parties now play a relatively small role in financing their candidates. To illustrate the marginal importance of parties, figure 3.1 shows that only a fraction of the money candidates raise during election campaigns comes from parties. Specifically, in the 2005–2006 election cycle, party support ranged from close to zero in states like Arizona, with a public financing system that strictly limits private sources of funds, to a maximum of 43 percent in Indiana, where the parties appear fairly strong financially. Figure 3.1 is arrayed for states with smallest (at top)

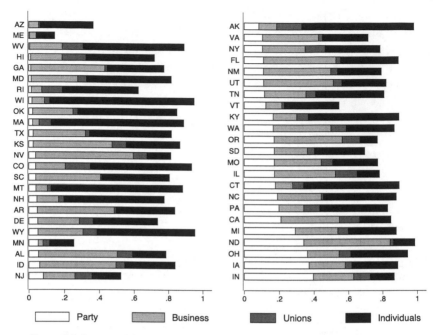

Figure 3.1. Source of State Legislative Candidate Funds for 2005–2006 Elections.
(*Note:* Figure includes proportion of all candidate receipts that could be
classified in one of these four categories using data from the National Institute
on Money in State Politics.)

to largest proportion of candidate funds that come from the party committee. As the figure makes clear, individuals and business interests provide the
vast majority of funds for campaigns in most states, and a small portion of
financing comes from other sources.

To be sure, political parties do more than just contribute to candidates.
Active parties help recruit candidates, advise them, mobilize voters, and
produce mass media. As we indicated in chapter 1, political parties have
tried to adapt to the candidate-centered nature of elections by providing
a range of "service" activities on behalf of candidates (Aldrich 1995; Cotter
1989; Herrnson 1988). But party organizations, for the most part, remain at
the margins in most states because they have lost control of nominations
and, at the same time, must compete with incumbents and partisan factions in raising money. To some extent, legislative campaign committees
(which we count as party committees in this study) have taken over some
of the activities once performed by central state and local party committees
(Shea 1995).[2]

As we show in the following analysis, the candidate-centered system that prevails in most states contributes to at least two adverse outcomes. First, it emphatically gives advantages to incumbents who can use the power of office to attract money. Second, it encourages the success of extreme candidates (extreme in comparison to the median voter in a district) because it allows ideological donors and factions to have disproportionate influence on which types of challengers and open-seat candidates run for office and win. To understand why candidate-centered laws have these consequences, we adopt a system-level perspective. Specifically, we look at the incentives and strategies of different types of donors.

Types of Donors in the Campaign Finance System

To illustrate how money flows into the political system, we begin by identifying how different types of groups tend to have different priorities when they invest in political campaigns. In our typology, there are four kinds of organizational donors—parties, business groups, unions, and issue groups. Table 3.1 describes how each of these groups prioritizes different goals in the political system.

The business sector—including firms and trade and professional associations—seeks selective *material benefits* from legislation, thereby reflecting narrow economic interests. The value of donations by business interests is that it allows these groups to build personal relationships with legislators and their staff on bread-and-butter matters that are highly specific to the interest group. Most of the time, such interests focus on shaping the technical aspects of policies (e.g., rules and regulations that might provide a competitive advantage), rather than changing the broad direction of policy. Considerable lobbying effort is simply spent on maintaining the status quo or tweaking it at the margins (Baumgartner 2009). These organizations invariably receive the most attention from the media because they are the biggest bloc of interest groups both in Washington and the state capitals, and because the pursuit of economic benefits through government lobbying raises suspicions about quid pro quo exchanges. Previous studies raised doubts about whether contributions change votes (Ansolabehere, deFigueiredo, and Snyder 2003), but there is consensus among practitioners and scholars that making contributions at the very least "gets your foot in the door" and that long-term relationships are valuable for having influence (Grossmann 2012). In our conceptualization, donors seeking material benefits use contributions to lubricate relationships with officeholders.

TABLE 3.1.   Differing Priorities of Political Donor Groups

Ranking	Parties	Business	Unions	Issue Groups
1st	Win elections	Material benefits	Broad policy	Broad policy
2nd	Broad policy	Broad policy	Material benefits	Material benefits
3rd	Material benefits	Win elections	Win elections	Win elections

Unions and issue groups both tend to prioritize *broad policy* change. These actors want to fundamentally reshape government policies on key social and economic issues. While unions seek laws that protect workers, issue groups include single-issue advocacy organizations that focus on issues such as abortion, guns, taxes, and the environment. Most of these factional organizations take positions that diverge significantly from those of the median voter. Rather than try to persuade moderate incumbents who might compromise on their policy goals, they instead make strategic contributions to support incumbents who strongly believe in their goals and give money to like-minded challengers to expand the number of legislators who support their minority viewpoints (Brunell 2005). This category also includes numerous individual donors who give directly to candidates who espouse their policy views.

Finally, political parties are generally associated with the goals of winning elections and holding power by fielding candidates for office and organizing partisan officeholders into a legislative caucus. In seeking control of government against rivals, these organizations stir electoral competition and public accountability as a by-product of the desire to win. These organizations are found at every level of government. In the statehouses, the most important organizations are the state central party committee (often referred to as the "state party") and the legislative campaign committee (often called the "caucus committee") that is controlled by the party leadership in the House and Senate chambers of the legislature. Our analysis focuses on financing at the state level, which includes the state central party, legislative campaign committees, and local party committees (district, county, or town). Based on our theory about the electoral motive that drives the pragmatists, we believe that legislative campaign committees are most likely among the layers of party organizations to help moderates in competitive seats because of the limited role of activists on these committees and the overriding concern of the caucus leadership to control majorities.

Regardless of level, however, winning is typically the main preoccupation of the party organization. In a series of interviews by Hassell (Hassell 2014), several insiders expressed this sentiment. As one former Republican state chair explained, "Higher up the [political] food chain, there's less idealism. It's more about winning. Not to say that there's not idealism, but it becomes pragmatic idealism." In the day-to-day activities of party organizations, insiders do not emphasize pursuing broad policy, even though "platforms" are useful for defining the identity of the organization. In fact, most policy development occurs outside U.S. party organizations through the work of partisan interest groups and think tanks.

We acknowledge that our typology of donor groups reflects stylized constructions of how different organizations behave. In reality, organizations may pursue several goals at the same time, and some groups blend across different categories of donors. Ideological interest groups, for example, behave like parties in that they tend to support candidates from just one party, and they invest in winning elections. Scholars currently refer to such groups as the extended party network (Bawn et al. 2012; Herrnson 2009), and we consider them the purist faction of the party because they push the party coalition to embrace their policy views. We also know that business firms can have strong preferences on broad policies (e.g., low taxes, minimal regulation) and may engage in partisan electioneering at times (Brunell 2005). Despite the mixing of goals for some groups, we see such goals as conceptually distinct and assign them to groups as their primary purpose in using campaign money.

Given this set of assumptions about donor goals, we can generate expectations about the types of contribution patterns we might expect to find among each donor group. Specifically, figure 3.2 indicates in stylized form how we expect the four types of organizations to distribute their money to candidates with varying ideologies. The *X*-axis displays candidate ideologies from liberal to conservative, while the *Y*-axis shows the proportion of group funds allocated to candidates based on their ideology.

In the first panel we expect political parties to send the greatest proportion of support to candidates in the middle of the ideological spectrum. This dynamic does not necessarily imply that party leaders naturally prefer moderate officeholders. In fact, all things equal, parties might very well prefer to elect noncentrist politicians to office. However, the overriding goal of the party organization is to win as many elections as possible and accrue power. To do this, parties will concentrate their resources on campaigns that are the most competitive, since their investments will have the highest payoff in these races. Given that competitive districts tend to be ideologically balanced, strong candidates in such districts tend to be those who are able to appeal to moderate "swing voters" or to the median voter (Ansolabehere, Snyder, and Stewart 2001; Canes-Wrone, Brady, and Cogan 2002).

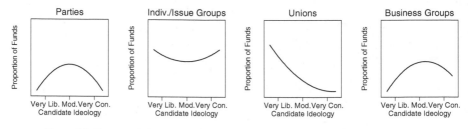

Figure 3.2. Expected Contribution Patterns among Four Types of Donors

Thus, when parties prioritize candidates running in competitive races, they also tend to be prioritizing an investment in candidates who are typically moderate.

Party organizations also are likely to fund challengers who have a shot at beating incumbents of the rival party. This is because party organizations want to gain seat share. In our framework, the emphasis on winning seats makes the party organization reflective of the pragmatist wing of the party. This faction will trim the sails of ideology to suit the median voter because its members reflect the pragmatists who want to gain and hold power. Such power confers status and the ability to dispense rewards to followers.

The second panel represents how we expect issue donors to distribute their funds across the ideological spectrum. These policy demanders will want to focus resources at the tail ends of the ideological distribution where candidates match their own preferences, depending on whether they are liberal or conservative policy groups. They ideally want to support a candidate who comes closest to their preferences but still has a good chance of winning. In choosing candidates who stray considerably from the median voter, policy donors are more risk-tolerant than party organizations, which put a premium on winning elections. The willingness of policy demanders to take electoral risks is precisely what contributes to the drift away from the median voter by the party coalition (to which they belong). Issue groups help to recruit and support candidates who agree with them despite their location relative to the views of the median voter. In doing this they help to create a party with a distinctive policy brand. Such groups are supported with contributions from highly ideological citizens who may also contribute directly to favored candidates.

Like parties, issue groups are also likely to finance challengers, so long as the challengers are like-minded on the issues that matter. They help challengers as a way of increasing the ranks of officeholders who agree with them and getting the legislature to adopt their preferred policies. Again, in contrast to party committees, issue groups are more likely to push for challengers with extremist views relative to the electorate. For this reason, issue groups are often active in party primaries to ensure that the party candidate who is most proximate to their preferred position gets the nomination (whereas the party organization will favor the party candidate who is closest to the median voter in the general election). The most aggressive issue groups might even participate in party primaries to support challengers against incumbents who have been unfaithful to the group's cause (Boatright 2013). The capacity to withdraw support (potentially or actually) helps policy purists hold party members in the legislatures accountable for their actions in office. In our framework, such issue groups constitute the purist faction that promotes partisan principles and ideals.

The third panel shows that we expect union organizations to focus their funds largely on liberal Democrats. In this way, unions behave similarly to issue groups, preferring to focus their resources on candidates who support their preferred policies over more moderate Democrats. And we expect that unions will rarely provide support for Republican candidates.

Finally, among business donors we expect a distributional curve that gives most resources to moderates who are amenable to bargaining and persuasion. Strong ideologues on either side can threaten the kinds of compromise that donors seeking special favors would like from government. Consider, for example, how Democrats and Republicans in Congress on the outlying left and right wings of the parties respectively combined in 2008 to take strong positions against the financial rescue plan crafted by the Bush administration, which was strongly supported by business interests.[3]

Despite the tendency of benefit-seeking donors to give to moderates, the fact that this group comprises mostly business interests means they are likely to have a bias toward conservative candidates who are more business-friendly (favoring free markets, limited regulation, etc.). For this reason, we expect to observe political contributions to be somewhat asymmetrical across the ideological distribution with a larger portion of funds going to conservative rather than liberal candidates.

Regarding incumbency status, we expect material-seeking donors to focus contributions almost exclusively on current officeholders rather than challengers. Incumbents are known quantities. They have produced a record, and thus are a more certain investment for donors with economic interests. In contrast, challengers are risky investments, not only because they are likely to lose, but because they might have a limited record and thus are not nearly as credible in their commitments as incumbents. Moreover, it would be risky for benefit-seeking donors to support challengers when such strategic behavior could incur the wrath of the incumbent who is more likely to win the next election.

Evaluating Our Expectations

To evaluate our stylized expectations about donor behavior we analyze how these four kinds of donors, as well as individuals, actually distribute their funds using campaign finance data from the National Institute on Money in State Politics (NIMSP). The NIMSP has collected data over several election cycles on donations to state legislative candidates. In the analyses that follow, we use all available data from the NIMSP for the period 1996–2010. Most contributions are categorized according to whether they originated from a political party, an issue group, a business organization, a union, or individuals.

The NIMSP data include information about whether each candidate is an incumbent, a challenger, or a contender for an open seat. This allows us to analyze which types of candidates are prioritized by different actors when allocating their resources. However, we have also formulated a set of expectations about contribution patterns based on the ideologies of candidates. While we cannot identify the ideologies of all candidates for state legislative office, Shor, Berry, and McCarty (2011) have created a set of ideological scores for incumbent officeholders over several years. Thus, we are able to examine which types of incumbent officeholders receive the greatest investment from parties, groups, and individuals. While we would preferably have data on all candidates for office, we believe the results would be similar if we had been able to include challengers as well.

Finally, it is important to note that the analysis that follows considers how each of these groups behaves in a context in which they are unconstrained in giving money (i.e., in states with no limits on their contributions). This allows us to examine how each actor would distribute funding under conditions where their decisions were not constrained by the legal regime.

Figure 3.3 demonstrates that our expectations about donor types (shown in figure 3.2) are generally quite accurate. The figure shows how parties, groups, and individuals allocated their funds across incumbents from different ideological backgrounds in elections held from 1996 to 2010. The line in each figure indicates the proportion of funds from that source being allocated to incumbents at each point in the ideological spectrum. In a sense, this is the ideological distribution of each sector's investment portfolio.

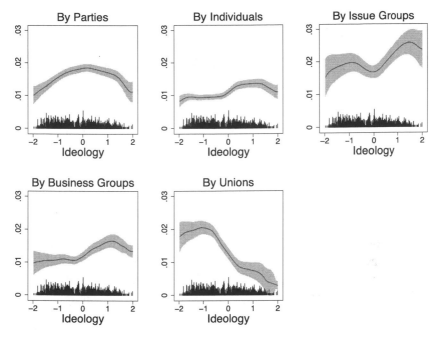

Figure 3.3. How Parties and Groups Distribute Their Funds across the Ideological Spectrum (1996–2010). (*Note:* Figure shows the proportion of funds given by each source to incumbent candidates for state legislative office from 1996 to 2010. X-axis ranges from most liberal [–2] to most conservative [2]. Grey shaded areas represent 95% confidence intervals and black bars show the distribution of candidates.)

The first panel shows the distribution of funds to candidates by political parties. Parties concentrate their funds on moderates rather than the extremes (we will examine subsequently whether this outcome results from parties putting money in the most competitive districts). The concave distribution clearly shows that parties give the most to moderates, with a sharp decline in giving to extreme candidates.

Individuals, on the other hand, contribute to candidates somewhat evenly across the ideological spectrum, though with a modest preference for more conservative candidates. The third panel shows how issue-based groups (what we call policy demanders) distribute their funding. The graph shows that these groups give a larger share of contributions at the liberal and, especially, conservative extremes. This convex distribution is counter to the pattern that political parties show.

The fourth and fifth panels also conform to our expectations. Business-related organizations tend to promote moderates with a decided tilt toward

TABLE 3.2. How Parties and Groups Distribute Contributions

	Parties	Business Groups	Unions	Issue Groups
Challengers	30%	5%	11%	27%
Incumbents	35%	77%	66%	43%
Open Seats	34%	18%	22%	30%

Note: Includes all contributions categorized by NIMSP from 1996 to 2008.

conservative moderates, but not the most extreme conservatives. Labor groups, on the other hand, demonstrate a strong preference for donating to candidates on the extreme liberal end of the spectrum.

Overall, the findings in figure 3.3 demonstrate that when parties and groups are unconstrained by electoral laws, they follow very different strategies with regard to ideology. Parties tend to favor moderates, while issue groups give more to extremists, and business groups favor conservatives. However, we also expect that these groups will pursue different strategies when it comes to the types of candidates they invest in. Table 3.2 shows the percentage of funds that different types of donors give to incumbents, challengers, and open-seat candidates. As we expected, of all groups, the parties give the largest share of funds to challengers (30 percent), which is nearly the same percentage as they give to incumbents. Open-seat candidates also receive a significant share from parties (34 percent). Not surprisingly, issue groups also give a large share of their funds to challengers (27 percent) and support open-seat candidates (30 percent). The groups that are clearly averse to supporting challengers are businesses and unions. Business groups give only 5 percent of their resources to challengers, while fully 77 percent goes to incumbents. Unions contribute just 11 percent of their funds to challengers and 66 percent to incumbents.

To summarize our findings thus far, we observe that parties, in their pursuit of electoral wins, give more than any other group to challengers and moderates. Issue groups, in pursuit of policy goals, give to challengers but prefer ideologues. Business groups (pursuing material benefits) strongly prefer incumbents—but focus on those who are moderately conservative. And unions (also pursuing policy) give largely to incumbents on the liberal end of the spectrum.

Incumbents Dominate in a Candidate-Centered System

Now that we have shown how different actors distribute their campaign funds, we will examine how the distribution patterns we have observed translate into the amounts of money raised from the different groups by incumbents versus

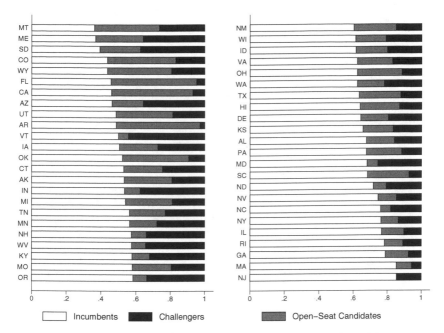

Figure 3.4. Proportion of All Funds Received by Different Types of Candidates (2005–2006). (*Note:* Based on authors' analysis of data from NIMSP.)

challengers and moderates versus ideological candidates. We argue that the contribution process is affected by campaign finance laws, which privilege one set of donors over others. For example, if donors seeking material benefits dominate the campaign finance system—as they do in the candidate-centered system—then we would expect that incumbents should do extremely well relative to challengers. And if donors with policy priorities dominate relative to donors focused on winning elections, then we would expect ideological candidates to receive more contributions than moderate candidates.

It is not surprising that incumbents do extremely well raising money throughout the United States. Groups oriented toward material benefits are the largest set of organizational donors to legislative candidates in the states,[4] and the candidate-centered system gives such groups a privileged position. At the federal level, in the wake of the 1974 reforms that institutionalized the candidate-centered system, business and trade organizations formed PACs at an explosive rate. It is reasonable to assume that this dynamic occurred at the state level as well where similar laws were adopted during this period.

Our analysis of the distribution of campaign money across the American states is unambiguous. Figure 3.4 shows the proportion of funds received by incumbents, challengers, and candidates for open seats in each state in

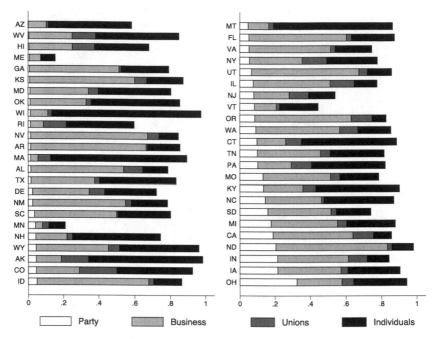

Figure 3.5. Fundraising Sources for Incumbents (2005–2006). (*Note:* Figure shows the proportion of incumbent funds that were categorized by NIMSP coming from each of four sources.)

2005–2006. We arranged the *y*-axis based on states in which incumbents received the smallest to largest share of contributions. Clearly, incumbents do extraordinarily well in the campaign finance system. The incumbent share of contributions ranges from a low of .38 in Maine to a high of .82 in New Jersey. If we compared only incumbents and challengers, an even starker difference in favor of incumbents would emerge. Nonetheless, this figure reveals strikingly how little money challengers receive across most American states. We should note that challengers tend to do better in less professionalized states, where elections are not as costly. In these states and in those with term limits, legislative turnover is above average, which increases the number of open-seat races.

Consider the next three figures that illustrate where each type of candidate gets campaign money. Starting with incumbents, figure 3.5 shows that in most states contributions come overwhelming from nonparty donors (businesses, individuals, unions, and various issue groups). In states where this is not true (e.g., AZ, WI, MA, MT) the numbers reflect very low contributions limits, which compel incumbents to seek contributions from individuals.

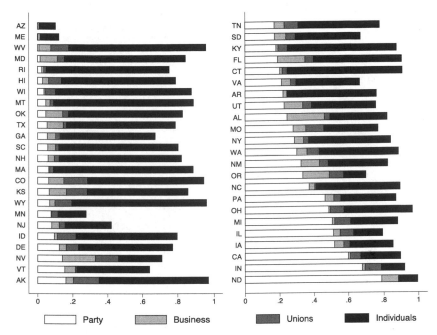

Figure 3.6. Fundraising Sources for Challengers (2005–2006). (*Note:* Figure shows the proportion of challenger funds that were categorized by NIMSP coming from each of four sources.)

A clear pattern that emerges from figure 3.5 is that incumbents do not rely heavily on political parties. The proportion that incumbents receive from parties is often close to zero, and only in Ohio does even one-fourth of an incumbent's war chest come from party contributions. In fact, often the flow of money is in the opposite direction. Incumbents give money to party committees rather than the other way around. When parties face low contribution limits, the party leaders call upon incumbents to raise money and contribute it to the party. In this way, the party will have money to pursue the collective goals of winning majorities. Ironically, this anticorruption strategy (of limiting the size of contributions to the parties) makes the money chase more fervid for officeholders because they must simultaneously raise money for themselves *and* the party (Heberlig and Larson 2012).

Turning to challengers, we observe an entirely different dynamic. Figure 3.6 illustrates that parties play a much larger role in financing challengers in many states. At the top end of the scale is a strong party state, Indiana, where party organizations provide roughly 70 percent of challenger financing.

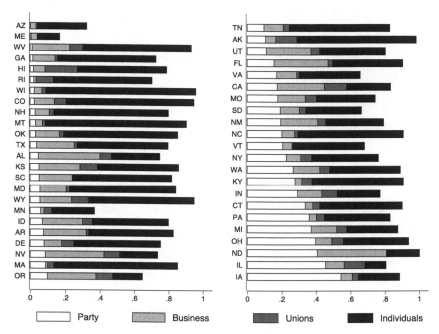

Figure 3.7. Fundraising Sources for Open-Seat Candidates (2005–2006). (*Note:* Figure shows the proportion of funds for open seats that were categorized by NIMSP coming from each of four sources.)

Other highly active party states include Iowa, North Dakota, Michigan, California, Illinois, Ohio, Oregon, and Pennsylvania. Individual donors, who, as we know, tend to be highly ideological, are an especially important source of funding for challengers in states where the party is not active. Noticeably, businesses, unions, and other groups make up a small fraction of financing to challengers in most states, and the groups that tend to give money are the issue advocacy organizations (not shown here).

Lastly, we show results for open-seat candidates in figure 3.7. This shows that the fund portfolios of open-seat candidates are similar to those of challengers, except that groups are more prominent for open-seat candidates. Groups that are too risk-averse to support challengers against sitting legislators are more willing to show partisan favoritism when the seat is openly contested (Brunell 2005). Note, however, that the party is a marginal participant in open-seat races for up to half the states. Some of this pattern is attributable to the fact that the party ignores open-seat races where one party is likely to win the district. It also reflects, however, the relatively weak position of parties in the campaign finance system within these states.

Ideological Candidates Benefit from a Candidate-Centered System

While we are not prepared to argue that candidate-centered campaign finance regimes drive polarization, we suspect that they serve as accessories because they give advantages to extremist donors in both major parties. Recall that we demonstrated previously the divergent incentives of donors and how differently they allocate their contributions. We can now show, from the candidates' perspective, which donors provide them with the bulk of their money.

Figure 3.8 shows how much of an incumbent's total campaign funds come from different sources, depending on the candidate's ideology. (Note that, because of the different sizes of the contributor groups, we have adjusted the scale of the vertical axis of each panel in order to "zoom in" on the different giving patterns.)

As with the earlier analysis of how different actors allocate their funds based on incumbent ideology, figure 3.8 includes incumbents running for reelection between 1996 and 2010. Beginning with party committees (top left), the data show that candidates who are moderates receive a larger share of their financing from the political parties. A candidate at the exact center of the ideological distribution relies on parties for about 8 percent of her funds, compared with much smaller amounts as candidates move left and right toward the ideological extremes. A distinct ideological asymmetry is also apparent in the data: highly conservative candidates show an uptick of support at the furthest right, approaching 7 percent for the most conservative candidates. This uptick is not mirrored on the left side of the graph, supporting the conclusion that highly ideological conservative donors are more ideological than their liberal counterparts.

The overall pattern is consistent with our argument that parties are a moderating force in electoral politics. Since incumbents typically get a smaller portion of their funds from parties than challengers, we expect the proportions that moderate challengers receive from parties to be even larger.

Now contrast this dynamic with the pattern for issue groups (top right), which is virtually the mirror opposite. Candidates at the extremes receive a larger share of their funds from issue advocacy groups. Note once again the ideological asymmetry: compared to liberals, conservative candidates tend to receive a greater proportion of their financing from such groups. To be sure, the sums are relatively small—the average amount never exceeds 2.5 percent. However, these groups tend to participate early in the campaign when money matters the most. Indeed, they are likely to become involved in the primaries when they can shape the candidate field (whereas parties and

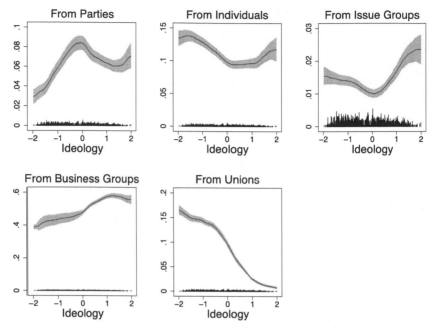

Figure 3.8. Relationship between Incumbent Ideology and Proportion of Funds Coming from Different Sources (1996–2010). (*Note:* Lines show the proportion of all funds raised by an incumbent depending on that incumbent's ideology. The scales of the vertical (*y*) axes have been adjusted to facilitate comparison of group contribution patterns.)

business groups rarely engage in contested primaries). In chapter 5 we will illustrate how these groups further expand their leverage through independent expenditures, a factor that is not captured here.

Additionally, the contributions by issue groups are likely to be indicative of a broader effort to mobilize individual contributions from like-minded citizens, who are often members of these issue groups (or, if not, who look to such groups for cues on giving contributions). We know that issue groups often advise their members on where to make individual contributions, using "scorecards" on voting records to indicate which officeholders are worthy of support. Because, as we noted in the previous chapter, individual contributors are ideological and favor giving to ideological candidates, it is not surprising that ideological incumbents also get a greater share of their funds from individual donors (top middle graph). Previous analyses showed an asymmetry, with conservative candidates being especially favored by extremist individual and issue donors. That pattern is not as clear here, because a large share of donations for conservative candidates comes from business groups rather than issue groups.

Indeed, because we are looking at incumbents it should not be surprising that much of the money that is contributed comes from donors seeking material benefits. Given that business-oriented interests tend to want limited government and minimal regulations, candidates on the conservative side get more money than on the liberal side. However, it is important to note that the most extreme candidates do not get a greater share of business contributions than candidates who are moderates. In other words, material benefit donors are a moderating element in the campaign finance system compared to policy-oriented donors, including both issue groups and individual donors (Barber 2013).

The Difference That Party-Centered Laws Make

Thus far we have shown that the prevailing candidate-centered system tends to help incumbents and ideological candidates. The one type of donor group that might counter this dynamic is the political party, and yet parties play a marginal role in most states in financing candidates. The mismatch makes us wonder if party-friendly laws might improve the situation. In other words, if laws allowed parties to raise and spend money more freely, might we expect challengers and moderates to do better financially?

Our argument is straightforward, based on these proven assertions. One, laws affect which donor groups play sizable roles in the campaign finance system. Two, groups have distinctive preferences for allocating their contributions. Three, parties have incentives to help challengers and moderates. And four, laws that favor parties should enable the flow of money to precisely these kinds of candidates. In this section we examine the proposition that "pro-party" laws actually increase the party role in financing campaigns, particularly for challengers and moderates.

To see if this is so, we compare states that have no limits on party contributions to candidates and states that have such limits. Figure 3.9 shows how campaign finance laws affect the proportion of funds that candidates receive from political parties and other funding sources in states with contribution limits on parties versus states without such limits. The figure shows that pro-party laws make a difference, especially for challengers and open-seat candidates. The first panel in the figure shows the proportion of candidate funds that come from parties in the two kinds of states. Without party constraints, challengers receive 20 percent of their money from parties, while

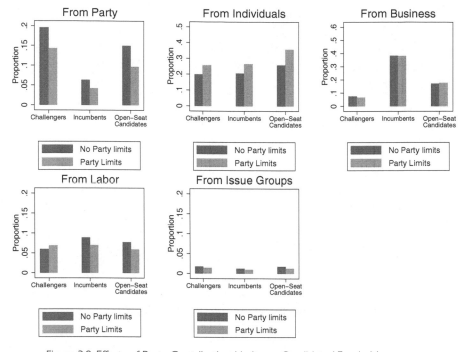

Figure 3.9. Effects of Party Contribution Limits on Candidates' Fundraising Portfolios. (*Note:* Based on authors' analysis of data from NIMSP. Y-axis is the proportion of funds received from each source.)

they receive less than 15 percent when parties are limited. Thus, removing limitations on political parties increases the share of funds that challengers receive from parties by a notable amount. Open-seat candidates see a similarly significant increase in support from parties in states where parties are unconstrained. However, note that incumbents' reliance on parties is less affected by limits on parties, a fact that is not surprising given that incumbents rely less on parties in general.

If parties can play a larger role in funding candidates because of laws that favor them, we logically expect other kinds of donors to play smaller roles. The data support our expectation. For example, the next panel in figure 3.9 (top middle) shows the proportion of candidate funds that comes from individual donors. Note that a high proportion of money that candidates receive comes from individuals across the board. With party limits in place, individual donors supply an even greater proportion of money to all kinds of candidates. Specifically, under party limits challengers receive 50 percent of funds from individuals, compared with 46 percent when parties can make contributions without restrictions. So when parties are constrained, challengers rely more on individuals, who tend to donate more to ideological candidates. Note also that incumbents become even more reliant on individual donors when limits are in place for parties. This is because limits are always imposed on interest groups when they are also imposed on parties (which typically do not give much to incumbents).

The Impact of Laws on Financing Ideological Candidates

So far we have seen that pro-party laws tend to encourage the provision of more resources to challengers and open-seat candidates. At the same time, however, we are interested in understanding whether pro-party laws would help finance more moderates. Our expectation is that, without limits, parties will focus their resources on moderates. In contrast, placing limits on parties will compel the parties to spread their financing more to other candidates who are at the ideological extremes. In figure 3.10 we show how much candidates rely on party contributions in states with and without party limits. As expected, when parties are unrestricted, moderate candidates, compared with ideologues, receive a higher proportion of their funds from parties. Again, the likely reason is that moderate incumbents tend to be in the most competitive districts where voters are ideologically balanced.

In states with party limits, the parties, limited in how much they can contribute to candidates in competitive races, spread their financing to more ideologically extreme incumbents. As the right side of figure 3.10 shows, the pattern is asymmetric, with the conservative candidates getting a higher proportion of their funds from the party. On the liberal side this dynamic does not appear to happen. While giving to moderates flattens, the money does not necessarily go to more extreme liberal candidates. We believe this pattern results from the fact that states with party limits tend to be more liberal and thus contain more Democrats in the legislature. Therefore, liberal (incumbent) Democrats do not have to rely as much on the party for funds.

These analyses suggest that laws affect the hydraulics of campaign money. When laws favor parties, the parties use additional resources to finance challengers and moderates. In this situation, candidates need to rely less on ideological donors, which should help to lessen partisan polarization. One possible criticism of this analysis is that our results might be plausibly driven by other factors (electoral, partisan, etc.) that are correlated with the presence or absence of party limits. For this reason, in the next section we introduce some controls to assess the independent effect of specific party laws on candidate reliance on party funds.

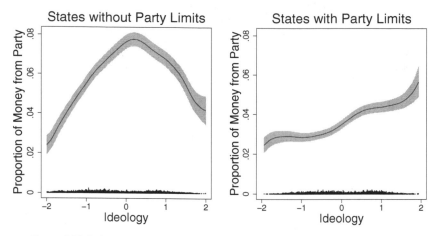

Figure 3.10. Relationship between Ideology and Candidate Reliance on Party Funds (2006–2010). (*Note:* Lines show the proportion of all funds raised by an incumbent that come from political parties depending on that incumbent's ideology.)

Explanatory Model

In this section, we provide a more complete investigation of the patterns we find above, using a multivariate analysis to examine the extent to which candidates rely on parties, individuals, issue groups, labor unions, or business interests for funding their campaigns. To do this, we include in our analysis 12,602 incumbent candidates for state senate in 39 American states across seven election cycles.[5] We focus on incumbents from state senate chambers, since competing for a senate seat requires candidates to raise more funds than are needed for campaigns for the lower chamber.

The five dependent variables in our analysis are the proportion of a candidate's total funds that come from each of the five sources. The independent variables in our models capture the finance laws in place in a state during the election cycle, the competitiveness of the race in which the candidate was running, and the incumbent's ideology. For campaign finance laws, we include three dummy variables capturing whether the state limited party contributions to candidates, individual contributions to candidates, and group contributions to candidates. Competitiveness is measured as the percentage point margin of victory in the election (Klarner et al. 2013); thus, higher values are associated with less competitive races. Finally, we include two ideology-related measures. The first is the senator's raw ideological

TABLE 3.3.   Factors Affecting Where Incumbent Senators Receive Campaign Funding

	Party	Individuals	Business	Unions	Issue Groups
Party Limits	−0.032*	0.029*	0.029*	−0.018*	−0.002*
	(0.003)	(0.004)	(0.004)	(0.002)	(0.001)
Org. Limits	0.010*	0.107*	−0.093*	0.013*	0.001
	(0.004)	(0.006)	(0.006)	(0.003)	(0.001)
Individual Limits	−0.010*	0.031*	−0.021*	−0.016*	−0.005*
	(0.003)	(0.005)	(0.005)	(0.003)	(0.001)
Margin of Victory	−0.002*	−0.001*	0.002*	0.001*	−0.001*
	(0.001)	(0.001)	(0.001)	(0.001)	(0.001)
Ideological Extremism	−0.010*	0.033*	0.001	−0.004*	0.002*
	(0.003)	(0.004)	(0.004)	(0.002)	(0.001)
Ideological Conservatism	0.001	0.004	0.086*	−0.063*	0.001
	(0.001)	(0.002)	(0.002)	(0.001)	(0.001)
Intercept	0.151*	0.137*	0.371*	0.087*	0.017*
	(0.004)	(0.006)	(0.006)	(0.003)	(0.001)
R-squared	0.108	0.073	0.155	0.241	0.013

Note: N = 12,602 incumbent senators running with opposition. Analysis conducted using seemingly unrelated regression. *$p < .05$.

score, with lower values representing more liberal senators and higher values associated with more conservative ones. The second measure is the absolute value of ideology—it captures the extent to which each senator is moderate (lower values) or extreme (higher values) in his or her roll call voting in the legislature.

Since the proportion of funds a candidate attracts from one source is naturally related to the amounts he or she is able to raise from other sources, we estimate the five models using seemingly unrelated regression, which accounts for the fact that the error terms in the five equations are related. Table 3.3 presents the results from our models.

The first column in table 3.3 presents the estimates for the factors affecting how much incumbents receive from political parties. Several significant patterns emerge from this model. First, not surprisingly, candidates running in states that limit party contributions tend to rely less on parties for their financing. On average, the effect of party limits is to reduce an incumbent's reliance on party funds by nearly 3 percentage points. The model also reveals that parties are sensitive to the competitiveness of the contest in which the incumbent is running. For every 10 percentage points that the margin of victory is larger (i.e., less competitive), an incumbent can expect to receive 2 percentage points less of their funding from political parties. Notably, however, once we control for margin of victory, we find only a small relationship between ideological extremism and reliance on party funds. This is because ideological extremism is correlated with competitiveness; that is, candidates in competitive races are much more likely to be ideological moderates. Thus, when parties invest in competitive races, they are typically investing in moderate candidates.[6]

The remaining models in the table show how these same factors affect the proportion of funding incumbents receive from other sources. For example, when a state limits party contributions to candidates, incumbent senators receive a higher proportion of funds from individuals and businesses, but slightly less from unions and issue groups. Incumbents in states with limits on other organizations tend to receive much more funding from individuals, but less from businesses. And candidates in states with limits on individuals actually receive less funding from all sources except individuals. The seemingly paradoxical fact that candidates in states with limits on individuals still tend to receive a higher proportion of funds from individuals can be at least partly attributed to the fact that all states that have limits on contributions from individuals also limit contributions from organizations.

The variable capturing a candidate's margin of victory is a significant factor that affects funds received from each source. Candidates in competitive races tend to receive more funds from individuals and issue groups, but those in less competitive contests tend to receive a higher proportion of their funds from businesses and unions.

Finally, ideology matters for most sources of funding. As incumbents vote in more ideologically extreme ways in the legislature, they tend to receive a higher proportion of their campaign funds from individuals and issue groups, but slightly less from unions. We found no significant effect for ideological extremism on funds received from business interests. The measure of ideological conservatism has a greater effect on funds from business interests and unions. More conservative senators receive a much higher proportion of funds from business interests, while more liberal senators receive a much higher proportion of funds from unions.

Overall, the findings presented in table 3.3 confirm the patterns we presented earlier in the chapter. Parties are largely unconcerned with ideology per se, but by investing in competitive races, they tend to support more moderate candidates. Individual donors are a more significant source of support for more ideologically extreme candidates. And business interests tend to support incumbents who are more conservative and who are running in less competitive districts, while unions tend to support only liberal candidates.

Summary of Findings

In this chapter we observed that political parties are fairly marginal players in financing candidates under the candidate-centered system that exists in most American states. The vast majority of money to candidates comes directly from either individuals or interest groups. We believe the source of money to candidates matters a great deal for the health of the political system. While most other studies examine whether the source of campaign money has a corrupting influence, in the sense of buying votes, we think that the source of campaign funding matters in other important ways. Specifically, we theorize that the source of money is tied directly to which kinds of candidates receive money in American politics.

We have adopted an institutional, system-level perspective to trace how the source of funds varies depending on the qualities of the candidates. We examined three types of donors that provide candidate financing, showing that these types have distinctive investment strategies. *Policy-oriented* donors (issue groups, unions, and individual contributors) tend to be ideological and prefer to back ideological candidates. Groups seeking *material benefits* (including economic interests such as business firms and trade associations) prefer to establish relationships with sitting officeholders, and so they support incumbents who tend to be slightly conservative. Finally, political parties primarily seek to *win elections,* and so they give money to challengers and moderates.

The candidate-centered system appears to privilege donors seeking either extremist policies or material benefits. The logical consequence of this system is that ideological candidates and incumbents do extremely well. Ideological candidates benefit because of the large role played by individual donors (and their affiliated issue groups), who tend to be ideological extremists. Incumbents dominate financing because of the large role played by business and trade groups seeking material benefits.

We cannot help but point out that these dynamics seem to be linked to widely perceived problems with the American political system. First, electoral competition is weak because incumbents rarely lose in legislative elections; this is in part because they dominate electoral financing (Abramowitz 1991). Second, officeholders are increasingly ideological and the major parties are deeply polarized. We believe this trend is related to the fact that highly ideological constituencies provide much of the financing in politics. We also believe that the lack of competition in legislative races, which is partially attributable to weakly financed challengers, allows officeholders to drift away from the median voter (Burden 2004).

For these reasons, we infer that a greater role for political parties might alter or at least attenuate these problems. As we demonstrated in this chapter, political parties are distinctive in that they choose to finance challengers more than other kinds of donors, and typically give money to moderates (largely because moderates are usually contesting the competitive races). Financing challengers could plausibly lead to greater competition, which should spur candidates in these contests to move toward the centrist median voter. And providing money to moderates should provide a counterbalance to a campaign finance system that stimulates the flow of money to ideological candidates.

The decision by parties to finance challengers and moderates is not due to the altruism of party leaders or their desire to improve the political system; it is because political parties put a premium on winning elections. As a by-product of their desire for power, party leaders will invest money in ways that could ameliorate what ails American politics. We have demonstrated that slight changes in campaign finance laws could improve the position of the political parties and allow them to pursue more intensively the strategies they are inclined to pursue. In the next chapter we will examine how these dynamics affect polarization in state legislatures.

CHAPTER 4

Ideological Polarization in State Legislatures

Our findings in the previous chapter—that political parties play a relatively small role in financing legislative elections in most American states and that parties behave differently than other kinds of donors, tending to support moderates and challengers—raise an intriguing institutional question. If campaign finance rules allowed parties to enjoy a larger role in financing candidate campaigns, would this tend to moderate politics and diminish ideological polarization between the political parties? Our findings also raise a more fundamental question regarding political representation. Would giving party organizations more clout to shape the field of candidates lead to officeholders who more accurately reflect the preferences of voters?

Addressing these questions bears directly on future policies for campaign finance reform. To this point, contemporary debates have framed reform as promoting either equality or liberty.[1] The egalitarians argue that laws should aim to reduce the ability of wealthy interests to dominate political financing, which they claim gives them an unequal voice in government. Those opposed to restrictions on political spending argue that such constraints diminish free speech. Differentiating ourselves from both egalitarians and libertarians, we suggest a third consideration. We posit that an "institutional" dimension has been overlooked in reform debates, to the detriment of representative government.

Addressing the Institutional Dimension

Our argument is that campaign finance laws shape the flow of money (what we have called the hydraulics of campaign finance) to political committees from various types of donors who have different agendas. In turn, the institutional flow of money affects the kinds of candidates who seek and win office, and also the ways in which they govern. Our main thesis is that money that flows outside party channels tends to promote ideological polarization between partisan officeholders. Conversely, money that is controlled by the party is more likely to moderate politics. Thus, the hydraulics of campaign finance have implications for political balance, stability, and the representation of majority interests.

In probing the policy question, we also raise related practical and theoretical concerns about the functioning of contemporary political parties in American democracy. From a practical perspective, our analysis in this chapter touches on whether party control over resources actually gives party organizations leverage in selecting who runs for and wins office. Since the early 20th century, the growing and widespread use of primary elections in the American states has removed the monopoly power that party officials once enjoyed in nominating candidates. The changes in the nominating process, coupled with other transformations in American society (including the rise of national-issue politics over the politics of regional interests), have given highly ideological candidates significant opportunities to pursue office with the help of like-minded partisan activists (Masket 2009). Given the importance of money in campaigns, it is entirely plausible that financially powerful factions will have considerable influence shaping the field of candidates, whether those factions are issue groups controlled by purists or formal party committees controlled by pragmatists.

From a theoretical perspective, our study helps advance our understanding about whether and how party organizations actually matter in contemporary politics. With respect to the financing of campaigns at the state level, one line of research suggests that parties have been mere conduits or empty vessels to funnel money to candidates (Krasno 2011; Rosenthal 1995). A second set of studies suggests a stronger if minimal role, arguing that party organizations are primarily technical organizations at the service of candidates who use them as addenda to campaigns (Aldrich 1995; Herrnson 1988; Kolodny 1998). Candidates, for example, benefit from the ability of party organizations to get wholesale goods and services at cheaper rates, including voter files, mailings, and even consulting services.

Finally, a third and emerging body of research claims that parties are much stronger than the conventional wisdom suggests, and that observers have missed this fact because they have been looking in the wrong places. These "network theorists" argue that the term *parties* actually includes not just formal party committees, but agglomerations of policy-demanding groups, consultants, and activists. And further, a significant amount of "party" campaign activity—such as the recruitment of candidates, fundraising, and mobilizing of voters—takes place by such actors outside the formal party organization (Bawn et al. 2012; Bernstein 1999; Bernstein and Dominguez 2003; Grossmann and Dominguez 2009; Herrnson 2009; Kolodny and Dwyre 1998; Kolodny and Logan 1998; Skinner 2007; Skinner, Masket, and Dulio 2012).

The network theorists might logically claim that the organizational form of political parties does not necessarily matter because contemporary parties are extended party networks comprising multiple interest groups and activists acting in concert to pursue partisan goals. The result of this dynamic is that the direction of the party reflects the aggregate of actions across dense partisan networks. Within the partisan network, the party committee can be a small or large node. But this does not matter because the "real" party combines the actions of all partisans. The implication of such theorizing is that, regardless of whether the traditional party committees are financially constrained or precluded from formally nominating candidates, the party thrives through the myriad linkages that bring partisans together for common goals.

We tend to disagree with this conclusion, even though we acknowledge the group-centered nature of partisanship. We do not object to the conceptualization of parties as consisting of networks of partisans, but we believe that organizational forms *matter* and that the "open systems" perspective can be pushed only so far. In our view, the party network reflects an assemblage of factions composed of various partisan interest groups, activists, consultants, and elected officials. Much of the time the factions row together. But the direction they tend to row depends critically on who controls significant resources. We argue throughout this book that money controlled by the formal party organization should give relatively more influence to an elected party leadership and the circle of pragmatists who tend to work through the party committees, rather than to the activists motivated mostly by issues and principles and operating principally from nonparty organizations.

To be sure, even the pragmatists have ideological views, which may slant their preferences toward particular kinds of candidates. But being pragmatists, they will focus primarily on winning elections by backing candidates who are not as extreme as the preferences of the ardent issue activists. We also acknowledge that not all party committees are controlled by pragmatists. Indeed, we suspect that many contemporary party leaders at the local level have been attracted to party operations precisely because they see the party as a vehicle to recruit and support candidates who favor their ideological positions. In contrast to 50 years ago, the party organization is much less a place for transactional politics than it was when traditional "bosses" controlled patronage to dispense to followers. For this reason alone the party organization will attract a more ideological leader than in the past. That said, we still maintain that local party leaders will adjust their ideological proclivities to advance electoral goals where there is two-party competition for office. Moreover, we believe that the higher the level of party, the more likely it will display moderating tendencies. State party officials will need to broaden the party appeal to ensure that the party brand does not hurt candidates statewide or in districts with moderate voters. Moreover, legislative caucus leaders want above all to win control of government; they will therefore be less inclined to impose purity tests on legislative candidates.

When laws constrain party organizations rather than affiliated partisan groups, the overall consequence is to diminish the centrality of the party organization as the venue for reconciling diverse factional interests (see chapter 1). And, more importantly for our argument, a diminished role for the party will reduce the influence of the pragmatists in party politics, who typically lead party committees precisely because they understand that it is in the interest of the organization to *balance* party factions. In other words, when resources for the party organization are reduced, influence moves away from pragmatists within party organizations toward the purist factions operating through policy-demanding organizations. Thus, the weakening of the formal party committee as a place to do partisan business means that collective partisan activity will be controlled more directly by financially well-off partisan factions, which get their funding from nationally based ideological constituencies. The "party" in this scenario exists as a dense network of policy demanders, but it is qualitatively different from one in which a financially strong central party organization is the major node. With weak party organizations, the ideological factions have greater leverage to recruit and support like-minded candidates at the expense of moderate party candidates (the kind favored by pragmatists) who might have a better chance of winning elections in competitive districts.

As noted in the opening chapter, our study challenges two dominant conceptions of political parties. One view sees parties primarily as controlled by "insiders"—mostly officeholders—who use the party to advance their ambitions (Aldrich 1995). The other view sees parties controlled mostly by "outsiders" who work through issue coalitions to advance policy objectives (Bawn et al. 2012). We tend to see political parties as controlled by outsiders, because our findings suggest that party organizations are not merely service providers assisting candidates, but entities that shape collective goals and electoral outcomes through the candidates they support. But we also view the "outsider" model as too basic, since it views the organizational form as of secondary importance. We demonstrate in this chapter that party organizations are of central importance because they generate *substantively different outcomes* when faced with more or fewer financial restrictions. In providing this empirical work, we hope to qualify the emergent school of theory expressed in the "extended party network" thesis by showing that party organizations matter. Their centrality in the network of partisan interests has the potential to moderate politics. In the last chapter of this book, we will say more about the positive outcomes that we believe will come from placing parties at the center of political networks.

Beyond parties, our analysis might also shed light on the million-dollar question: does money buy policies? Most studies look at whether donations influence votes on legislation (Ansolabehere, deFigueiredo, and Snyder 2003) or legislative effort (Hall and Wayman 1990). This approach reflects the view that the relationship between donors and candidates is essentially dyadic. Our lens is broader. We think that money has an impact at the system level. We focus on how the flow of money shapes the ideology of officeholders in the legislature. Their ideological predispositions potentially affect a whole array of specific policy choices they pursue, and shape institutional patterns that affect governing. Research shows, for example, that ideological polarization affects how parties organize themselves in legislatures, the amount of power they give leaders, and the degree of bipartisanship shown by legislators (Rohde 1991). Our study looks further back in the chain of influence. We try to show that the polarization we observe in legislatures is linked, in part, to how campaign finance regulations affect the relative power of groups engaged in elections, including party organizations, partisan factions, ideological donors, and a variety of interest groups. The electoral power these groups accrue—partly due to campaign finance laws—affects who is likely to run for office, who gets supported, and how they behave once in office.

In sum, this chapter combines our interest in understanding both political parties and campaign money using a system-level approach. Our analysis is ultimately about representation. Our goal in this chapter is to examine whether party-centered laws might create the kind of ideological moderation in legislatures that would be more reflective of the preferences of the majority of voters.

Partisan Polarization and Representation in the American States

In the opening chapter we pointed out an apparent disconnect between American voters and the people they send to office. At the federal level, representatives in Congress are much further to the right or left than voters in their districts (Bafumi and Herron 2010). One consequence is that the congressional parties are polarized ideologically, with few moderates in either party to help stitch together compromise legislation. The absence of moderates in Congress does not mean there are no districts where moderate voters prevail. Such districts are often represented by either liberal Democrats or conservative Republicans, a dynamic that Bafumi and Herron (2010) have referred to as "leapfrog" representation. This situation leads us to believe, like Fiorina, Abrams, and Pope (2005), that it is not necessarily the voters who are ideological but the choices being offered to them.

Most discussion about partisan polarization focuses on the national level. Recent research, however, indicates that polarization is also a fact at the state level (Shor and McCarty 2011). Table 4.1 uses data from Shor and McCarty (2011) to illustrate the distance between party ideological medians in the state legislatures (combined chambers). The states are arranged from most to least polarized based on voting patterns in the 2010 legislative sessions. The level of polarization of each state in 2010 is also compared with its level in 1997. The "Change" column shows the amount and direction of change that each state has experienced over those 13 years (negative numbers mean decreased polarization and positive numbers increased polarization).

First, note the wide variation in states. The California legislature stands out as representing the highest level of polarization, followed by Colorado. California is now heavily tilted toward Democrats, which enables the state to avoid some of the gridlock that the U.S. Congress faces. At the other end of the scale, some states are not very polarized because both parties are fairly liberal (like Rhode Island and Delaware) or mostly conservative (like Louisiana and Arkansas).

Table 4.1 also reveals that the distancing between the parties has increased over time in most states. Over this period, 31 legislatures have seen some increase in polarization, 14 have become less polarized, and 4 have neither increased nor decreased. (This is a total of 49 states; Nebraska is once again omitted from our analysis because of its political structure.)[2] The data provided by Shor and McCarty provide an excellent resource to assess the impact of campaign finance laws on legislative party polarization. We can observe interesting variation in polarization across states and over time, which can be assessed against institutional variation—namely campaign finance laws—across and within states.

In our view, a critical problem emerging from partisan polarization is that the ideological distancing of legislators is not typically reflected in the communities they represent. If increasing polarization were mirrored by the preferences of district constituents, then it could be argued that the legislatures

TABLE 4.1. Average Legislative Polarization and Change, 1997–2010

Average Polarization of States (in Order of Polarization [Most to Least] in 2010)

State	Polarization 1997	Polarization 2010	Change
California	2.61	3.01	0.40
Colorado	1.81	2.30	0.49
Arizona	1.69	2.20	0.51
Washington	2.13	2.13	0.00
New Mexico	2.01	1.98	−0.03
Idaho	1.16	1.94	0.78
Texas	1.67	1.91	0.24
Michigan	2.00	1.89	−0.11
Montana	1.56	1.85	0.29
Wisconsin	1.72	1.83	0.11
Missouri	1.23	1.80	0.57
New Hampshire	1.86	1.79	−0.07
Minnesota	1.74	1.77	0.03
Maryland	1.47	1.74	0.27
Ohio	1.41	1.70	0.29
Oregon	1.31	1.70	0.39
Georgia	1.30	1.60	0.30
Virginia	1.42	1.60	0.18
Utah	1.30	1.55	0.25
Maine	1.42	1.54	0.12
Iowa	1.47	1.50	0.03
North Carolina	1.55	1.48	−0.07
Florida	1.31	1.44	0.13
Alaska	1.59	1.38	−0.21
New York	1.38	1.38	0.00
Connecticut	1.34	1.34	0.00
Indiana	1.21	1.30	0.09
Tennessee	0.95	1.29	0.34
Alabama	1.05	1.27	0.22
Oklahoma	1.18	1.26	0.08
Pennsylvania	1.23	1.26	0.03
Vermont	1.28	1.25	−0.03
Kansas	1.25	1.24	−0.01
South Carolina	1.10	1.22	0.12
Wyoming	1.48	1.17	−0.31
Mississippi	0.85	1.17	0.32
Illinois	1.18	1.16	−0.02
Nevada	0.93	1.15	0.22
Kentucky	1.37	1.12	−0.25
South Dakota	1.08	1.08	0.00
North Dakota	1.16	1.06	−0.10
Hawaii	0.48	1.01	0.53
Massachusetts	0.95	1.00	0.05
New Jersey	0.96	0.99	0.03
West Virginia	0.77	0.93	0.16
Delaware	0.63	0.71	0.08
Louisiana	0.60	0.58	−0.02
Rhode Island	0.52	0.49	−0.03
Arkansas	0.53	0.46	−0.07

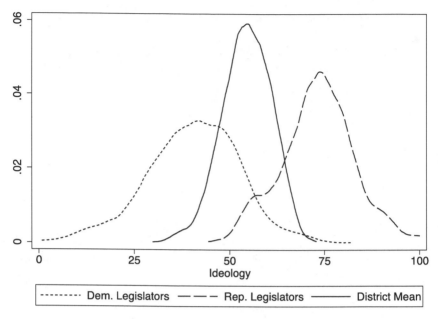

Figure 4.1. State Legislator and District Ideologies. (*Note:* Graph shows the distribution of state legislators and state legislative districts across the ideological scale.)

were merely being responsive to voters. But this is not the case. Examining data on voter ideologies from Catalist, we can see that state legislators tend to be far more polarized than the districts they represent. Figure 4.1 shows the distribution of Democratic and Republican state legislators across the ideological spectrum (the short and long dashes, respectively), compared with the distribution of the median ideologies of the districts those legislators represent (the solid black line). For legislators, the ideological scores are determined by their roll call votes in the state legislatures. For the districts, the ideological score is the ideology of the median adult in the district, as determined by Catalist.[3]

The figure is presented in terms of the ideology scale used by Catalist, so that 0 is the most liberal value and 100 is the most conservative. The figure clearly indicates that people in the legislative districts are not polarized in the same way that legislators are. While state legislators are distributed bimodally, with most Democrats falling clearly on the more liberal side and most Republicans falling clearly on the more conservative side, the distribution of districts is unimodal and centered in the middle of the ideological spectrum. Thus, if state legislators are polarized along party lines, the explanation does not appear to be that this is so because they are closely representing their districts.

The implications of these trends do not appear good. We observe at the national level problems associated with polarization, including partisan rancor and policy gridlock under divided government. The ongoing policy battles between the parties on immigration, health care, and other policies seem to be predicated on false policy choices that entirely lack a middle ground. The failure to act when public opinion supports a reasonable compromise raises essential questions about the ability of institutions to represent voters and function adequately. Some recent research even indicates that policy extremism appears to make voters less able to choose candidates who reflect their views. When candidates take extreme positions, they emit very strong partisan cues, which makes it harder for voters to recognize when a candidate in the opposing party might actually be closer to their own preference (Rogowski 2014).

How Party-Controlled Money Increases Moderation in the Legislature

As should be clear by this point, we maintain that strengthening party organizations by improving their finances might temper the ideological extremism of candidates. We outlined in the opening chapter the inherent pragmatism of party organizations and the mechanisms through which the moderating dynamic works. We also noted that the party organization, through its governance structures and historical label, is the broadest representation of the party and is therefore less likely to be dominated by narrow issue factions.

We described several mechanisms by which party leaders and party officials can temper extremism among the party ranks in the legislature. One direct way is by their choice of whom to support in elections. As we showed in chapter 3, pragmatists in the party organization tend to support candidates whose views are closest to the median voter and who logically have the greatest chance of electoral success in a general election. A second way party committees moderate politics is by substituting party money for purist contributions. After all, it is candidates, not parties, that receive the bulk of their donations from purist donors, and as we show in the next chapter, the candidates in the most competitive seats receive significant support through "independent" spending by issue groups. Our argument has been that a greater reliance on party support will lead to decreased reliance on ideological sources of money, which might influence how officeholders campaign and govern. If the party were a primary source of support, legislators who are fearful that straying from purist positions might hurt their fundraising prospects could take more moderate positions, knowing that the party will support them in any competitive election. This is because, as we have seen from studies of party allocation strategies, there is no relationship between the degree to which officeholders vote with the party and how much money they get from the party committees (Bianco 1999; Damore and Hansford 1999; Herrnson 1989; Leyden and Borrelli 1990; Nokken 2003, but see Jenkins 2006). In other words, the party does not necessarily use its funds to enforce party discipline, particularly for officeholders who come from moderate districts where a vote against the party might serve them well electorally. Any incentive for party leaders to use their resources to whip a particular vote will be balanced against concerns about losing seats.

A third plausible party mechanism for moderating politics comes at the prenomination stage. To the degree parties control a disproportionate share of resources, they have latent power to shape candidate recruitment and influence who gets on the party ticket. We call this the "800-pound gorilla in the room" argument. It is more speculative than the previous claims because we have not examined in depth how or whether this happens. We infer this dynamic from previous research and interviews with state party leaders. What we are arguing is that, despite the fact that political parties have legally lost control over the nomination process due to the increased reliance on primaries, partisan elites can have influence over who eventually wins a party nomination through their use of endorsements and other key electoral resources (Cohen et al. 2008; Masket 2009). While formal parties in many states cannot typically give money to primary candidates, the mass of party resources should at least allow party leaders to make credible offers of support to prospective candidates in trying to recruit them. All things being equal, party leaders will want to pledge their electoral backing to candidates who have the best chance of winning in closely contested races—usually those who are more centrist.[4] Toward that end, party officials can also informally "clear the field" by discouraging others from running, backed by the weight of their campaign war chests. Ultimately, a strong party organization can choose simply to ignore an undesirable candidate in the general election. According to the director of the well-financed Florida Democratic Party, "We basically do all the recruitment . . . so we don't have many truly contested primaries. And we stay away in the general election if a wacky candidate wins who does not reflect the district. It's a waste of money to help them anyway."[5]

Finally, a fourth way party organizations might encourage moderation is indirectly by enhancing electoral competition. Such competition tends to encourage candidates in both parties to take positions closer to those of the median voter (Burden 2004). As we noted in chapter 3, compared with other types of donors, party organizations are more generous to challengers. In supplying challenger financing, parties plausibly increase the tightness of contests, which incentivizes candidates to fight for voters in the middle.

Expected Outcomes of Party-Centered Campaign Finance Systems

Given the contrasting array of incentives offered by party organizations and factional groups, we can set forth clear hypotheses about how a party-centered campaign finance system will affect outcomes. We will then examine those hypotheses in the light of data gathered from state governments.

In states with a relatively strong party role in financing elections, we hypothesize the following:

1. *Officeholder ideological preferences will be less extreme* in party-centered states because well-funded parties will support moderates and challengers.
2. *Legislative chambers will appear less extreme and more open to compromise* under a party-centered campaign finance system because party-induced moderation will increase the number of legislators who might cross party lines.

Hypothesis 1: Legislators Are More Moderate in Party-Centered States

In the first analysis, we would like to understand whether states with party-centered (i.e., party-friendly) laws tend to elect politicians who are more centrist than states where parties lack these advantages. Using data on officeholder ideological scores from Shor and McCarty, we can make direct comparisons of legislators elected in states that allow parties to raise and contribute unlimited sums (15,026 legislators) to those running in states that have limits (35,149 legislators).[6] Figure 4.2 shows the distributions of the scores of the Republican and Democratic legislators in these two sets of states. The *x*-axis is a legislator's ideology score, with negative values indicating more liberal legislators and positive values representing more conservative legislators. The *y*-axis simply shows the relative number of legislators at each point along the ideological spectrum. The solid and long-dashed lines reflect legislator scores in states where parties have no limits

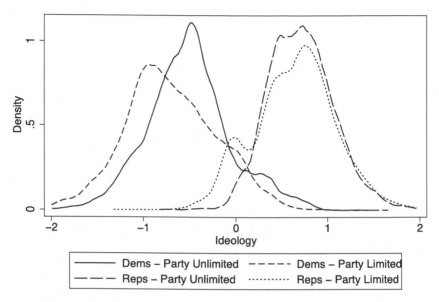

Figure 4.2. Ideological Distribution of Legislators in States With and Without Limits on Party Fundraising/Contributions. (*Note:* N = 18,573 Democratic and 16,576 Republican legislators in states with party limits. N = 7,350 Democratic and 7,676 Republican legislators in states without limits on parties.)

on contributions to candidates and no limits on what they can raise from individuals. The shorter dashed lines represent states where parties are limited in either raising or contributing money (or both).

First, the figure highlights the importance of party labels in the American states. Most Democrats fall on the left side of the spectrum and most Republicans on the right. Officeholder preferences clearly reflect a strong bimodal distribution based on which party they belong to.

At first glance, the effect of party limits seems minimal, even though the distribution shifts toward the middle as we expect. Observing the solid and long-dashed lines, it appears that a larger proportion of legislators in party-centered states are moderate. This effect is larger on the Democratic side, which shows a peak for party-centered states that is noticeably closer to the center compared to the peak for states where parties are highly constrained. On the Republican side, the shift is less pronounced, but nonetheless shows the same moderating dynamic. Note that there is more overlap between the parties in party-centered states, suggesting that the two parties plausibly have more opportunities for policy compromise. We will address that dynamic subsequently.

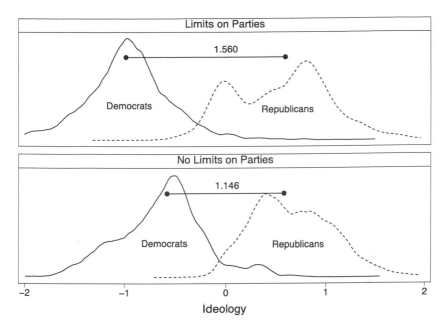

Figure 4.3. Ideological Distribution of Legislators in Professional State Legislatures With and Without Limits on Party Fundraising/Contributions. (*Note:* N = 8,086 Democratic and 6,967 Republican legislators in states with party limits. N = 2,852 Democratic and 2,939 Republican legislators in states without limits on parties.)

Figure 4.2 includes all states in the data compiled by Shor and McCarty, but we expect to find that campaign finance laws will have their biggest impact in states where money matters a great deal. Those states tend to have professional legislatures where the value of office is quite high and competing for a seat tends to be more resource-intensive. Because money matters more, those who have control of it should have considerable leverage in the electoral process. By this reasoning, if parties are key players in financing elections in professional legislatures, we should see a more dramatic impact on the ideological moderating of officeholders. And indeed this is what we find.

Figure 4.3 shows the same kind of analysis as the previous one, but for only those 20 states that rank highest on professionalism. To determine whether a state has a professional legislature, we use the Squire Index, which classifies legislatures based on factors such as the amount legislators are paid, how many days the legislature is in session, and how many staff are employed by the average legislator (see Squire 2007). We take the 20 most professional legislatures and classify those as our "professional legislatures" in figure 4.3.[7] For additional clarity, we separated the presentation into two figures, with the top showing the distribution for states with contribution or fundraising limits on parties and the bottom showing the distribution for states without either of those limits. There are significant differences, with legislatures in unlimited states showing considerably less polarization. Specifically, in states with limits, the distance between median members is 1.56, while this distance is only 1.15 in party unlimited states. The disparity between the two sets of states is like going from one competitive legislature that experienced considerable bipartisanship such as Indiana (which is less polarized than Congress) to another that is as polarized as Oregon (which is even more polarized than Congress). We also note that the shift toward the ideological middle appears similar for members of both parties in states with party-centered laws. The ideological distribution for both Republican and Democratic parties in unlimited states reflects a normal curve that skews asymmetrically toward the center, which is not true of the distributions for states with restrictive party laws, which show high peaks skewing toward the liberal or conservative poles.

Overall, these results suggest to us that a stronger role for the party in financing elections has the potential to increase the presence of moderate legislators, especially in states with professional legislatures. Of course, one concern with these results is that the states we examine may differ on some other dimensions that tend to be correlated with how partisan or polarized they are likely to be. However, recall from chapter 1 that we compared states that enacted limits on parties to those that did not and found no observable differences on a range of factors that might be associated with the probability that a legislature would polarize. Thus, we have reasonable confidence in the patterns presented in figures 4.2 and 4.3. Nevertheless, in the analysis that follows, we conduct an even stronger test of our expectations by taking advantage of the fact that the data we have collected cover a considerable passage of time.

Hypothesis 2: Party-Centered Campaign Finance Reduces Polarization in Legislatures

We next explore our second hypothesis: that a party-centered campaign finance system will make legislatures less polarized, which could improve the governing process. In Congress and many states the politics of compromise, which seems necessary in a separated system of powers, appears to be hard to practice because party members are so far apart on their preferences. But if the distance between parties could be lessened, it seems conceivable that a legislature might become more fertile ground for transactional politics and the kind of across-the-aisle bargaining that leads to bipartisan legislation.

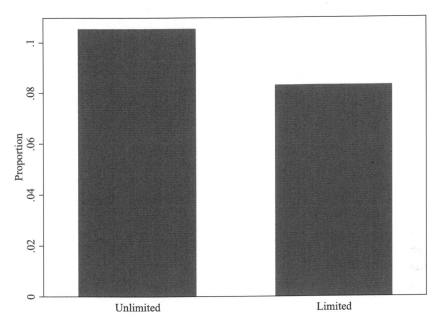

Figure 4.4. Partisan Ideological Overlap in States With and Without Party-Centered Campaign Finance Laws (1996–2008). (*Note:* Figure compares the proportion of legislators whose ideology overlaps with at least one member of the opposite party in states with no limits on party fundraising and spending to the proportion in states where parties do face such limits. Includes nearly all chambers during the period 1996 to 2008.)

First, we consider the prospects for finding common ground. We think this is more likely to happen when some members of both parties share ideological preferences. In times of divided government, moderates in the legislature often form the core of bargaining agreements between branches of government (Trubowitz and Mellow 2005). Moderates reflect the "pivot," and the greater the number of legislators who occupy the pivot, the stronger their leverage to forge bipartisan agreements. We measure bipartisanship as the percentage of legislators whose ideology overlaps with at least one opposing party member's ideology. In figure 4.4, we compare the ideological overlap between states with and without campaign finance restrictions. (Our measure simply reflects the area in figure 4.3 where the Democratic and Republican distributions overlap.) It is clear that ideological overlap is greater in states where the parties have no restrictions on making contributions and raising money from individuals. In these states, about 10.5 percent of legislators overlap in their preferences with at least one member of the opposing party, whereas in states with limits only about 8 percent do. While the difference does not appear to be large, in percentage terms the move from 8 percent to 10.5 percent reflects more than a 20 percent increase in bipartisanship.[8]

Finally, we seek to directly test our expectations that party-centered campaign finance laws would attenuate, and perhaps even reverse, legislative polarization in the states. While our earlier analyses used individual legislators as our units of analysis, in this case we look at the legislatures themselves. Our dependent variable is simply the distance between the median Democrat and the median Republican in each legislative chamber. When that distance is greater, it means that the parties are more polarized in the legislature; when the distance is smaller, it means that there is less polarization. The mean level of polarization during the years of our study was 1.33 (standard deviation of .47). The levels of polarization ranged from 0.42 in the Rhode Island Senate in 2003 and 2004 to 3.21 in the California House in 2007 and 2008.

Our key independent variable is, once again, an indicator of whether a state limited the extent to which parties could raise and spend money on legislative campaigns. When a state was limited in either the amount it could raise from individuals or the amount it could give to candidates, the variable was coded as a 1. When there were no such limits, the variable was set to 0. As we have in other models, we also control for whether the state limited the amount individuals or organizations could contribute to candidates.

One important note regarding these variables is that they are often highly correlated. Among all states, the prevalence of party limits is correlated with the existence of individual limits at .81 and with limits on other organizations at .46. This high correlation makes it more difficult to determine the effects of limits on political parties, especially relative to the effects of limits on individuals. However, it is important to note that the existence of different types of limits is less correlated among the 20 most professionalized legislatures. Among this group of states, the party limits variable is correlated with the individual limits variable at .66 and with the organization limits variable at just .31. In addition, of the 20 states that we identify as having the most professionalized legislatures, 11 had different laws on party versus individual limits during at least part of the time under study. While this amounts to about 11 percent of the cases, we believe that because so many different states have an experience of having different laws on the books at some point during our study, the inferences we draw from the analysis that follows are valid.

In addition to these variables indicating the type of campaign finance laws that were in place, we also include a one-year lag of the dependent variable of polarization. Including the lagged value of polarization as an independent variable in the model means that we are introducing a more stringent test for the impact of campaign finance laws. We attempted other lag structures, but these did not result in a good fit with the data and, in any event, these alternative operationalizations did not alter our main findings. We do, however, include a variable indicating the year of the observation. This information is included since polarization has been known to be increasing nationally during the period covered by our study. Accordingly, we expect the coefficient for this variable to be positive and statistically significant.

In conducting this analysis, we use cross-sectional time series regression. We include chamber fixed effects to attempt to control for any unmeasured differences across the states and chambers. Again, this choice is made to provide for the strongest possible test of whether campaign finance laws matter. Essentially, the results we show below are the effects of campaign finance laws after controlling for other differences across chambers and over time.

Results

Table 4.2 presents the results from two models—one examining the effects for all state legislative chambers in our dataset and the other focusing on just professional legislatures. We focus first on results presented in the first column. Not surprisingly, the coefficients for both the lagged value of the dependent variable and the year are statistically significant and positive. This indicates that the amount of polarization in a chamber at a given point in time is a function of the amount of polarization during the previous year and that polarization is increasing over time. Interestingly, only the coefficient for limits on individual contributions is statistically significant. This indicates that among all chambers, placing limits on contributions by individuals tends to increase the amount of polarization there is in the legislature.[9]

The second model in the table limits the analysis to the 20 most professionalized legislatures. The lagged value of polarization is again significant in this model, as is the variable for year. Notably, when it comes to professionalized legislatures, only the indicator for party campaign finance limits appears to matter for polarization. States that limit what parties can raise and spend appear to experience more polarization than those that do not have such limits. The coefficients for individual and group limits are small and lack significance in this model, indicating that they do not appear to be associated with polarization in professional chambers.

TABLE 4.2.   Models Estimating Effects of Campaign Finance Limits on Polarization in State Legislative Chambers (1993–2013)

Independent Variables	All Chambers	Professional Chambers
Lagged Polarization	0.798*	0.833*
	(0.015)	(0.019)
Year	0.004*	0.002*
	(0.001)	(0.001)
Party Limits	0.017	0.063*
	(0.012)	(0.020)
Individual Limits	0.054*	0.048
	(0.020)	(0.028)
Organization Limits	–0.008	–0.003
	(0.022)	(0.027)
Intercept	–7.484*	–3.967
	(0.944)	(1.298)
N	1,530	653
R-squared	0.791	0.829

Note: Each model includes chamber fixed effects. The Professional Chambers model estimates the effects for the 20 most professionalized legislatures. $*p < .05$.

To gain a sense of the magnitude of the effects of limiting party contributions on polarization, we use the estimates from the professional chambers model in table 4.2 to plot predictions for a counterfactual comparison in figure 4.5. Specifically, we imagine a state with an average amount of polarization in 1995 (which would amount to a difference of 1.48 in the party medians). We imagine that this state had no limits on parties, individuals, or organizations. We then use our regression model to set this hypothetical state on two different paths. In one path, we imagine that the state continued to set no limits on parties; in the alternative scenario, we imagine that the state enacted limits in 1996. Figure 4.5 shows what would happen to polarization in that legislature depending on which of these paths the state chose to take.

Figure 4.5 demonstrates the important implications that party finance laws have for polarization in state legislatures. In our hypothetical scenario, the state that chose to impose party limits sees polarization increase over the subsequent decade, whereas the state that continued with no limits on parties sees a decline in polarization during that same period. Within 10 years, the decision of whether to place limits on parties produces a 0.3 difference in polarization in legislatures that had identical levels of polarization 10 years earlier. That difference amounts to three-fourths of a standard deviation in levels of polarization; it is a sizable effect. In short, states with parties facing few restrictions tend to see less polarization of parties.

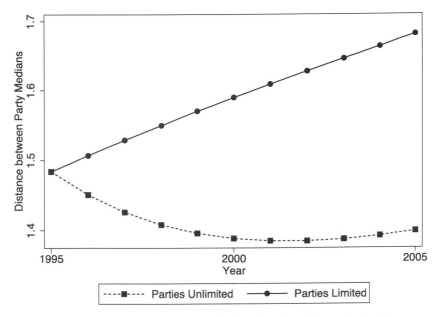

Figure 4.5. Projected Levels of Polarization Based on Party Finance Limits. (*Note:* Projections in this figure based on model estimated in table 4.2.)

While these are hypothetical estimates derived from our model, simple bivariate tests reveal a similar story. We can compare the change in polarization from 1997 to 2007 in 36 professional legislative chambers that had the same laws on party limits across that entire period. We show this comparison in figure 4.6. Among this group, the increase in polarization was nearly three times as large in the 28 chambers that limited party contributions as it was in the 8 chambers that allowed for unlimited contributions. Specifically, in the states where parties were limited, the distance between the parties increased by .12, on average. However, in the states where parties could raise and spend unlimited amounts, polarization increased by just .04.

Summary So Far

In this book we have been making the argument that the institutional flow of money affects the ideological direction of political parties. In previous chapters we showed that campaign finance laws alter the flow of money, putting money in the hands of pragmatist or purist factions of the party, depending on whether the laws are party-centered or not. We then showed

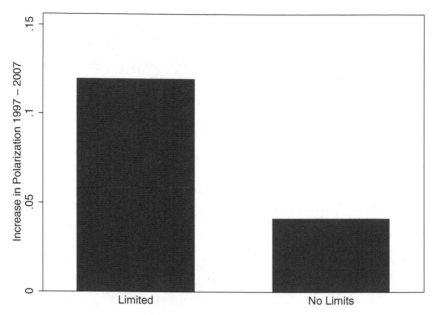

Figure 4.6. Average Increase in Polarization in Professional Legislatures Based on Laws Limiting Party Contributions/Fundraising (1997–2007)

how these laws affect which candidates get money and from whom. In this chapter we observed the real consequences of this flow of money on representative institutions. We were able to demonstrate how the ability to raise and give money by the party organization affects state legislatures. Campaign finance laws appear to confer resource advantages (or disadvantages) on pragmatists in the party organizations, which then affect their capacity to shape the composition of preferences in legislatures.

At the individual level, we showed that officeholders in states with unrestricted party spending are decidedly more moderate than their counterparts in states that restrict party financing. This dynamic is true for members of both parties, and especially so in professional legislatures, where money matters most in campaigns. Based on this finding we were able to show that legislatures in states with "party-centered laws" achieve greater ideological overlap between members of the two parties. This overlap plausibly provides a firmer foundation for creating legislative compromise across parties.

At the institutional level, we demonstrated that there is less polarization in the legislatures of states where parties are able to raise and spend money without limits, even after controlling for other factors that might contribute to polarization. To the degree that legislatures close the distance between the parties, these bodies should become more representative of citizens in the state who, in aggregate, have preferences that fall mostly between the party medians.

The findings in this chapter have important theoretical and practical implications, which we will address in the next two chapters. For now, we simply note that our observations cast doubt on a view that party organizations are simply conduits to pass money to candidates. We observe that well-financed parties generate substantively different outcomes than weakly financed parties. This alone suggests that party organizations matter as institutional actors. Based on this study, we cannot be certain of the degree to which party actions affect the selection of candidates or the voting behavior of officeholders. But we certainly observe changes in the composition of preferences of members in legislatures, and we see how this affects polarization of a legislature over time.

Our results should refute any oversimplified theory of political parties as networks of policy-demanders, with little account for how a well-financed party organization might alter the direction of the party. If parties are merely networks of policy demanders, we should not observe differences in states where formal party organizations have a robust financing role in elections.

And to make a broader point, we have demonstrated that money matters, although not necessarily in the ways that most people think it does. The flow of money does indeed shape the preferences of officeholders, but not necessarily as a quid pro quo or as exerting unequal influence on wealthy donors. What we show is another kind of bias—one that is rooted in the incentives of actors *within* partisan coalitions who contend for control over the goals of the broader party coalition. For this reason we think it imperative to pay attention to the laws that affect the hydraulics of campaign money. At the very least, the findings in this chapter should dampen the momentum of a reform agenda that focuses solely on an anticorruption approach to regulating money in politics. Such a limited reform agenda would have the effect of clamping down on the financing of party organizations, with potentially toxic consequences for the party system and democratic governance.

CHAPTER 5

The Hydraulics of Campaign Money

We wrote this book not only because of our academic interest in political parties and elections, but for a practical reason. We share with many U.S. citizens widespread concerns about the consequences of growing ideological polarization between the major political parties. Like many scholars we are intrigued by the underlying dynamics that have been pushing the political parties into polar ideological directions. Our main purpose in this book, however, has been a practical one. We seek to shed light on whether the design of campaign finance laws encourages or discourages ideological polarization.

In this chapter we summarize our findings from the previous chapters and highlight the effects of campaign finance laws on ideological polarization of the political parties. We will also provide some insights about the growing importance of "independent" spending, which we view as an outgrowth of overzealous efforts to clamp down on contributions to candidates and especially to political parties. At the federal level, independent spending has soared, but it has also been prevalent in the American states where political parties have been financially constrained.

We begin by recapitulating two of our main themes: the differences between pragmatists and purists, and their implications for American politics, and the effects on our polity of what we call the hydraulics of campaign finance reform.

Pragmatists and Purists Revisited

At the outset we made the claim that campaign finance laws that restricted the party organizations might have the effect of giving greater clout to ideological elements—the purists—in both party coalitions. In our framework, the "party" is a broad mix of groups, activists, and professionals who help recruit and support candidates for office. In this sense we agree with the "group-centered" approach of the UCLA school, which conceives of the party as a constellation of partisans who coordinate their political activity across a network of interest groups. The UCLA school, however, tends to dismiss the organizational form as an epiphenomenon—a kind of side issue—with little or no bearing on such partisan matters as who gets elected and what the party stands for.[1] To adherents of this perspective, the party organization—strong or not—is not where the real action is, since coordinated decisions are made throughout a dense network of partisan groups, with or without the guidance of the formal party organization.

As we have made clear in our analysis, we disagree. We think the organization of the party matters significantly in shaping the direction of the party. In our view, the party organization is the natural venue of the pragmatists.[2] And laws that limit the flow of resources to the party organization correspondingly weaken the pragmatist faction. We argued at the outset that the several factions in the party have different priorities, and we maintain that these factions are in a constant state of natural tension. Our view differs from that of the UCLA school, which tends to characterize coordination within the network as essentially frictionless.

We have called the pragmatists the materialist Hobbesians of the party. They pursue power for status and very tangible benefits. Their ranks include the Karl Roves, the James Carvilles, and a host of lesser-known party officials, including many of the leaders in state offices, who thrive on the game of politics. To be sure, the pragmatists have ideological preferences, but these are sublimated to the aim of winning elections as a path to reaping the benefits of power. Because they keep this aim in sight, pragmatists are averse to embracing extreme policies that might make them lose votes or that might create the kind of ideological gridlock that would prevent the flow of benefits to them and their followers.

On the other side of the coin are the purists who operate primarily outside the party structure. These policy-demanding partisans engage in politics primarily for a cause rather than for an individualistic benefit. They make politics a principled quest for the ideal, rather than the merely realistic; for this reason, we think of them as the idealist faction of the party. Understandably, purists want government policies to reflect their values—gun rights, abortion rights, limited government, expansive government, or whatever distinctive worldview they espouse. The purists give the party a principled spine and make politics more than just horse-trading. Thanks to them, the parties have distinctive policy positions that give voters genuine choices.

Thanks to them, political elites are held accountable. And unlike the pragmatists, the purists are willing to stake out strong positions even if this puts the party at electoral risk. In their view, compromising on principles undermines the legitimacy of their cause and demoralizes followers. Politics for the many purist donors is as much an expressive form of participation on behalf of causes as it is an instrument for helping the party gain power.

In our framework, the pragmatists and purists constitute two broad elements of the party that contend for influence. The degree of power either faction holds depends primarily on the context of the period. For example, in a nation divided by major policy disagreements, such as slavery, the purists are bound to have more influence, since they provide moral clarity on the issues that grip the public. We would argue, however, that the conferral of power on one faction over the other is also dependent on rules that favor one or the other. And given the relative importance of money in politics, campaign finance rules matter for allocating power. The money whose flow such rules govern is not, of course, the only critical resource in politics, but those who have access to money exercise influence because politicians will naturally depend upon them.[3]

Another Look at the Hydraulics of Money in Politics

Our research agenda moved beyond the usual analysis of political contributions. Rather than look at one-to-one relationships between donors and candidates, we gave attention to the larger flows of money in the political system. Experience with campaign finance reform suggests that trying to stop the amount of money in politics is not very effective, and that political spending is rather inelastic. Like water, money finds a way to get around obstacles. The hydraulic theory of money in politics makes us attentive to how campaign finance laws channel money to (and through) different political actors. And we want to be clear about the very different incentives and behaviors of the actors in the political system. When money flows to one set of actors—the purists—it is likely to be used in different ways than when it flows primarily to the pragmatists.[4]

Based on our hydraulic theory, campaign finance rules affect which factions control relatively more money. When well-intentioned reformers pass laws that limit contributions, the amount of money in politics does not change significantly, but its flow migrates to either the purist or the pragmatist faction. In other words, the rules do not necessarily create effective "dams" that block money from entering politics, but instead expand or carve new "canals" that channel its flow in other directions. And this rechanneling of money empowers different elements in the political system.

For this reason, we observe heated political battles over campaign finance reform. Not surprisingly, skirmishes over the rules occur not only between the parties, but often *within* the parties (La Raja 2008). For example, in lengthy deliberations over passage of the McCain-Feingold Act in 2002, which banned party soft money, Democrats were highly divided. The more liberal members embraced the legislation for ideological reasons, and the more moderate members were concerned that eliminating party soft money would hurt the party's electoral prospects. Based on our theory about how campaign finance laws negatively affect party organizations, we think the McCain-Feingold Act benefited the purists outside the formal party structure at the expense of the pragmatists closely affiliated with the party organization.[5]

When the pragmatic party organization has a restricted role in elections, the opportunities expand for more ideological elements to support party candidates. As candidates rely increasingly on the purists for their campaigns, the collective party becomes more ideological and distinctive. The shift can be subtle and can play out over several election cycles before significant change can be observed. But it is a process that can gradually affect every decision of who runs for office, because ideological donors are key gatekeepers in the party. People may choose to run or not based on signals they get from party activists about their "fit" for office (Thomsen 2014).

This factional dynamic between pragmatists and purists inspires a central paradox in our conceptualization of political parties. While political scientists have traditionally posited a tight link between strong party organizations and strong programmatic parties, we do not think such a link is necessarily forged in a two-party system (APSA 1950). In fact, we speculate that the relationship might be inverse rather than direct. Parties that are weak organizationally might end up stronger programmatically, because the purists operating outside the formal party structure are able to influence the selection of candidates and the behavior of officeholders through direct contributions and in-kind support from affiliated interest groups. Purists might castigate incumbents publicly for being disloyal to the party, and might even campaign against them in the primary. In contrast, a financially strong party organization will use its resources to finance candidates who hew more closely to the views of the median voter. And pragmatists in the party organization will not want to risk a seat by pushing members to vote in unity with the party for a highly ideological candidate, when a vote for such a candidate, who might be distant from the district median, would put them at risk electorally.

We have shown in our analysis that, in light of the differences between purists and pragmatists, campaign finance laws that favor party organizations have a dampening effect on ideological polarization. Pro-party laws tend to shift resources to the pragmatist faction in the party organization whose main goal is to win elections rather than to make the party ideologically liberal or conservative.

To be sure, there are much deeper currents driving party polarization than campaign finance rules. Research shows that activists in both parties have become more ideologically cohesive over time (Baldassarri and Gelman 2008; Layman et al. 2010), and that activists have disproportionate voting power in nominating party candidates (Fiorina, Abrams, and Pope 2005). The wealthier partisan activists might also pull the coalition in their direction by helping to finance influential think tanks and foundations. Other activists attend party meetings and conventions, lobby government officials and elected members persistently, mobilize core constituencies at critical governing moments, recruit candidates (often from their own ranks), and generally promote in the media a national set of policy issues at all levels of government.

Notwithstanding the multipronged influence of activists within party coalitions, we think campaign money matters for polarization. Much of the impact takes the form of direct contributions to candidates or, increasingly, is exerted through independent spending by partisan groups. But power is also granted through the latent capacity of activists to punish politicians by withholding group endorsements and hampering the mobilization of financial resources. Such endorsements help politicians attract donations from voters who closely follow such cues when deciding where to give money.

Perhaps more critical than the elite individual donors who might give up to $5,000 to a candidate are the mega-donors who now finance super PACs or 501(c)4 organizations with millions of dollars.[6] Mega-donors, be they individual or groups, draw the attention of politicians and anoint their issues with credibility. Consider, for example, the fervor with which prospective Republican nominees for the 2016 presidential election attended a meeting convened by casino magnate Sheldon Adelson, who spent close to $100 million financing 34 different candidates and groups in the 2012 election.[7] In that cycle he gave $20 million alone to "Winning Our Future," a super PAC backing the failed candidacy of Newt Gingrich.[8] The ability of a donor like Adelson, who has highly conservative positions on Israel and taxation, to personally finance a super PAC gives him disproportionate influence in national party politics.[9]

Summary of Key Findings

Our claims about the campaign finance system are based on arguments developed, and information presented, primarily in the analytical chapters of this book (chapters 2, 3, and 4). In those chapters, we carefully examined who gives money, who receives money, and how these dynamics affect ideological polarization in U.S. state legislatures. Through that analysis, we illustrated how financial constraints on party organizations actually shift power from pragmatists to purists because laws that hamper parties make candidates more reliant on ideologically driven donors. We focused our analysis on state legislative elections because an effective comparative analysis would not have been possible if we had focused only on federal elections.

In the following sections, we summarize our main findings.

1. Candidates rely overwhelmingly on nonparty sources of funding.

Candidates receive on average 25 percent of their funding from individual donors and 32 percent from nonparty organizations. In contrast, they receive just 9 percent from political parties. The party financing of candidates varies from virtually 0 percent in Arizona to a high of 40 percent in Indiana. These findings illustrate the candidate-centered nature of American elections and contrast noticeably with the party-centered financing systems in many other democracies. The conclusion is inescapable that parties play a relatively limited role in funding legislative elections in the United States.

This situation is relatively recent. Historically, political parties were less constrained in making contributions relative to other organizations. But this changed considerably in the past two or three decades, precisely during a period of increasing polarization. In 1990, only one in five states limited the amount that party organizations could contribute to candidates. By 2010, that proportion increased to half the American states. The tightening of regulations on political parties has occurred at the same time that partisan organizing has become more important because competition for government control has increased and party programs have grown far more distinctive. With constraints on party finances, however, partisans have sought independent campaign tactics to help favored candidates win. Those who have exploited independent spending the most are the ideological factions and entrepreneurs with the means and motive to step into the breach left by the weakened party organization. We maintain that this dynamic contributes to the palpable ideological distancing of the parties.

2. Individual donors are highly ideological.

Americans who contribute money in state legislative elections are much more ideological than the average American voter. These donors can be separated decisively into two ideological camps: one squarely on the left and the other just as clearly on the right. In contrast, the vast majority of American voters have policy preferences that are mostly in the middle, just a bit left of center.[10] While others have demonstrated similar findings at the national level, our study reveals identical patterns in state-level elections. We contend that the heavy dependence of candidates on highly ideological donors—who provide two-thirds of the donations received by state legislative candidates—is related to the kind of candidates who emerge in elections and enter office.[11] Donors serve as party gatekeepers who help shape the field of party candidates through their decisions to give or withhold contributions.

3. Small donors are as ideological as large donors.

Our analysis of individual donors also shows that the much-heralded small donors (those giving less than $200) are just as ideologically divided as the large donors. This finding raises a paradoxical situation. Recent efforts to encourage small donors as a way of diminishing the potentially corrupting influence of large donors could end up reinforcing the ideological divide between the parties' donor populations. We see little evidence that a strategy of encouraging candidates to raise more money from small donors will broaden the pool of donors to include more moderates. In fact, other research indicates that contributions from small donors, in comparison with those from Americans in the top .01 percent of wealth, go disproportionately to highly ideological candidates (Bonica et al. 2013). And in support of our arguments about how business interests tend to be pragmatic, this same study shows that executives from *Forbes* 400/*Fortune* 500 companies give disproportionately to candidates who are *closer* to the center than the party ideological mean for all candidates, while small donors give disproportionately to candidates at the ideological extremes.

We also observed that the donor pools in states with low contribution limits do not differ in demographic makeup from donors in states with no contribution limits. One argument for low contributions is that they will compel politicians to seek donations from a broader swath of the electorate. Yet, even in states with low contribution limits, donors remain overwhelmingly wealthy, white, male, and married. This finding suggests that the imposition of contribution limits is not an effective strategy to broaden either the ideological or demographic profile of donors.

4. Individual donors prefer to contribute to ideological candidates.

Donors typically prefer to give money to candidates rather than to parties or groups because the candidates share their ideological views. While some donors are strategic, focusing their giving on candidates in close races, we mostly observe behavior that suggests that donors are mostly exercising a strongly expressive form of participation. We think this reflects the political passions of donors and their sense of ideological kinship with candidates. A highly liberal and popular officeholder, such as Democratic U.S. senator Elizabeth Warren of Massachusetts, raises significant amounts of money from very liberal donors because of the causes she champions, even though she is unlikely to face a serious electoral threat.

Tellingly, our analysis shows that as a candidate moves from the center to the ideological extremes (controlling for political competition and other factors), she relies more heavily on individual contributors as opposed to political parties. In fact, ideological orientation makes little difference in how much money parties give to candidates. The logical implication is that candidates who want to attract individual donors (who make up the largest source of financing in almost all states) must leave the middle of the ideological spectrum or already occupy a policy position compatible with those donors.[12]

5. Party asymmetry is noticeable.

We see significant partisan differences in the behavior of individual donors. Conservative donors appear reluctant to give funds to the party because they view the party as too moderate. In contrast, candidates are viewed as closer to their position. These perceptions lead to unique, ideology-based donor strategies. The more a donor self-describes as a conservative, the more he or she focuses heavily on giving directly to conservative candidates and like-minded issue groups. In contrast, liberal donors appear just as willing to give money to candidates as to political parties. That is, liberals do not tend to see ideological differences between candidates and the political party, viewing both as relatively moderate. For this reason, we observe the same proportion of very liberal donors saying they give to candidates and parties.

The differences in behavior on the left and right may account, in part, for the fact that the Republican party appears to have moved further to the right in the past decade than the Democrats have moved to the left.

As we demonstrated in chapter 3, individual contributors tend to give to highly conservative candidates. And these same highly conservative candidates receive a larger share of their contributions directly from issue groups in comparison to candidates on the left. While issue groups provide only a small portion of a candidate's total funds, their contributions can indicate broader levels of support. Not only do such groups tend to give early in campaigns when contributions matter most, but they also mobilize members and like-minded individuals to give directly to candidates. The stronger presence of issue groups in financing the campaigns of highly conservative candidates might be one reason for the strength of an extreme conservative faction in the Republican Party.

6. Party organizations support moderate candidates and challengers more than other institutional donors do.

When parties and groups are unconstrained by electoral laws, they follow very different strategies with regard to ideology and incumbency status. This has everything to do with the motives of different sets of donors. Political parties, which focus primarily on winning, generally favor moderates because moderates tend to be situated in competitive districts that the party wants to win. The pragmatists ultimately choose to support candidates close to the median voter. This strategy contrasts directly with that of the partisan issue groups. They champion narrow policies, and this causes them to give a greater proportion of their funds to officeholders at the ideological extremes. Labor unions follow a similar pattern by giving most of their contributions to the liberal extremes of the Democratic Party. In this way, unions behave strategically like ideological activists, seeking major policy change through electoral replacement rather than legislative compromise by working with legislators in the middle.

Business groups, in contrast, tend to favor moderate to conservative officeholders (but not extreme conservatives). We believe this is so because businesses are far more interested in bargaining with legislators over material benefits than trying to transform major policies. The conservative tilt of business groups reflects an interest in having governments that do not regulate their industries and professions.

The differences in institutional support of candidates can affect the ideological makeup of state legislatures. All things being equal, a greater role for political parties should help moderates raise money. Similarly, a greater role for business PACs might do the same, but with a tilt toward conservative candidates (and incumbents).

Therein lies a central paradox of regulating money in politics. Efforts to keep business-related money out of politics may help avoid problems of corruption or rent-seeking by interest group lobbyists, but could stimulate greater ideological polarization as candidates come to rely more on ideological donors. Barber's research at the federal level, for example, notes that candidates have relied increasingly over the past three decades on individual rather than PAC contributions (Barber 2013). He speculates that this is one reason for the heightened ideological polarization of members of Congress. Given these dynamics, we reluctantly acknowledge a potential zero-sum dilemma with regard to the goals of campaign finance reform: laws can be designed to limit either corruption or polarization, but not necessarily both. (We will propose new strategies that may address this dilemma in chapter 6.)

While our study focused on ideology, we also found different levels of support across donor groups based on incumbency status. Among institutional donors, parties give the largest share of funds to challengers (38 percent), compared to business groups (7 percent) and labor unions (11 percent). Issue groups typically want to increase the number of members who think like them, so they give more to challengers than other groups (31 percent). The implication of these findings is that political parties, which are most concerned with winning elections, are likely to spur political competition through their strategy of financing challengers. By helping to finance challengers, political parties might indirectly encourage movement toward the median voter as races get more competitive. Issue groups will also help challengers, but these candidates are more likely to be very ideological compared to the ones that parties support. Challengers are likely to do worse under campaign finance systems that rely heavily on PACs (most of which are business-related) and individual donors, because these two sets of donors heavily favor incumbents.

7. Moderate candidates benefit disproportionately from party financing.

Moderate candidates fare best with political parties. There is a direct relationship between being a moderate candidate and receiving a greater proportion of funds from the party. In contrast, the most ideological candidates receive a greater proportion of funds from individuals and issue groups, while moderates fare worst with these donors. Again, our argument is not that parties prefer moderation, per se, but that the pragmatists who operate the political parties focus money on close races where there are mostly likely to be moderate candidates. We were able to show that moderate-to-conservative candidates also benefited disproportionately from business-group contributions. (The benefit to conservative candidates is not surprising, given the business preference for candidates who favor limited regulation and taxes.)

These findings clearly match our expectations based on the underlying motivations of different donors. The most ideological candidates get a larger share of money from individuals and issue groups with strong policy preferences. Ideological candidates are the darlings of the purists. In contrast, moderates benefit from the party organization, with its pragmatic orientation toward winning elections regardless of ideology. The implication for policy is that moderate candidates would benefit in elections if money came through the pragmatist faction, which is located primarily within the party organization.

8. Laws affect the flow of money going to moderates versus ideologues.

Our study shows that campaign laws matter but not the way people typically think they do. The use of contribution limits—a very popular reform tool—does not affect the total share of ideologues who give money, or even change the demographics of donors very much, including factors such as race, gender, or wealth. Instead, these laws follow the hydraulic principle of money in politics, affecting what kind of candidates receive money and from which sources. We were able to demonstrate how the design of campaign finance laws promotes or deters a larger financial role for political parties. And, specifically, we were able to show how increasing the role of the party had positive consequences for the political system.

First, our comparative analysis showed that *laws favoring parties stimulated additional contributions to the party organization*. When there are no limits on the amounts that parties can receive (and there are limits on candidates), the number and sum of donations to the parties increase by an average of 57 percent. Testing our theory that parties can serve as "filters" for ideological money, we found that laws that limited money to candidates but not parties had the effect of enticing more ideological donors to give to the parties, rather than giving directly to candidates. We believe that enabling the party to mediate these funds should help to diminish ideological polarization (see finding No. 9 below).

Second, we found that *laws favoring parties increased the financial role of political parties relative to other donors in the electoral system*. In states with no limits on party organizations, the party provides a greater share of resources to candidates. This shift toward the parties makes candidates less reliant on ideological sources of funds (and less reliant on business groups too). We also note that this shift makes candidates less reliant on the transfer of funds from other candidates in the party. When parties are comparatively strong fundraisers, there is no need for the entire membership of the party caucus to be pressed intensively into the service of raising money for candidates who need it.

Not only do we think that having to effect such money transfers is a highly inefficient way of partisan organizing, but we are concerned that the reliance on colleagues for support increases the importance of money in the legislative routines of elected officials. Members who are not even in close races find themselves continually asking for contributions that they can pass on to others in the caucus. The emphasis on raising money for others in the party caucus makes this practice a chief means of building bargaining power with colleagues and advancing into leadership (Heberlig, Hetherington, and Larson 2006; Heberlig and Larson 2012).

We do not think that the additional time that legislators spend on raising money is good for representative government: fundraising takes away from time that could be spent on building policy expertise, developing working relationships with other members, and interacting with district constituents (Francia and Herrnson 2003; Tokaji and Strause 2014). We also speculate that having to raise money constantly leads candidates to spend a disproportionate amount of time with a tiny slice of wealthy Americans, which can skew the perspective of legislators. At the federal level, according to freshman U.S. senator Chris Murphy (D-CT), fundraising has become "soul-crushing" and threatens to distort his view of the public's concerns. He says that "you're hearing a lot about problems that bankers have and not a lot of problems that people who work at the mill in Thomaston, Conn., have."[13] At the state level, the experience is surely less intense, but it is no less true that politicians in need of campaign money spend more time with those who can make contributions than with other, more typical constituents.

Third, *when the laws allow parties to play a stronger financial role, moderate candidates get a larger share of money from parties.* We found that parties were able to concentrate their funds among moderates when they did not face constraints on political contributions. In contrast, in states with party limits, the state parties appear compelled to spread their funds to more ideologically extreme candidates. This was particularly true on the Republican side. In party-limited states, candidates relied more heavily on individuals as their source of funding, and individual donors tend to reward ideological extremism: for every one point farther from the center an incumbent is, 5 percent more of that candidate's funding comes from individual donors.

Fourth, *challengers fare better financially when states have pro-party laws.* The removal of limits on political parties increases the share of funds that challengers receive from parties by 50 percent. (Keep in mind, however, that they still only get, on average, 16 percent of total money from parties in states without restrictions on parties.) There are several potential implications of these dynamics. In the candidate-centered system, challengers tend to be poorly funded relative to incumbents. A shift toward a party-centered system might improve the financial situation of challengers and their prospects in elections. With respect to our main focus on ideology, we also suggest that raising the salience of party funds should make challengers less beholden to ideological activists, who typically provide them with the most support.

Overall, our results indicate that laws can create a stronger role for parties in financing elections. By allowing parties less restricted access to donors, the ideological sources of money (from individuals and issue groups) can be filtered through the party to support moderate candidates in closely contested districts. In this way, the parties have a potentially "cleansing" effect on the ideological money that is given directly to candidates.

9. Legislatures are less polarized in states with pro-party laws.

The two major parties are ideologically distinctive in each of the 50 states. We see a clear bimodal distribution for ideology among state legislators based on party, in comparison with the rest of the electorate, which displays a normal, unskewed distribution. Our findings suggest that carving a larger financial role for the party organization could attenuate the polarization in state legislatures. We demonstrate that in states with party-centered campaign finance laws, the distance between the party ideological medians in the legislature is considerably shorter than in other states. Over time, our model predicts that removing financial restrictions on parties should lead to less polarized parties, while the reverse is true if parties are restricted. If the distance between parties diminishes and ideological overlap between the parties increases, additional opportunities for bipartisan compromise on policy are likely to arise.

When candidates get money from the party, the dynamics of polarization shift. Officeholders who get money from the party should become less beholden to the ideological partisans who typically fund campaigns. Pragmatist party leaders will tend to be more lenient with members than issue groups on votes that might offend district constituencies. Money controlled by party leaders will enable caucus members to vote in ways that decrease their electoral risk. The availability of party funds may also make it easier for the parties to attract moderate candidates who would otherwise have to pass through ideological donor gatekeepers. We do not argue that party financing will cause partisan legislators to converge inexorably toward the median voter. The ideological positions will remain distinctive because of other powerful forces pushing the parties apart. Indeed, interviews with partisans and scholars in many states suggest that the party leaders in legislatures are more ideological than in the past.[14] But these leaders are responsible to multiple constituencies and must work to preserve their majority status. These incentives predispose them toward pragmatism even if they have strong policy preferences.

The Relationship Between Laws That Limit Parties and Independent Spending

We have focused on political contributions in our analysis. But in the past decade there has been an explosion of campaign spending, particularly at the federal level, which does not involve direct contributions. This financial activity is called by many names, depending on statutes in the American states, but the characteristic that ties them together is that the spending is done *independently* of the candidate's campaign. Those who engage in such campaigns cannot legally coordinate with the candidate, and so these activities are commonly referred to as "independent expenditures" or "IEs."

Independent expenditures are not new. At the federal level IEs have been used from time to time by interest groups, at least since the passage of the FECA amendments in 1974. And if one takes a broader definition of independent spending, it plausibly includes all the efforts in American political history when interest groups advertised in support of favored candidates. In the early part of the 20th century, for example, the United States Brewers' Association frequently engaged directly in campaigns against politicians who favored Prohibition or local taxation of alcoholic beverages (Odegard 1928).

What has changed about independent spending is its pervasiveness. We could readily predict the surge in IE spending based on hydraulic theory and our group-centered conceptualization of political parties. Partisans have strong incentives to find alternative ways to support candidates when financial constraints are imposed on the party organizations, especially during a period when control of government hangs in the balance, as it does in Congress and many state legislatures.

The incentive to deploy independent expenditures is strengthened by contemporary First Amendment jurisprudence, which thwarts efforts by the government to regulate such spending. A foundational court decision, *Buckley v. Valeo* (1976), created a key distinction between contributions and expenditures. The Supreme Court argued that government could restrict the source and size of contributions to candidates and parties because of a sufficiently compelling interest in preventing corruption. But such logic did not apply to expenditures made independently of candidates and parties. Without the explicit exchange between donor and candidate, the threat of a quid pro quo (or its appearance) was greatly diminished.

Subsequent court decisions reinforced *Buckley*, including the infamous *Citizens United v. FEC* (2010), which allows any organization to spend unlimited money in politics.[15] At the federal level, corporations and labor unions were previously barred from such spending (but not individuals).[16] In the aftermath of *Citizens United*, similar laws in states barring any kind of independent organizational spending are now unconstitutional. Nonparty groups have been buoyed as well by an appellate court decision, *SpeechNow.org v. FEC* (2010), which invoked the logic of *Buckley* to disallow contribution limits on organizations making IEs. The reasoning was this: if candidates cannot be corrupted by independent expenditures, then any contributions to organizations making such expenditures should not be corrupting. At this point, *any* nonparty groups deploying IEs can raise money without restrictions (based on *SpeechNow.org v. FEC*) and spend unlimited sums in elections (based on *Citizens United v FEC*).[17]

To demonstrate our argument that tight restrictions on parties cause dramatic increases in independent spending, we once again compare states with and without limits on party organizations. We observe IE data in state legislative elections from 2006 to 2010 gathered by the National Institute on Money in State Politics. NIMSP collected reports filed by individuals and committees with state disclosure agencies in the 20 states that provide relatively robust disclosure.[18] While the data do not cover all the states, we do capture the variety of campaign finance laws in American states, particularly as they apply to political parties. For example, the data include four states that place no limits on parties (IA, MO, NC, and TX), two states that limit contributions to parties (CA and OH), seven states that limit contributions from parties to candidates (AZ, ID, ME, MI, MN, TN, and WA) and seven states that limit contributions to and from parties (AK, CO, CT, MA, OH, OK, and WI). Moreover, the data show conservative totals because some states do not require disclosure of electioneering communications, which target voters before an election but do not explicitly tell them whom to

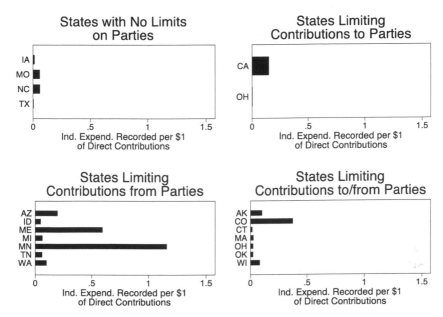

Figure 5.1. Independent Expenditures Relative to Total Contributions in States Depending on Party Contribution Laws (2010–2012). (*Note:* Based on data from NIMSP.)

vote for. Despite some of these limitations, the data provide the best portrait available of IE activity in the American states and allow us to observe whether laws that constrain parties tend to increase the amount of IEs.

Figure 5.1 reports IE spending per $1 of total contributions to candidates in a state. We adjust the figure relative to conventional contributions because we do not want amounts in a large state like California to swamp the analysis. The figure arrays states from top left to bottom right based on the stringency of laws restricting parties. At the top left are states that allow unlimited contributions to and from political parties; the top right shows states with limits on contributions to parties (but no limits on party contributions to candidates); the bottom left shows states limiting contributions from parties (but not contributions to parties); and the bottom right shows states that limit both contributions to and from the parties.

The pattern of IEs illustrates exactly what we expect, namely that IEs are greater when parties are limited, precisely because partisans choose to finance campaigns outside the formal party structure. In states with no limits on parties at all, we observe very few independent expenditures relative to traditional contributions. We note that three of these states—Iowa, Missouri, and North Carolina—are highly contested for control of the legislature, so the pressure for partisan organizing is critical. Yet, partisan organizing tends not to embrace the kind of outside spending that is now pervasive in congressional elections. Moving to the right we see a fairly similar situation in two states that limit contributions to the parties. Both these states have relatively high contributions to the parties (California and Ohio were both roughly $65,000 in 2010), and yet in highly expensive California we observe minimal outside spending and in highly competitive Ohio there is virtually none. Turning to the bottom left graph, with limits on contributions from parties, we observe particularly high spending in Arizona, Maine, and Minnesota. Not coincidentally, these are all states with public financing rules for candidates that limit the amount of money they can spend. The incentives for outside spending are truly significant in such states. Finally, in the bottom right chart we observe states where parties face limits on contributions to and from them. We see particularly high independent spending in highly competitive states such as Colorado, and to a lesser extent in Wisconsin.

Figure 5.1 reflects a snapshot of spending in 20 states, but it suggests at least two additional conditions that increase outside spending beyond the constraints on parties. First, limiting how much candidates spend will generate outside spending. These rules are in place in public financing states that require candidates to cap their own campaign spending in return for getting subsidies. Second, competitive states where control over the legislature is at stake tend to see somewhat more independent spending. In the next section, we turn to *who* is making these independent expenditures.

Why Independent Spending Contributes to Partisan Polarization

Our group-centered view of political parties leads us to believe that IEs contribute to political polarization. In a campaign finance system with limits on contributions to candidates, we expect partisan factions of both purists and pragmatists to exploit IEs as a strategy to support favored candidates. Nonetheless, we anticipate that IEs will tend to benefit the purist factions for at least four reasons.

1. Purists exploit independent expenditures more than pragmatists.

IE spending is risky because groups must be willing to take strongly partisan positions in campaigns that could create political backlash from the electorate. The groups most likely to spend money independently are ideological factions who are willing to take these gambles to promote a cause or candidate. Issue/ideological groups are less concerned than pragmatic benefit seekers, such as business interests, about public backlash resulting from IEs, because voters are not necessarily familiar with the groups sponsoring the ad and the public has limited means to sanction the group for ads it does not like. Some purist partisans may view IEs as an opportunity to set the campaign agenda around their favored issue positions and rally behind candidates who champion them.

To be sure, the pragmatist faction in the party will also exploit IEs by splitting apart an "independent expenditure party committee" that operates in the final months of a campaign without communicating with officials in the traditional party committee. Alternatively, to take advantage of unlimited fundraising allowed by the *SpeechNow.org* decision, party professionals might establish nonparty organizations (some call them "shadow parties") that are not affiliated in any legal sense with the traditional party committee. We have observed this dynamic at the federal level with party establishment figures such as Karl Rove managing two groups since the 2010 elections, American Crossroads and Crossroads GPS, which run campaigns ads in targeted races.[19]

In the emerging realm of independent spending, the pragmatist faction competes directly for IE financing with purists. As we have pointed out, wealthy ideological donors tend to prefer giving their money to groups that highlight the issues they care about. So when IEs become institutionalized in the electoral system as a "normal" way of campaigning, many wealthy donors will be inclined to use nonparty groups rather than the party organization (or the shadow party) to advance their policy goals.

The potency of ideological super PACs is compounded by the shrinkage of nonideological money in the electoral system. Most of that nonideological financing comes from business interests, who stick primarily to the conventional campaign finance system by making contributions to candidates and parties through business PACs. In states with low limits on PAC contributions, however, the ideological money—both from individuals and super PACs—takes up a larger share of total campaign money in the electoral system, with consequences for polarization (Barber 2013). Increasingly, IEs are another way for ideologically sourced funds from individuals and issue groups to help candidates. One of the great ironies of *Citizens United v. FEC* is that corporations have not exploited the ruling to the extent that advocacy groups and labor unions have (Fenton 2014). And yet the media galvanized public attention around the idea that *Citizens United* would make corporations an unstoppable force in Washington.[20]

The highly pragmatic orientation of most corporations makes them refrain from being so publicly partisan. The experience of Target Corporation, a leading retailer, provides a telling example of how highly partisan political activity is not good for business. In the immediate wake of the *Citizens United* decision, Target made a $100,000 contribution to MN Forward, a Minnesota business coalition airing TV ads in support of a Republican gubernatorial candidate who championed lower corporate taxes. However, the fact that the candidate also opposed same-sex marriage drew highly publicized calls for a boycott of Target from civil rights organizations and progressive groups. This publicity hurt Target's image with many customers and compelled the company to make a public apology to employees (Mullins and Zimmerman 2010).

For most business groups, there is greater safety in contributing to candidates and parties directly rather than to IE groups. For this reason, business interests gave soft money to national parties in the years before passage of the BCRA, but we do not observe them giving similar amounts to IE groups. A primary goal of reformers was to put an end to party soft money, and they have largely succeeded. But the consequence has been greater influence for the polarizing tendencies of ideological groups that have not hesitated to exploit IEs. When the campaign system imposes low contribution limits on parties, it diminishes the supply of nonideological money that typically comes from benefit-seekers such as business firms and trade associations. Hence, the trade-off between corruption and ideological polarization: low contribution limits on PACs might restrict the kind of rent-seeking from business interests that Americans deplore as corrupting. But laws to reduce PACs' influence appear to elevate the prominence of ideological groups that are least likely to embrace compromise in politics.

To demonstrate that constraints on party organizations lead to greater dominance of ideological interests through IE spending, we look closely at the groups that engaged in this strategy between 2006 and 2012, using the same data cited above, collected by the National Institute on Money in State Politics. Figure 5.2 includes IE spending by 5 groups in the 3 states *without* party limits (on the right side), and the same groups in the 17 states *with* party limits (on the left side). The groups we identify include: Democratic Party (black), Republican Party (dark gray), labor unions (white), business (light gray), and issue groups (with the broken line). First, note on the left side of the graph that both Democratic and Republican party organizations try to get around constraints by using IEs, and they do so fairly equally.[21] Democrats spent just over 4 cents per dollar of total political contributions made by all donors to state legislative races; Republicans spent roughly 3.5 cents per dollar of contributions.

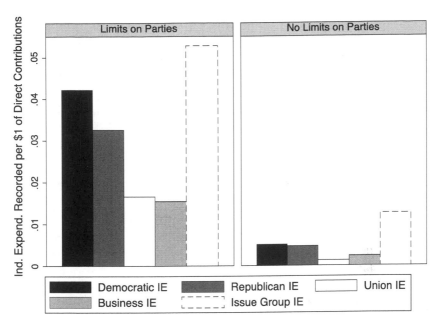

Figure 5.2. Independent Spending by Groups in States With and Without Party Limits (2006–2012). (*Note:* Based on data from NIMSP.)

Of greater significance is the amount of IE spending by issue groups. Between the years 2006 and 2012, issue/ideological groups spent more than 6 cents per dollar of total political contributions made by all donors. Further analysis reveals that 61 percent of these contributions benefited Democratic candidates, while 39 percent benefited Republicans. Overall, the amount spent by issue groups reflects 36 percent of IEs in these states. Some of the largest spenders among issue groups were the Greater Wisconsin Committee, the Michigan Coalition for Progress, the Civil Justice Association of California, the California Alliance, and Twenty First Century Colorado.

Labor unions are also very active in the states with limits on parties, and entirely on behalf of Democrats. They spent 2 cents per dollar of contributions in those states. Recall our analysis in chapter 3, which showed that labor unions tend to support the most liberal candidates in the Democratic Party, a strategy that aligns them closely with very liberal issue groups in the Democratic Party coalition. We also observe about the same amount of independent spending sponsored by business interests, which appeared to come mainly from the various state chapters of Chambers of Commerce, realtor groups, and trade or professional associations.

The findings in figure 5.2 indicate that the IE strategy is dominated by issue/ideological interests. If we also include labor unions, which tend to support the most liberal candidates, then the bias toward the polar edges of the party is even more pronounced. Note in the graph on the right side of figure 5.2 that IEs constitute a very small amount of election spending when political parties are not limited in financing their candidates. IE spending is low because the parties can support their candidates directly and transparently through the conventional campaign finance system. And yet, even in states with pro-party laws some issue groups will use IEs. This is not surprising because such groups may want to shape the campaign issue agenda and put weight behind favored candidates. But the IE amounts are small compared to those in states where party organizations are constrained. When parties are constrained, opportunities arise for issue groups to fill a vacuum by helping candidates who would otherwise rely on party support.

2. The prevalence of IE groups allows ideological donors to avoid the moderating mediation of the party organization.

The availability of IE groups provides additional opportunities for ideological donors to finance ideologically like-minded groups while shunning the party organization that is willing to support moderate candidates. We are not opposed to donors exercising their First Amendment rights by supporting groups or candidates of their choice, but we argue that the political system should incentivize donors to support party organizations, which help build broad-based partisan coalitions. Recall our finding in chapter 2 that pro-party laws can encourage ideological donors to send money to the parties, even when that is not necessarily their first choice. And in chapter 3, we showed how party organizations will then invest these ideologically sourced contributions to finance moderate candidates in close races. This dynamic allows the party organization to serve as an institutional filter to reduce the influence of ideological money in the political system.

The IE groups that tout ideological causes make them attractive venues for donors who might see the party as too wishy-washy. The wealthy donor can have more say in how his or her dollars are spent with an IE group that is highly focused on a few issues and candidates. This situation contrasts sharply with that of a party organization, which often has obligations to multiple candidates and constituencies in towns and counties throughout the state. The nature of a broad party coalition necessitates compromises among factions. Such compromises may upset a major donor who is pushing a cause. The availability of IE groups gives purist contributors an attractive alternative to working with the party organization. In a recent election, a disgruntled major donor to the Minnesota Republican Party chose to stop giving to the party organization because its leadership did not take an uncompromising position on right-to-work laws and other conservative positions (Shaw 2012). Instead he gave to the highly conservative Freedom Club State PAC that supports like-minded state legislators and members of Congress, including Michelle Bachmann (Richert 2012). Meanwhile, the Minnesota Republican Party faced a $2 million debt at the close of the 2012 election. Raising money has become increasingly challenging for the parties thanks to constraints on fundraising, their broad focus, and requirements for highly transparent reporting of donations. According to Ken Martin, chair of the Minnesota DFL, "If you're a donor and you can write a million-dollar check to an outside group with little or no disclosure and focus it on very specific activity and have no [regulatory] urgency or burdens in terms of disclosure hanging over your head, why wouldn't you go that way and give a contribution?"[22]

The increasing importance of these outside groups puts pressure on members to toe the line on specific policies that are out of the mainstream among the electorate. At the federal level, members of Congress talk of "trimming their sails" in anticipation of outside spending for which they might be criticized in the next election (Tokaji and Strause 2014, 79). A former chair of the National Republican Congressional Committee, Tom Davis (R-VA), places part of the blame on the weakened state of political parties. He says, "[C]ampaign finance laws, as well-intentioned as they may have been, have pushed money away from the political parties—centering forces—and out to ideological interest groups. Politicians face more pressure to please these extreme interests" (Davis 2012).

3. Pragmatists lose the strategic benefit of direct connection to candidates and the broader party structure.

While pragmatists in the party organization can also exploit IEs, they forego many advantages when they are forced to avoid communicating with their candidates as they normally do as party officials. To be sure, we know that professional campaigners have become adept at coordinating messages under rules requiring "independence" (Tokaji and Strause 2014). But it is undoubtedly more challenging for independent groups to craft nuanced strategy and shift quickly as events on the ground change in the final days of a campaign. Not only is it more difficult to coordinate media campaigns with candidates, but grassroots efforts to mobilize voters suffer as well. According to an election lawyer for Democratic state parties, Neil Reiff, the IE vendors tend to focus on highly polarizing ads rather than broad voter mobilization: "Most [consultants] just want to run ads and collect their checks. They don't care about the labor-intensive, low-cash returns on grassroots work."[23]

From a purely budgetary standpoint, we can expect problems managing campaigns efficiently when funds are not fungible across partisan groups. There are times in a campaign when it might make more sense to spend money on voter contact rather than TV ads. But decisions about the best use of the marginal dollar cannot be made when campaign organizations are legally cordoned off from one another and each IE group has already allocated its money to be spent on a particular activity. Substitution that might take place within the formal party organization in the heat of the campaign is likely to be minimal. In this way, the pragmatist faction of the party loses a valuable strategic asset when the party organization cannot be the venue for such decisions.

The emphasis on IEs also entails an emphasis on TV and individual candidates. This is not typically the way party organizations operate. Instead, parties consider the broader candidate slate and balance TV with grassroots efforts. One state party executive says, "The super PACs have, frankly, an easier sell. . . . Invest in us, and we're going to go on television and say these horrible things about Republicans." He added, "We do voter registrations, we do vote-by-mail campaigns. We do a lot of things that are a little bit less sexy but no less important."[24] Others have noted that the ads made by outside groups do not always resonate with local voters.[25] In effect, the campaign finance laws that limit party organizations appear to have encouraged a fragmented partisan campaign that short-circuits the combination of local coherence and broad partisan perspective that traditional party organizations might have conferred on campaigns.

4. National groups displace the role of state parties.

A related problem is that the state party organization loses power to national issue groups that have the wherewithal to raise money from national constituencies. Recent research shows that partisan groups organized at the national level are using IEs to influence the outcome of state-level races (Hamm et al. 2014). These groups do not necessarily work with local parties and groups the way state parties do. Groups like the Republican State Leadership Committee (RSLC) are not integrated into the broader party structure that includes national, state, and local committees, all of which have broad-based leadership of officeholders and activists. A good example of the power of national groups over local and state parties is Wisconsin. In a battle with the Republican governor over his effort to take away the collective bargaining rights of public unions, local Democratic party officials appeared willing to negotiate a compromise but nationally based outside groups running ads were not.[26] Notably, the state parties in Wisconsin did not have much money to back up their arguments while outside groups did. In federal elections, the parties formerly played a major role in coordinating voter mobilization for races across the ticket, but many experienced campaign professionals no longer view the state parties as effective or as a place to build a career. The best talent flows to super PACs (Tokaji and Strause 2014).

The loss of power for state parties will likely accelerate because many state parties face contribution limits, while super PACs do not under the Court decision in *SpeechNow.org*. At the same time, state parties have been severely restricted from campaigning for the entire party ticket because of the federalization of campaign finance law.[27] Under BCRA, any grassroots activity that includes support for federal candidates must abide by restrictions on the federal definition of soft money, even if state laws are less restrictive. This obstacle increases the incentives to use nationally sponsored super PACs to make up for the weakness of state parties; super PACs have begun to do some of the things that state and local parties used to do, such as building grassroots infrastructure, recruiting volunteers, and supporting full-time staff. In comparing the importance of different groups in federal elections, interviews of political consultants revealed, according to one scholar, that "the overriding theme was that the state and local parties are just not the important players that they used to be in federal elections. On some occasions, we got laughs or chuckles when we even mentioned state or local parties" (Daniel Tokaji, as quoted in Overby 2014).

Even if some state parties are adept at IEs (as they are in Minnesota, for example), the arrangement in which parties are legally cut off from their own candidates makes no logical sense. Allowing parties to raise and spend more money in coordination with candidates would make them more important to candidates and give them a more powerful voice in recruitment and in setting the direction of campaigns. Drawing on the group-centered model of parties articulated by the UCLA school, we believe the formal party reflects a key faction, with its own set of demands on the coalition.

To the degree pragmatists in the party organization dominate the resource game, they have a bigger say in how to craft messages and where to invest campaign funds. The money allows parties to use carrots and sticks with other elements of the party outside the organization. State parties can invest in local parties and activist groups in ways that encourage them to avoid giving a free path to extremist candidates. In short, the ability to give and withhold resources is a significant source of power.

The institutionalization of IEs is moving quickly at the federal level and is already a common campaign strategy in states such as Arizona, California, and Minnesota. We expect the growth of IE groups in state legislative elections unless campaign finance laws carve out a greater role for parties. As we have shown in the preceding analysis, IE spending is most robust in states that limit the parties. These are the same states where polarization between the parties in the legislature appears greatest (as we demonstrated in chapter 4). Party organizations may attempt to get around these laws by using IEs, but this adaptation is a weak substitute for having laws that give the parties greater freedom to support candidates. Indeed, if the IE strategy were an effective substitute for party organizations, we should not observe the differences we see between limited and unlimited states with respect to ideological polarization. The fact that we see different outcomes in these states implies that having campaign money inside the traditional party organization matters. This dynamic suggests that the UCLA school and other proponents of party network theory are overly optimistic in assuming that parties easily adapt organizational forms to achieve similar outcomes.

Lack of Transparency

Aside from their impact on polarization, IEs present another problem: heavy use of IEs undermines financial transparency in politics. IEs are often funded by groups with names that the public does not recognize, with little reference to whether they are Republican or Democratic partisans. At the federal level, for example, we observe super PACs such as "Crossroads America" or "Freedom Works" or "Citizens for a Working America." To make matters even more challenging, some of these groups do not even have to report information on their donors because they are classified as "social welfare" organizations under section 501(c)4 of federal tax laws.

Reformers have been focused on imposing disclosure requirements on groups that run campaign ads independently. This strategy hardly addresses the larger problem: voters simply do not know these groups, which makes it a daunting challenge to bring broader accountability to their actions. Unlike party organizations, the vast majority of these groups have short histories and the kind of bland labels that give no indication of who is behind them. We do not believe that an emphasis on disclosure of outside groups, while laudable, will significantly advance the goals of political transparency and accountability.

Our theory suggests a different approach to improving transparency and accountability. Our hydraulic theory implies that funds now being spent by IEs would diminish greatly if the party organizations played a larger role in financing politics. The findings shown in figure 5.2 suggest that we are correct that removing the fetters from parties might eliminate much of this spending. With this in mind, we turn to our suggestions for campaign finance reform in the next chapter.

CHAPTER 6

The Future of Reform: Build Canals, Not Dams

Our findings about the relationship between partisan donors and campaign finance laws have important implications for reform aimed at reducing ideological polarization between the parties. Given the moderating tendencies of pragmatists in the party organization—particularly the leadership in the legislative caucus—we feel strongly that more money should flow through parties. This goal can be achieved by allowing parties greater freedom to finance elections, without many of the regulatory constraints on contributions and expenditures that now pertain. For this reason we urge reformers to consider a "party-centered" campaign finance system that would boost the influence of the pragmatist wing of the party by making party organizations more salient in elections.

To accomplish this strategy, reformers would have to give up on long-held assumptions about the value of imposing relatively low contribution limits on parties as a way to thwart corruption. Low contribution limits, or even *any* contribution limits, on parties distort the campaign finance system in ways that tend to benefit partisan purists. In many ways, the distortion in the campaign finance system that tilts influence toward purists is no less problematic for democratic politics than the distortion attributed to wealthy rent-seeking interests. In either case, political representation is strongly biased toward the preferences of the wealthy interests. Indeed, low-income Americans may suffer as much from polarization in the party system as from quid pro quo corruption; but it is this latter transgression that is currently the target of campaign finance regulations. Partisan polarization tends to exacerbate problems of economic inequality because political stalemate makes government less responsive to the needs of poorer citizens (Hacker and Pierson 2010; McCarty, Poole, and Rosenthal 2006). If party organizations had more freedom to raise and spend money in election campaigns, we believe that legislatures would be less polarized and more likely to find the compromises necessary for governing in a separated system of powers and for forging deals that serve the broader electorate.

Recalibrating campaign finance laws will require a shift away from the anticorruption framework that puts an emphasis on limiting money in politics. Instead, we urge that reformers conceive of their task as "building canals, not dams." In other words, reformers should think broadly about the institutional flow of money into politics, rather than focusing on one-to-one transactions between donors and candidates.[1] For too long, political reforms that were intended to clamp down on political contributions have been predicated on the seemingly unassailable notion of "one person, one vote" (Feingold 1988). But policy is not made by counting votes; it is the product of contestation between well-resourced groups with intense policy preferences (Cain 2014). The current campaign finance system (and nominating system) gives advantages to small factions that influence the direction of the party coalition through their control over campaign resources and other political assets.

To put it plainly, erecting dams—constructing contribution limits to hold back money—not only does not work, it actually favors a relatively small group of purists. The purists are willing to go to great lengths to influence the outcome of elections, even when contribution limits constrain how much they can give to candidates. When candidates face low contribution limits in a regulatory context that prohibits parties from supporting candidates generously, purist factions mobilize donations from their members, manage voter mobilization campaigns, and may even run independent advertising to advance their favorite candidates. In this way, the anticorruption approach to reform tends to purge the campaign finance system of benefit-seekers (e.g., business interests) while elevating the issue-oriented, ideological financiers of American elections. We argue for an honest acknowledgment—and skillful balancing—of the trade-off between combating corruption on the one hand and mitigating ideological polarization on the other.

Let us be clear that we are not criticizing purist factions for trying to influence elections. Such activity is their constitutional right, and we believe members of such groups act as solid citizens by engaging in politics to promote what they see as the good society. And as we said previously, we recognize the value that purist factions add to the party system by helping to clarify the policy positions of the parties, which in turn helps voters make decisions. At the same time, we highly value the role of pragmatists in mediating diverse interests within and between the major parties. Their work helps make governing possible in a large republic with a constitutional system of separated powers. The pragmatic leadership of party insiders provides the glue that binds diverse interests, and this glue, by preventing fragmentation, helps to lessen policy gridlock (Pildes 2015).

What a Party-Centered Campaign Finance System Would Look Like

We propose four relatively simple steps to improve the campaign finance system. Our reform proposals are minimalist for two main reasons. First, we are concerned that prevailing approaches to regulating money in politics lead to complicated rules with layers of details about what political committees can and cannot do. We have not addressed these complexities in this book, but it seems clear that the profusion of regulations surrounding financial reform adds perversely to the cost of politics and gives advantages to those with the legal resources to overcome them. Our focus has been the impact of laws on ideological polarization but, given space, we could have written about the dampening effect of such complex laws on legitimate political activity (see, for example, Bauer 2013). We want more political activity, not less, and we would like much of it to be channeled through accountable organizations such as the political parties, which have a remarkable history of creating broad governing coalitions that respond to majority sentiments in the electorate. Our approach is very much rooted in a pluralist tradition that pays attention to challenges of collective action for less well-off citizens and values fair contestation among groups (Cain 2014).

Second, we think our minimalist approach, which focuses on strengthening party organizations, also advances other worthy goals of political reformers, but in less conventional ways than most proposals. Critics of the campaign finance system, for example, claim that incumbents control most of the campaign money, which makes them hard to beat. From our perspective, strengthening the party should address this problem, because the parties are in fact the most likely sources of support for challengers intent on competing against incumbents.

Another concern of reformers is the lack of transparency in campaign money, and our proposal helps here as well. At the federal level, there have been intense efforts recently by reform advocates to require nonprofit organizations that engage in any activity that resembles electioneering to reveal the names of their donors.[2] Some of these proposals would require the involvement of agencies such as the Internal Revenue Service and the Securities and Exchange Commission, which have limited experience in dealing with political regulation.[3] We think that encouraging the flow of money through parties would greatly improve disclosure and accountability, since parties regularly report all their finances in great detail to the Federal Election Commission (FEC). This would obviate the need to engage other federal agencies in elections in ways that are controversial and often delegitimizing to the proper work of those agencies (Mayer 2014).

Given our concerns about the overcomplexity of regulations and our findings about the positive impact of party organizations on the electoral system, we propose four basic rules to create a party-centered system of campaign finance:

1. Limits on contributions to the political parties should be relatively high or nonexistent. A chief goal of reforms should be to channel more money through accountable and moderating party organizations. Parties should be treated differently than PACs and candidates. Our study examined many states that had no limits on contributions, and we observed decreased polarization in these states. There might be good reasons to have some limits, so long as they are not so low as to cause the distorting effects we illustrated. Such limits would also prevent party leaders from "shaking down" interest groups for very high contributions. A reasonable limit would set some boundaries on such behavior. This limit should depend, of course, on the cost of elections in a particular state.

2. Modest limits should be imposed on contributions to candidates. In conjunction with raising limits on contributions to the parties, we think it is important to place reasonable limits on the amounts that candidates can raise from nonparty contributors. Doing this will prevent interest groups and ideological donors from simply focusing their largesse on favorite candidates. As we showed in chapter 2, placing limits on candidate contributions encourages donors—including ideological donors—to give to the party instead. The combination of high or no limits on parties, with modest restrictions on candidates, will help channel the flow of money through party organizations.

3. No restrictions should be imposed on party support of candidates. Political parties should be permitted to help their candidates as much as desired with direct contributions or in-kind support. This is a critical aspect of attenuating polarization, because parties tend to target moderate candidates in closely contested districts. Not only will this dynamic help finance more moderates, but it will encourage the financing of challengers to face incumbents. Currently most state parties—including the caucus in the legislature—play a very limited role in financing candidates. The leadership that controls the legislative party, especially in highly competitive states, has powerful incentives to finance challengers and moderates. We would not think it unreasonable if parties could provide at least half of candidate resources for a political campaign.

4. Public financing should support party organizations. Many proposals seek to subsidize elections as a way of reducing the influence of big money in the political system. We support public financing of elections because we believe that elections are an underfunded public good, and that providing more resources for elections might lead to improved voter information and participation. But we think that most popular public financing proposals would tend to exacerbate problems of polarization because they ignore the vital role of political parties.

Two recent efforts in particular come to mind. First is the so-called "matching system" approach, which seeks to encourage small donors by having the government match each small donation with a multiple of that amount in public subsidies. In New York City, for instance, a donor might choose to contribute $50 to a candidate. The city government will then match this amount by a multiple of 6, which provides the candidate with a total of $350 ($50 from the individual and $300 from the government).[4] This strategy encourages candidates to mobilize small donors, which is why reform advocates would like to adopt this matching program for state and federal elections (Malbin 2013).

We are concerned, however, that participants in matching programs are not necessarily representative of the broader electorate. As we showed in chapter 2, small donors are as ideological as large donors. For this reason, if matching programs simply mobilize the same demographic of potential donors, this dynamic might reinforce polarization.[5] To avoid these polarizing tendencies the matching system must truly expand the range of small political contributors beyond the intensely ideological donors who give money, and also encourage donations to broad-based organizations, including political parties and other kinds of multicandidate campaign committees.

The second approach to public financing that we call into question goes under the name of "Clean Elections" reforms. These have been implemented in Arizona, Connecticut, and Maine. Under Clean Elections, candidates must raise small sums of money from individuals to qualify for a lump sum of public funds for use in both the primary and the general election. Those who participate cannot accept any contributions from other entities. In theory, this political reform opens elections to a wider range of candidates (an important goal sought by reformers), but research suggests that candidates who win elections tend to be more extreme than candidates who emerge under the private system of financing (Hall 2014).

The reason ideological candidates appear to do better is related to a main argument we have been making in this book. Namely, anticorruption laws, such as Clean Elections, tend to purge pragmatic money from the electoral system. These programs essentially filter out party organizations and benefit-seeking donors (e.g., business interests, trade associations) who tend to provide financing for moderate candidates. To the happiness of some, Clean Elections reform appears to reduce the influence of these much-reviled benefit-seeking groups who pursue favorable treatment on regulations and technical aspects of policies in order to enhance their profits. But in purging self-interested money from the campaign finance system, the policy purists appear to gain influence in electoral politics (Bonica 2013; Bonica et al. 2013). Without parties and business PAC money, candidates become more dependent on ideological small donors and independent spending groups that seem to proliferate under public financing systems like Clean Elections. While such public finance programs may increase competition by putting incumbents in peril—not such a bad thing—these officeholders can be replaced all too easily by ideologues (Hall 2014; Masket and Miller 2014).

Of greater concern to us is that public financing schemes rarely consider how to enlarge the role of parties. This is regrettable because subsidizing the parties is one of the few proven ways to address both the concern about corruption and the concern about ideological polarization. We have initially characterized these twin problems as zero-sum, but public financing of the parties has the potential to address them simultaneously.

Some states already provide subsidies to parties, but the amounts are rather small. According to the National Conference of State Legislatures, 10 states provide public grants to political parties. State residents are typically given an option on tax forms to "check off" stating that they want some of their tax payment to go toward the political parties (without increasing the filer's tax liability) or add-ons (which do increase the filer's tax liability), ranging in amounts from $1 to $25. In 8 of these states the tax filer can request which party gets the funds, which are often used to defray the expenses of party conventions.[6] Political parties also benefit from lower postal rates for direct mail than other political committees. But we think that public subsidies to political parties should be larger than they are now, which would strengthen the parties' roles in elections. Properly designed, these programs could dilute the negative impact of both ideological and rent-seeking donors.

Another potential public financing proposal would provide public subsidies to each voter in the form of a voucher worth $50–$100 (Ackerman and Ayres 2002; Hasen forthcoming 2016; Lessig 2011). During each election cycle, citizens would have the option of either directing this voucher from a state or federal treasury to a candidate of their choice, or delegating this power to an intermediary group, such as a political party or political action committee (PAC). The virtue of the voucher system is that funding decisions are made through individual choices rather than statutory formulas, which plausibly enhances public deliberation and participation. Should a voucher system be attempted, we think voters should be nudged with incentives to give vouchers to political parties and multicandidate committees. One possibility is to simply make the political parties—including a minor party—the default option for voters who would rather not spend time choosing a candidate. Privileging parties in a voucher program might advance some of the positive dynamics associated with party activity (e.g., moderation, support for challengers, transparency). To be sure, the details of such a proposal would have to be worked out clearly, and an experimentation period in local elections should be included to provide insights about the consequences of this reform.

At the very least, if public financing schemes leave out the parties, these rules should not prohibit parties from using private money to support their candidates. To do otherwise invites large amounts of independent spending by issue groups with limited accountability. In Connecticut, the legislature recently changed its Clean Elections law to allow parties to support candidates with private funds.[7] We believe this is a wise change. In Minnesota, another favorable wrinkle has been added to a public financing law, allowing parties to play a strong role in elections: under the Minnesota public finance laws, candidates are required to limit their own spending, which makes them rely heavily on the party in campaigns. Notably, the Minnesota parties face their own limits on private financing, but unlike the national parties, they are allowed to coordinate with outside groups to help their candidates.[8] According to the chair of the DFL, this helps them serve as the "central hub that drives the campaign agenda."[9] And when parties drive the agenda, they typically steer it toward the median voter.

Will a Party-Centered System Work?

To summarize our argument, we predict that our reform strategy will contribute to three positive dynamics in the campaign finance system. First, it will reduce the direct reliance of candidates on ideological sources of money.

This will especially affect the individual donors who provide the bulk of money directly to candidates. The party, instead, will be able to serve as a filter for these ideological donations to reduce their power to influence electoral politics. Second, the party will use its money to finance more moderates who have the best chance of winning competitive elections. To be sure, many races are in lopsided one-party districts, but the party's ability to redistribute funds from ideological and material-minded sources to moderates should, over several election cycles, enhance moderation in the legislature. Third and finally, our party-centered strategy should diminish the importance of independent expenditures, which are often polarizing, nontransparent, and unaccountable.

These three claims are supported with evidence, but we foresee at least two reasonable objections suggesting that our proposal will not work. Let us attend to these before addressing the challenges to implementation.

Objection 1. The political parties will serve merely as conduits if they have no financing limits. This is an important concern. If a candidate faces limits and the parties do not, then the party could plausibly become an empty vessel through which candidates can avoid restrictions on their own fundraising. The classic anticircumvention approach is to impose limits on parties as a way to preclude the conduit strategy. And we believe it is precisely this party-limiting strategy, taken to unreasonable bounds, that has been so detrimental to American politics. To give one example, the federal Bipartisan Campaign Reform Act of 2002 tried to prevent federal candidates from benefiting from soft money by imposing a $10,000 limit on soft money donations to state parties (which under state laws often have no restrictions on soft money). As we explained in the previous chapter, this rule effectively "federalized" state party financing, making it extremely difficult for the state parties to run large voter mobilization campaigns for the entire party ticket (Reiff 2012). The results have been nearly catastrophic for many state parties. Not only does this rule limit their ability to help federal candidates in the state, but it impacts their voter contact efforts to help candidates in state elections.[10]

The anti-circumvention approach leads to a "whack-a-mole" dynamic in which regulators keep adding new statutes in a vain attempt to close new loopholes as they crop up. We think a better strategy would be to simply enforce rules that prohibit donors from earmarking contributions to the party. This would mean that donors could not tell the party where they want their contribution to be spent and that candidates could not legally compel the party to turn over funds on the basis of a claim that particular donations were intended for themselves.

A surer way to prevent parties from serving as conduits is to encourage their institutionalization as well-bounded, complex organizations with professional norms for decision making. One way to do this is to make them desirable organizations for offering positions of leadership to ambitious individuals. In the legislative caucus, this comes naturally because the legislative leadership usually takes control of party finances. Legislative leaders might also recruit talented members to serve on the party committee and hire professional staff to help win elections. For state committees outside the legislative caucus, it would help if parties had more autonomy over the conduct of their internal affairs, instead of being regulated heavily by state governments. One critical change would be to allow party organizations a greater role in nominating favored candidates; such an enhanced role could include the ability to provide campaign support in primary elections. This practice is currently forbidden by some state laws and, more importantly, by local political norms. Nonetheless, we would like to see the party organization become, once again, an attractive venue for the contestation of candidate nominations, rather than yielding so much power to issue activists outside the party structure who can mobilize their factions behind preferred party candidates in local primaries.

We have no illusions that our recommendations for strengthening the parties will all be cheerfully accepted. Some of the most powerful people in the party—incumbent officeholders—do not particularly like having strong party organizations because robust organizations threaten their autonomy. But, more critically, any pro-party legislation can be perceived by an incumbent as giving ammunition to the rival party as it runs a candidate to challenge the incumbent's reelection. Despite such misgivings, partisans understand the necessity of organizing collectively to win elections, particularly in states with intense competition for control of government. As we have argued throughout this book, the party committee could become more institutionalized as the central node for partisan organizing if campaign finance laws and other statutes did not inhibit party organizational development.

Objection 2. Giving party organizations more resources will not prevent ideological partisans from having significant power. Let us be clear. We do not claim that ideological partisans will be thwarted from influencing the party. If laws become more pro-party, many of the same actors, both purists and pragmatists, will continue to participate in party affairs. However, we argue that a shift in the legal terrain will tilt power *toward* the pragmatist faction. And with relatively more resources to work with, the pragmatists will have additional influence to shape the direction of the party coalition.

Directing more money to parties will not "solve" polarization. But we believe it could diminish the extremist tendencies in the system because pragmatists will have more leverage than they have now. The formal party organization is an "interest group" too, and to the degree that its loyalists dominate the resource game, they have a bigger say in how to craft messages and where to invest resources. Having financial resources would enable the formal party to defend its own interests and preferences. The party organization may not even generate more moderates in the legislature, but by having abundant campaign resources, its leadership maintains a stronger position to challenge extremists and to broker deals. As one longtime political consultant in North Carolina observed with respect to money flowing to nonparty groups, "There's nobody refereeing the fights. We're not seeing party bosses or strong chairs that can try to work out deals behind closed doors to keep it from breaking out into the public."[11]

Having control over resources means more than being able to give campaign contributions. Resource control provides the means for leadership to offer carrots and sticks (mostly carrots, we think) to encourage members to take a tough vote for a party position that is more moderate than the purist faction of the party might prefer. A leadership that lacks leverage over the far right or left wing factions of the party has little means by which to generate bipartisan support for legislation. In legislative battles, members fear that purist factions will attack them in the next election or, at the very least, refuse to give them valuable campaign support. But having the party organization to rely on as a very large source of campaign support could give legislators more confidence to buck the purist faction. Of course, a stronger party alone will not always be able to stave off challenges from the far left or right in party primaries. No amount of money or party support would have helped Eric Cantor when he lost the 2014 primary to a little-known, underfunded Tea Party candidate. But backlash from the purists might be minimized when the party organization can easily defend the reelection of officeholders who are willing to compromise despite the wishes of the purists.

As we demonstrated in the previous chapter, pragmatists are disadvantaged when the campaign finance system becomes hospitable to independent spending. While pragmatists can use nonparty organizations to wage campaigns, our analysis shows that IEs are dominated by purist groups. This arrangement gives the purists additional leverage in setting the campaign agenda and shaping the behaviors of politicians. Like the UCLA school, we view purist policy-demanders such as the NRA or MoveOn.Org as essential elements of the party coalitions. But there are dangers as these purist factions augment their power within the coalition by controlling a disproportionate share of campaign resources in elections.

Our argument is not absolutist. The parties will always rely on ideological money, which will influence their direction. Party polarization will not disappear anytime soon because polarization stems from so many other factors besides campaign money. We have also drawn attention to the strong asymmetry between the parties. The Republicans have many more highly conservative donors who view the GOP as too moderate for their liking and much prefer to finance very conservative candidates and groups. But party leaders, like John Boehner in the U.S. House, tend not to be ideologues. We think the same dynamic is mostly true at the state level. Leaders of party coalitions cannot afford to be overly ideological if they want to stay in power.

The impact of our pro-party laws should be greatest in states with professional legislatures and in states where control of the chamber is tightly contested. It is precisely here where money matters so much and where collective partisan organizing is imperative. Well-financed party organizations, particularly legislative parties, should have the power to tamp down the more ideological elements of the party coalition.

Will It Work for Congress?

Despite our theoretical expectations and our empirical analysis, we remain realistic about whether a shift to party-centered campaign finance laws will affect election dynamics at the federal level. We expect that our findings will generalize to Congress, particularly given that the strongest results we uncover are for the most professional legislatures (those that are most closely comparable to Congress). In some ways our remedy of changing campaign finance laws may be "too little, too late" to lessen the ideological divide. Nonetheless, we believe strongly that the national committees of the political parties should have fewer restrictions on financing elections. Even if the impact of financially stronger parties on polarization is minimal, we think the advantages of transparency and accountability make a powerful case for channeling money through the party committees.

The post-Watergate reforms of the 1970s passed by Congress were insufficiently flexible to adjust to the new realities of a strengthened party system (La Raja 2013). The Federal Election Campaign Act (FECA), particularly its 1974 amendments, enshrined a candidate-centered system that, in effect, treated political parties as if they were interest groups. The law did this by treating parties and PACs identically in the limits it imposed on contributions to candidates. Even the limits on party-coordinated expenditures with candidates turned out to be fairly ungenerous as the cost of elections mounted. The inefficient campaign finance system, which channeled money mostly to incumbents, started to break down in the 1990s as the party system became truly competitive for control of Congress, and the party programs diverged significantly. This situation raised the stakes for all partisans to organize collectively.

Regrettably, the constraints of FECA on parties made it implausible for them to play a significant role in organizing campaigns. And because the party limits were not adjusted for inflation, the situation only got worse as time went on. The consequence was that partisans started experimenting with soft money in the late 1980s as a way to circumvent the party limits. Soft money, including funds without source and size limits, could be used only for "party-building" purposes. In the 1990s, the parties began to spend a large portion of these funds on television ads. The parties claimed that these were issue ads to promote the party, when in reality any reasonable person would acknowledge that they were intended to help targeted candidates.

The response to party soft money by the reform community and many liberal members of Congress was the conventional anticorruption approach. The reformers pushed to ban soft money in the hope of returning to the candidate-centered campaign finance system of the 1970s, even though the party system had changed dramatically. In 2002, Congress passed a typically populist reform measure, the Bipartisan Campaign Reform Act, which banned party soft money for the national parties and created a surfeit of anticircumvention rules to prevent state party committees from using it as well. The new rules made it arduous for parties at all levels of government to organize partisan campaigns across the ticket and weakened their position vis-à-vis outside interests.[12]

As hydraulic theory would predict, partisan money began to flow in great abundance to outside organizations, some already existing (e.g., unions) and some made up on the fly. Supreme Court jurisprudence, from *Buckley v. Valeo* (1976) through *Citizens United v. FEC* (2010), consistently guaranteed, invoking First Amendment protections, that these nonparty groups would be relatively unfettered in their actions to raise and spend money. The courts, however, permitted the ban on parties, invoking the reasoning that parties, because of their close ties to candidates, might otherwise be tempted to engage in quid pro quo corruption. This reasoning stands as the only basis on which the courts currently allow restrictions on financing elections. Post-BCRA, the political parties cannot even coordinate with partisans outside the party who rely on soft money, even though these nonparty groups (many of them representing purist partisans) can coordinate with one another. The cumulative effect of populist reform has been to fracture campaign spending and disperse partisan influence, giving partisan and highly ideological interest groups greater leverage, compared with the party insiders who operate through formal party committees.

Outside spending in federal elections is now firmly institutionalized and is unlikely to dissipate any time soon. Super PACs and 501(c)4s have attracted the intense support of very wealthy individuals and prominent national issue groups. These political actors will continue to focus their considerable resources on targeted races, even if the parties become financially stronger. The potential for exerting national-level influence, even when races are lost, is simply too enticing for them to resist. A casino magnate like Sheldon Adelson surely understands that he advances his cause with a gamble on targeted races, even when his candidate loses.

We are therefore pessimistic about a return to an era in the 1980s when candidates controlled the electoral environment with their own committee resources. The purist factions in either party have strong incentives to challenge party pragmatists with the threat of running their own campaigns rather than cooperating within the party structure. Even if pragmatists running the national party committees gain more financial power under a more pro-party system, the purist factions will see benefits in running advertisements to set the campaign agenda on their own terms. For this reason, the leaders of issue groups such as the Club for Growth or NRA on the right, or Sierra Club and NARAL on the left, will continue to mount narrow issue campaigns in selected races throughout the country.

Despite our pessimism about using enlightened campaign finance law to turn back the clock on polarization at the federal level, we think that the reforms we advocate are worth pursuing for the other reasons we mentioned. First, changes at the state level should create consequences that bubble up over time to the federal level, since candidates who run for the state legislature are the main pool of candidates for Congress. Second, implementing pro-party laws at the federal level will also increase accountability as an increased flow of money would have to be routed through highly transparent political parties. Third, by pushing more money back to traditional campaign organizations, the FEC would have the appropriate role of regulating a greater portion of money in politics, rather than involving "amateur" agencies such as the IRS or SEC.

Fortunately, there is some movement in the direction of pro-party laws, although this has resulted from the handiwork of the Supreme Court rather than Congress. As a result of the *McCutcheon v. FEC* (2014) decision, contributors no longer face the aggregate contribution limits that were imposed by the 1974 FECA. Before this decision, they would have been allowed to give a maximum of $123,200 to all political committees in the 2013–2014 election cycle.[13] The new ruling enables limitless contributions, meaning that parties do not compete as much with candidates for contributions. This allows them to set up joint-fundraising operations to raise money for both the party and its candidates. States have also begun changing their laws to comply with the ruling.[14] The problem in most states, however, is that when they adjust contribution limits, they typically focus only on raising the limits for contributions to candidates and not those going to parties (which is not surprising, since such changes tend to help the incumbents who write the laws). In the 2013 session, for example, of the nine states that raised or eliminated contribution limits, only two states—Connecticut and Maryland—raised the limits on donations to parties (and these were very modest increases).[15] The other seven states reemphasized the candidate-centered approach by raising limits only on individual and PAC contributions to candidates.[16]

Can Pro-Party Reforms Be Implemented?

We said at the outset of this book that our position regarding greater financial autonomy for the political parties would not be popular. We are arguing for strengthening party organizations by allowing them a greater role in funding political campaigns. This recommendation comes at a time when much of the public disdains a party system that has generated considerable antagonism and gridlock at the federal level and in many states. But it is precisely because of the polarized nature of the party system that we are making our proposals.

Our paradoxical argument is that fortifying party organizations should make the parties less shrill and more open to compromise. We know, however, that this argument may not resonate with the broader public, even if it has the support of many expert scholars in the field (Cain 2014; McCarty 2013; Persily 2014; Pildes 2014; Wallison and Gora 2009). Some of the findings that buttress our arguments seem flatly counterintuitive. To take one example, those who believe the solution to better democracy is increasing the number of small donors may regard with suspicion our finding that expanding the number of small donors is likely only to intensify the problems of polarization. To be sure, the push for a greater number of small donors seems to accord with arguments favoring equity and opposing corruption, but the effort to increase the number of small donors is unlikely to create a less ideological population of donors. In fact, the pursuit of small donors will simply reinforce a strong bias in the political system toward highly ideological policy positions at the expense of moderation and compromise.

True, this kind of policy distortion is different from the kind we associate with corruption, but it is no less a form of representational bias in favor of wealthier and more educated segments of the public. As Larry Bartels has argued in his book, *Unequal Democracy*, the chief distortion in policymaking is not corruption but elite ideology, which is reflected in the donor class (Bartels 2008). Another seminal book by McCarty, Poole, and Rosenthal, *Polarized America* (2006), notes that the distancing of party elites and ensuing gridlock prevent government from adjusting policies to changing economic and demographic circumstances in order to dampen growing inequalities. Not surprisingly, the least fortunate suffer when policy compromises cannot be forged to effect policy adjustments.

Our reform proposal to strengthen parties financially will be met with considerable skepticism because it challenges the prevailing populist narrative about the malign effects of money in politics. We have put forth a pluralist framework for understanding the campaign finance system that asks concerned observers to focus less on the one-to-one exchanges between donors and candidates, and more on the institutional flow of money in politics though different kinds of political groups. We see institutional mediation of party organizations as a partial means to dampen the factional power of political donors who tend to pull the party coalitions to the extremes on social or economic issues. The wealthy Americans who donate money have policy positions and priorities that are sometimes (but not always) at odds with the preferences of the broader population (Gilens 2012; Rigby and Wright 2013). Our recommendation to facilitate the flow of money through political parties will not necessarily change this imbalance in power; however, we believe that the pragmatic orientation of the leadership of the party organizations will help to prevent the worst excesses of extremism that thwart the proper functioning of government, to the detriment of the most marginalized citizens.

We turn to political parties to help dampen the power of financially strong ideological interests. Our pluralist solution of channeling more money through parties is imperfect, of course, because the party organizations will remain vulnerable to capture insofar as they come to rely on narrow financial constituencies (which would imply very thin pluralism within the parties). But given the imperative to win elections and secure the rewards of elective office, the pragmatists who typically control the party organizations are likely to appreciate that kowtowing to narrow interests puts at risk the party's control of government. We believe that the pragmatic ambition for power and status, which is inherent in human nature, will prove ample to balance the passion of the purist factions for causes that may lead to intolerance for rival opinions, delegitimizing of the opposition, and gridlock. This is not a cynical view, but it affirms the Madisonian perspective that democracies cannot rely on virtue alone to ensure effective functioning.

Knowing that we face skepticism regarding our fundamentally novel approach to campaign finance, we lay out three challenges relating to the practicality and feasibility of our proposal in anticipation of future debates about actually implementing reform. Briefly, these challenges are:

1. Prevailing narratives in the reform community about reform goals and solutions may not countenance reform policies that do not emphasize the prevention of corruption and/or the increase in equity and democracy in our political system;
2. Strategic calculations about how reform affects partisan outcomes will make one party or the other refuse to compromise on a policy; and
3. Mass opinion about campaign finance will be inimical to our "pro-party" reform proposals.

We discuss these challenges in the following sections.

I. The Prevailing Narrative: "Money Is the Root of All Evil"

A common trope among advocates for political reform is that money is the genesis of all problems in a democracy. By "money," most reform advocates are referring to the political contributions given to candidates for office (thereby ignoring or downplaying the greater sums spent on lobbying, think tanks, and foundations that propose policies). The call for reform of the campaign finance system is almost entirely rooted in a narrative about political corruption. This is a story that is readily grasped by the public, and it has been exploited cynically at times by some political reformers, even though they acknowledge, in private, that the problem of money in politics is infinitely more complex.[17]

There are legitimate concerns in any democracy that the wealthy may use their resources to bend policies in their favor and undermine the principle of political equality. At the nation's founding, fears of corruption of government by moneyed interests (bankers especially) pervaded the arguments of antifederalists against the establishment of a strong national government that would be vulnerable to capture by such groups. The focus on corruption was reinforced at the turn of the 20th century when the power of large corporate trusts to shape state and federal policies threatened the basic democratic principle of equality. Progressive reformers attributed the inability of government to address problems associated with monopolies, urban blight, and immigration to the corrupting influence of corporate interests (railroads, mining, steel, etc.) that bought off party bosses and politicians. The problems of democracy, according to Progressives, could be traced directly to the use of money to buy votes and the related party spoils system that distorted public policy to advance private interests (Croly 1963; McGerr 1986; Milkis 2009). With the fervor of a moral and religious crusade (Rosenblum 2008, 117; Underkuffler 2013), the Progressives helped pass a raft of reforms that aimed to cut the ties between the political parties and wealthy interests.[18] These reforms included direct primaries, nonpartisan elections, and campaign finance reform. A major assumption was that *more democracy*—with people making political decisions directly—would decrease the importance of money in politics.

A powerful argument of Progressive reformers continues to resonate today. This is that the nation would be "a more perfect union" without the action of money in politics. We see this argument in its most articulate form in two recent books: *Republic, Lost* by Larry Lessig (2011) and *Corruption in America* by Zephyr Teachout (2014). These heirs of the Progressives view the problem as an "economy of influence" fueled by the relentless pursuit of campaign money for reelection. The insidious dynamic of the endless chase after money distorts the genuine expression of public purpose and even taints the efforts of good people trying to do the right thing (Lessig 2011). Like the Progressives before them, these reformers believe that the campaign finance system is chiefly to blame for the failure to enact good policies on pressing issues such as banking regulation, environmental protection, and immigration.

Not surprisingly, the corruption narrative powerfully shapes the design of campaign finance laws. The focus of most reforms is to keep money out of politics by limiting the source and size of contributions. Enactment of limits is routinely accompanied by a raft of anticircumvention statutes that attempt the Sisyphean task of trying to prevent money from sluicing its way into campaigns through backdoor channels. Strategies of this sort have constituted the foundational approach of American campaign finance reform, as exemplified at the federal level by the BCRA of 2002.

We think this approach is largely futile, given the hydraulics of the system, and even detrimental to the political system. Experience since the passage of the BCRA has proved our point; the act has occasioned the explosion of nonparty groups that now spend as much on elections as parties and candidates. At the state level, we demonstrated in chapter 5 a similar dynamic, revealing that independent spending by issue groups has increased dramatically precisely in states where campaign finance laws have limited contributions to and from political parties.

The consequence of the anticorruption, populist approach, then, has been to elevate parties of principle over parties of interest. David Hume, the great 18th-century British political philosopher, admired parties of principle but preferred parties of interest because they were reasonable and capable of compromise.[19] The flexibility of such parties is essential in a society that can be divided on irreconcilable issues (such as, in Hume's day, religion and today, social or economic dogmas). We have argued throughout this book that parties include both the purists, who are motivated by causes, ideologies, and virtue, and pragmatists, who are motivated by status, power, and material benefits. Campaign finance laws to date have been more effective at curbing contributions from pragmatic interests, specifically the party organizations and business interests, than from ideological, purist interests.[20] The purists benefit because they are typically willing to take greater risks to circumvent the laws and are constitutionally protected more than are political parties with respect to First Amendment jurisprudence.

The impact of pro-purist campaign finance rules is a different kind of distortion in the political system than the kind lamented by traditional reformers. The party system tilts toward ideological extremes in each party coalition. In the rhetoric of reformers, giving money for issue causes appears morally praiseworthy, while giving for materially self-interested reasons is tantamount to sin. The argument is specious: the issue causes espoused by ideological donors tend to be unrepresentative—they do not reflect the priorities and preferences of most American voters. Such giving is not morally praiseworthy if it biases a democratic polity.

The concern of many contemporary advocates for reform is that money in politics distorts equal representation, even though they tend to use the vague term of "corruption" to make a case for laws that they believe would minimize representational bias. Legislators have a challenging task as politicians because they must try to represent multiple constituencies, which include district voters, issue groups, partisan activists, and yes, donors.[21] But we would argue that their primary constituency is the local district voters, and the best approximation to reflecting the positions of those voters is to be close to the median voter. In this way, legislators should maximize, or at least balance, district representation; and the legislature as a whole should also become aligned more closely with the median voter in the state (see, for example, Stephanopoulos 2015). As we have demonstrated in this book, pro-party campaign finance laws will tend to align members of the legislature more closely with the median voter.

The desire to limit the power of wealthy donors in the system is understandable. But the regulatory axe does not fall equally on all wealthy donors. The guiding approach of contemporary reforms puts too much emphasis on the prevention of corruption when it might more profitably cultivate a system that encourages integration and balance of interests (Cain 2014). This is the kind of Madisonian pluralism that is difficult to achieve but imperative to cultivate if a society is committed to both fairness and the capacity to govern. Pluralism and political integration are served by enabling party organizations to play a robust role in financing elections and campaigns. The fact that pragmatists reconstitute themselves through "shadow parties" via super PACs is a decidedly poor substitute for having campaigns operate with the clearly identifiable party labels of the Republican or Democratic organizations. The UCLA school may argue that the partisan pragmatists reconstruct their power by campaigning through super PACs, but it is decidedly a power in which the collective party is *less responsible* to the public.[22]

In the future, we think the reform narrative on campaign finance should emphasize fairness, stability, and accountability more than corruption. To achieve these goals we favor the pluralist approach, which has been neglected in debates on reform (Cain 2014). The prevailing populist approaches overestimate the capacity of citizens to participate in small donor programs or to organize themselves to challenge the power of entrenched and ideological interests. Instead, we see a vital role for intermediaries such as political parties, which have traditionally played a strong role in aggregating interests, forging consensus, and allowing for fluid coalitions. While pluralism has its flaws in representing less well-off constituencies (and we try to address some of them here), its pathway reflects the reality that citizens are often best represented by interested organizations and individuals.

2. Strategic Partisanship to Game the System

There is no doubt that partisans will ask themselves how any proposed political reform will affect their ability to wage successful campaigns. No one, particularly an incumbent officeholder, wants to change the status quo if he thinks the new rules will hurt him electorally (Samples 2006). In a similar way, partisans will seek rule changes that they believe will give them strategic advantages over rivals (La Raja 2008). So an important question to consider for implementation of our suggestions is whether a proposal to make parties financially stronger will advantage Democrats or Republicans. To the degree that partisans see an advantage to the other side, they will resist reform.

Our sense is that Democrats may be more concerned than Republicans with a policy that allows additional money to flow through the parties. One reason is that the Democratic activists in the party are more likely to hold ideological views that are antithetical to our party-centric approach. Given a commitment to equality, liberal activists among the Democrats often espouse a Progressive-era mindset that money in politics favors policies for the self-interested rich. Democratic strategists have even wielded campaign finance reform as a populist campaign issue that they believe burnishes their Jacksonian image as the party of the common citizen.[23] Meanwhile, conservative activists in the Republican Party tend to espouse the values summoned by the word *liberty*, and they are more inclined to support laissez-faire policies on money in politics.

From a strategic perspective, the elected leadership of the political parties will worry about the impact of laws on the electoral prospects of the party. Democrats, for example, may fear being swamped by corporate support flowing disproportionately to the Republican Party. This concern is not mere speculation. We noted in chapter 3 that business interests tend to favor right-of-center candidates, which would locate them closer to the Republican Party. On the other hand, business interests are typically strategic: they give to both parties, and even show favoritism to Democrats when they are in power (Herrnson, Shaiko, and Wilcox 2005). Moreover, in a previous study that we conducted, we found no difference in partisan outcomes in states that allow corporations to make unlimited contributions or to spend money in politics without restrictions (La Raja and Schaffner 2014).

Democrats may also worry that the Republicans will benefit from having a larger number of wealthy individual donors who support Republicans. We know of no studies that have shown this to be true. Wealthy liberal donors have been quite generous to Democratic candidates and parties. Indeed, our analysis in chapter 2 suggests that liberal donors have been more willing to give to the Democratic Party than conservative donors to the Republican Party. Historically, we should note that Democrats have tended to rely more heavily than Republicans on large donors because their share of middle- and upper-middle-income donors willing to give donations to the party was not as large the Republicans'. Indeed, the average contribution to Republicans has typically been lower than the average contribution to Democrats (La

Raja 2008). This historical pattern may be changing as social media sites attract liberal donors of modest means who are professionals in the education, marketing, and technology-based sectors.

Democrats may also believe that the current system that punishes party organizations and encourages outside spending is favorable to their party. Indeed, we have shown that a large fraction of independent spending comes from labor unions, which almost always support Democratic candidates. The organizational structure of labor organizations may advantage them over major business groups in waging such campaigns. Labor unions appear less averse to taking strong public positions in campaigns because these actions will not affect them as negatively as such positions affect corporations, which generally try to maintain a nonpartisan image among customers. However, the historical advantages of labor unions as independent campaigners may be waning: our analysis at the state level indicates that business interests and conservative groups are now equally engaged in independent campaigning. As the use of nonparty groups become more institutionalized through super PACs and 501(c)4 groups, the relative strength of labor unions in campaigns may erode.

To Democratic partisans who fear our pro-party proposals, we say that we have found little evidence in our research that making the parties financially stronger will preferentially benefit Republicans. In electorally competitive states, including states that allow unlimited contributions to parties, we observe financial parity between the parties. And state party leaders insist that having additional resources available to the parties would allow them to invest in building out the long-term infrastructure of sophisticated voter lists, and to develop grassroots networks in legislative districts throughout the state.[24] At present, state parties are being eclipsed by national-level groups and are losing the capacity to support local parties, which rely on volunteers to do most of the work (Overby 2014). We are also convinced that a pro-party campaign finance system will make it easier for third parties to play a role in elections when grassroots support exists for minor parties. With easier access to funds, third parties can launch voter signature drives to get on the ballot, advertise their party, and support candidates.

3. Can Public Opinion on Campaign Finance Reform Be Changed?

One considerable challenge will be persuading the public that political parties should be larger players in financing campaigns. Americans appear to dislike the party system and may not fully appreciate the important role of political parties in a democracy. On the other hand, our own research into public opinion reveals that voters do, in fact, acknowledge the unique relationship between candidates and parties, and they see a legitimate and robust role for parties in financing elections. As we demonstrate below, voters seem more inclined to grant the parties greater freedom to raise and spend money compared to other groups. This suggests the plausibility of making a persuasive argument to pursue party-centered reforms in the campaign finance system. The timing is especially appropriate now, as voters are concerned about "dark money" being spent by groups they do not recognize. If the public could be convinced that the campaign system would be more transparent and accountable, they might be willing to support pro-party reforms, particularly if such reforms *also* address ongoing concerns about corruption in the financing of elections. This strategy would entail civic education about the value of political parties and the potential impact of reforms in improving governance. Americans tend to have a romanticized view of democracy that overvalues the power of individuals, acting alone, to achieve the common good (Pildes 2015).

Perhaps because of this highly individualized conception of how democracy works, Americans strongly believe that the campaign finance system should first and foremost prevent corruption. When asked to rank the importance of promoting certain outcomes in the campaign finance system, "reducing corruption" lands at the top of the list for voters, regardless of party (see figure 6.1). The next most important category is "preventing unequal influence," which citizens affiliated with both parties ranked almost equally (party data not shown here). The third highest goal that citizens want policymakers to pursue is "ensuring transparency." This concern might help policymakers frame an argument for having a party-centered system, since party control of campaign funds would make disclosure of campaign finance much more stringent than the current situation in which mystery groups spend independently without strong disclosure requirements.

The last two goals are, in ranked order, "promoting competition" and "preserving freedom." In elite debates, preserving freedom is *the* central argument claimed by opponents of campaign finance regulation. Yet the public does not appear as committed to this value when considering the purpose of campaign finance rules. Among the options we offered in our survey, preserving freedom was ranked last by respondents, including Republicans whose leaders tend to champion freedom in contentious battles over reform.[25]

Given the overriding concern of the public to focus on the prevention of corruption, it is not surprising that citizens intuitively like the idea of

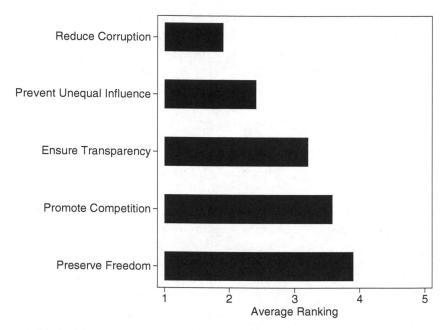

Figure 6.1. What Goal Is Most Important for Campaign Finance Reform? Average Rank Ordering of Preferences among Respondents (Scale: a high of 1 to a low of 5). (*Note:* Wording of question: "There are many values that policy makers must take into account when deciding what kinds of laws they should enact regarding political fundraising. Please rank the following values in terms of how much weight you think they should be given." Reponses are: Preserve freedom to contribute and spend money, Ensure no individuals or groups have unequal influence, Reduce corruption in the political system, Ensure competition in elections, Help public know who contributes and spends money on elections. Data collected by the 2012 Cooperative Congressional Election Survey (postelection). Number of observations = 785.)

imposing contribution limits on giving to candidates and parties. Putting a limit on contributions—including very low limits—seems like the right way to address the problem of big money in politics. But as we demonstrate in this book, limiting the parties creates unintended negative consequences such as ideological polarization and reduced accountability for independent spending. A public that pays scant attention to the details of campaign finance and has less-than-expert knowledge of how the political system actually works cannot be expected to understand the full implications of funding limitations across the spectrum of donor and candidate types. In fact, the vast majority of Americans hardly care about campaign finance as an issue.

In an annual Gallup Poll about "the most important issues," Americans consistently rank campaign finance near the bottom. In a 2012 poll conducted by Pew Research, the typical respondent listed campaign finance as 22nd out of 23 issues listed, with just over 1 in 4 saying it should be a "top priority" for the president and Congress. Sadly, it barely nosed out "global warming," which filled the last spot.[26] Nevertheless, despite the low salience of this very complex issue, conventional reformers continue to present low contribution limits to the public as an essential remedy to fixing the problems with the campaign finance system and restoring public trust.[27]

As far as we can tell there is no research that demonstrates a clear link between low contribution limits and reduced corruption or greater trust in government. In fact, studies appear to suggest that no relationship exists between various kinds of campaign finance laws and levels of trust or efficacy (Cordis and Milyo 2013; Persily and Lammie 2004; Primo and Milyo 2006). We believe that reform advocates do a disservice to the public when they make claims that are lacking in empirical support while pushing for reforms that research shows cause pathologies in the campaign finance system. For this reason, we encourage a cautious approach to reform that builds bipartisan consensus around common values and incremental solutions that have demonstrable outcomes. We think it inappropriate to make reform a partisan issue, or to attempt such sweeping changes as a constitutional amendment, which would add manifold complexities to regulating money in politics.[28]

Our proposal to strengthen party financing of elections is both incremental and compatible with public understandings of the unique role that parties play in a democracy. Voters appear willing to grant more discretion to the parties in financing elections if they can be reassured that the problems of corruption are being addressed. To understand public sentiment we asked voters to what extent they think various groups should be allowed to contribute to political candidates. We asked this about four groups: political parties, advocacy groups, labor unions, and businesses. The response choices were (1) Not at all; (2) Should be allowed to contribute a small (but limited) amount; (3) Should be allowed to contribute a large (but limited) amount; (4) Should be allowed unlimited contributions.

Our findings, presented in figure 6.2, show that voters are most willing to grant parties greater freedom to support candidates. The highest segment of each bar (black) indicates the proportion of voters who believe that a particular group should *not* be allowed to contribute money to a candidate. Only 23 percent said this about political parties, which is less than for any other group. But of greater importance is the willingness of many citizens to lightly regulate party finances. In our sample, almost half of respondents

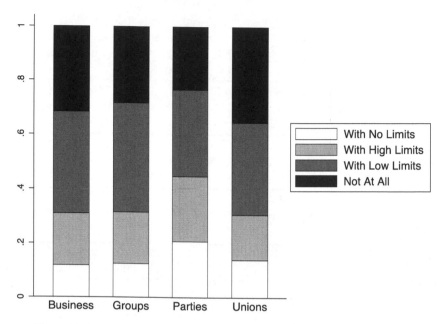

Figure 6.2. Support for Contribution Limits to Candidates for Different Types of Contributors. (*Note:* Based on results from a survey of 1,000 American adults conducted in October 2014 by YouGov.)

would allow parties to contribute without limits (the lowest, white, segment) or very large amounts (the second lowest, or light gray, segment), a figure that outstrips what they would allow for other groups. This comparison includes issue groups, which are the party's principal competition for shaping the ideology of the party coalition.

Support for imposing few restrictions on parties varied by the ideology of the respondent, with liberals being somewhat less in favor of no limits or high limits, but the differences are not that large. Almost 40 percent of liberals would like to see no limits or high limits, while just over 50 percent of conservatives feel the same way. We conclude that the public seems amenable to having pro-party laws, and a sustained educational campaign about the benefits of a party-centered system could increase support beyond existing levels.

In building the case for policy change, the traditional reform community will need to alter its anticorruption approach and raise awareness of other problems in the campaign finance system. Shifting away from the dominant corruption narrative will not be easy, because that narrative is familiar and readily graspable by the public. Moreover, the conventional advocacy strategy generates passion among loyal reform constituencies and financial contributions to the organizations that promote anticorruption reform. But reframing the debate is imperative and might begin by acknowledging that robust democratic politics requires a significant amount of political spending. Even grassroots campaigns require money for building voter lists, training volunteers, and sustaining the organizational infrastructure. The essential question is how does such money *enter* the political system? A good reform argument will elucidate the best institutional pathways for bringing money into politics, including forms of public financing. We encourage a debate that raises the salience of political parties as part of the solution for making the campaign finance system less dysfunctional. This debate would make a clear connection between the growth of "dark money" by outside groups and the unrealistic constraints on political parties.

We note that prominent commentators in major national newspapers have made compelling logical arguments for allowing parties to play a larger role in financing elections as a means of avoiding the worst pathologies of the federal campaign finance system (Brooks 2014; Rauch 2014). We hope our empirical work gives additional credibility to such arguments. Others have framed an argument for reform in ways that resonate with broader concerns about inequality and the chaos of a system without apparent rules. Thomas Edsall, for example, writing in the *New York Times*, argues that the system has become a "two-class structure of election financing": one that is accountable and promotes broader participation, and the other that is opaque and dominated by a few wealthy individuals. He writes: "Policing the hodgepodge of regulations, statutes and rulings governing elections has become virtually impossible. A kind of lawlessness prevails that is incompatible with the goals of democracy."[29]

We agree that the campaign finance system is in disorder in many states and especially at the federal level. For this reason, political elites need to make a credible case that pro-party laws would bring coherence and accountability to the system. It will be essential to emphasize the important role of parties in making the broader system work adequately and to remind voters that they have the power to hold parties accountable in ways that are not possible with interest groups. The reforms should build on the fact that voters understand the legitimacy of parties and candidates working together. This strategy to promote a party-centered system will work if reforms also address overriding concerns about corruption. For this reason, reforms should be specific about how parties would disclose their financial activity, and how the rules will make it difficult for parties to be merely cash conduits for their candidates.

Proposals might also consider providing generous subsidies to parties—minor parties too—so they do not rely exclusively on private money.

Based on the findings in this book, we hope to underscore to the public that the prevailing campaign system advances the politics of the extreme elements in the major parties. This kind of bias seems as unfair as the notorious kind of rent-seeking pursued by wealthy interests at the broader expense of the public and its governing institutions. By restoring the party organizations to positions as central players in campaigns, we expect greater coherence in political campaigns, better balance in the representation of interests, and more effective governance. By reinvigorating party organizations, we hope that the party-centered campaign finance system will help shift highly contentious debates in the nation's legislatures toward areas of common ground and fertile policymaking.

Notes

Chapter 1

1. Rassmussen Report, "53% Think Neither Political Party Represents the American People," April 24, 2014. Accessed September 11, 2014. http://www.rasmussen reports.com/public_content/politics/general_politics/april_2014/53_think_neither _political_party_represents_the_american_people.

2. Washington's Farewell Address 1796, The Avalon Project, Lillian Goldman Law Library, Yale Law School. Accessed September 14, 2014, at http://avalon.law.yale.edu /18th_century/washing.asp.

3. Prior to 2002, "soft money" referred to campaign funds given to political parties with no limits on the source or size of the contribution. Under the Bipartisan Campaign Reform Act of 2002, however, the national parties were banned from financing federal elections with soft money. See Public Law 107-155 (March 27, 2002). http:// www.gpo.gov/fdsys/pkg/PLAW-107publ155/pdf/PLAW-107publ155.pdf.

4. The issue of buying votes in the legislature has been studied extensively. The findings are at best mixed, and most studies suggest there is no relationship. For a review of the research on this topic see Stephen Ansolabehere, John M. deFigueiredo, and James M. Snyder, "Why Is There So Little Money in U.S. Politics?" *Journal of Economic Perspectives* 17, no. 1 (2003): 105–30. The most sophisticated work on political influence indicates the process is more complicated than campaign contributions. See, for example, Frank R. Baumgartner, *Lobbying and Policy Change: Who Wins, Who Loses, and Why* (Chicago: University of Chicago Press, 2009).

5. Super PACs are a new kind of political action committee (PAC) that emerged in the wake of the federal court case *SpeechNow.org v. Federal Election Commission.* Based on this decision, PACs are allowed to raise and spend money without constraints so long as they spend the funds independently of the candidate they are supporting.

6. For a review of the literature on causes of polarization see Geoffrey C. Layman, Thomas M. Carsey, and Juliana Menasce Horowitz, "Party Polarization in American Politics: Characteristics, Causes, and Consequences," *Annual Review of Political Science* 9, no. 1 (2006): 83–110.

7. Alex Isenstadt, "GOP Could Pay a Price for Gerrymandering," *Politico*, July 1, 2013. Accessed July 3, 2013, at http://www.politico.com/story/2013/07/gop-could-pay-price -for-gerrymandering-93597.html?hp=t1. For evidence against this viewpoint, see John Sides, "Gerrymandering Is Not What's Wrong with American Politics," in Wonkblog, *Washington Post*, February 3, 2013. http://www.washingtonpost.com/blogs/wonkblog /wp/2013/02/03/gerrymandering-is-not-whats-wrong-with-american-politics/.

8. For a perspective on resource dependency theory as it relates to parties, see Panebianco (1988). For a broader application of the theory, see Pfeffer and Salancik (1978).

9. In their heyday of the mid-19th century, the American political parties were a provider of social services and sponsor of entertainment during elections. See Michael E. McGerr, *The Decline of Popular Politics: The American North, 1865–1928* (New York: Oxford University Press, 1986).

10. See William P. Riordan, ed., *Plunkitt of Tammany Hall, by George Washington Plunkitt*. Made available online by Project Gutenberg, release date December 29, 2008. Accessed September 14, 2014, at http://www.gutenberg.org/files/2810/2810-h/2810-h .htm.

11. Subsequent theoretical research has helped demonstrate why parties find it electorally beneficial to be distinctive, showing that voters prefer parties that convey solid information about their platforms compared to those that remain opaque, even if the latter party is closer to voter preferences. See James M. Snyder and Michael M. Ting, "An Informational Rationale for Political Parties," *American Journal of Political Science* 46, no. 1 (2002): 90.

12. See Edmund Burke, "Thoughts on the Cause of the Present Discontents" (1770). Accessed September 14, 2014, at http://www.ourcivilisation.com/smartboard/shop /burkee/extracts/chap2.htm.

13. The 1950 APSA report on political parties recommended that the finance limits on parties be removed and that they should receive government financing as well. This recommendation never came to pass, and the parties at the national level remained handicapped by, among other laws, the Hatch Act (1940), which put a $3 million cap on party spending. See American Political Science Association, "Toward a More Responsible Two-Party System," *American Political Science Review* 44, no. 3 (1950): Supplement.

14. These views have been made most provocatively in Bawn, Cohen, Karol, Masket, Noel and Zaller (2012). It should be noted that party scholars not affiliated with UCLA have made similar conceptual arguments about networked parties. See, for example, Paul S. Herrnson, "The Roles of Party Organizations, Party-Connected Committees, and Party Allies in Elections," *Journal of Politics* 71, no. 4 (2009): 1207–24. Accessed September 16, 2014, at http://www.people-press.org/2014/06/12/political-polarization -in-the-american-public/. Other scholars include Jonathan Bernstein, Casey Dominguez, Matthew Grossman, and Richard Skinner.

15. A good example of this kind of coalition building took place among conservatives in the Republican Party. See John Cassidy, "The Ringleader: How Grover Norquist Keeps the Conservative Movement Together," *New Yorker*, August 1, 2005, p. 42.

16. Above and beyond political spending, the candidate benefits from the cumulative effect of coordinated support. When a party coalition converges on a candidate, it sends a strong signal to attentive voters that the candidate supports the party agenda

and stands a good chance of winning. These voters may have ties with such groups and compose a significant portion of the electorate, particularly in primaries and low-turnout general elections.

17. See Michael Dimock, Jocelyn Kiley, Scott Keeter, and Carroll Doherty, "Political Polarization in the American Public" (Washington, DC: Pew Research Center, 2014). Accessed September 16, 2014, at http://www.people-press.org/2014/06/12/political-polarization-in-the-american-public/.

18. See Wilson (1962).

19. We thank Jonathan Bernstein for several of these insights about the two differing approaches.

20. This point is not addressed sufficiently in the UCLA model. The UCLA theorists argue that factions differ on issues, but that the issues are so unrelated as to not affect the willingness of disparate factions to form a coalition. The implicit theoretical argument is that factions agree to take on coalition members so long as a new issue faction does not undermine the policy goals of any particular factional member. We believe this is an unrealistic assumption, especially given the importance of agenda setting in accomplishing policy goals.

21. Jenna Portnoy and Robert Costa, "Eric Cantor's Tea Party Opponent in Va. Primary May Be Picking up Momentum," *Washington Post*, May 13, 2014. http://www.washingtonpost.com/local/virginia-politics/eric-cantors-tea-party-opponent-in-va-primary-may-be-picking-up-momentum/2014/05/13/1a2d92d0-d9d7-11e3-b745-87d39690c5c0_story.html.

22. See Jennifer Medina, "California's Nonpartisan Primary Shows Independents to Be in Short Supply," *New York Times*, June 6, 2012. http://www.nytimes.com/2012/06/07/us/politics/independents-falter-in-california-primary.html.

23. Cameron Joseph, "Untamed Cruz Refuses to Play Nice with GOP Campaign Arm," *The Hill*, July 8, 2014. http://thehill.com/blogs/ballot-box/senate-races/211641-untamed-cruz-refuses-to-play-nice-with-gop-campaign-arm.

24. In the American party system, the party committees are typically separated according to the two elected branches of government. Each chamber in the legislature has its own party. At the national level the Democrats have the Democratic Congressional Campaign Committee (DCCC), the Democratic Senatorial Campaign Committee (DSCC), and the Democratic National Committee (DNC). The Republican counterparts are the National Republican Congressional Committee (NRCC), the National Republican Senatorial Committee (NRSC) and the Republican National Committee (RNC).

25. We believe our analysis about how campaign finance laws change the substantive character of political parties provides an important corrective to recent scholarship that too easily embraces an "open-system" organizational model of political parties, suggesting that parties are entirely malleable "shape shifters" in response to changes to the campaign finance laws or other regulations. See, for example, Bawn et al. (2012); Gerken (2014); Issacharoff and Peterman (2013); Skinner, Masket, and Dulio (2012).

26. Phone interview on June 11, 2014, with Neil Reiff, Washington-based election lawyer at Sandler, Reiff, Lamb, Rosenstein, and Berkenstock, who serves as counsel for Democratic state parties.

27. A clear example of this is the use of "social welfare" organizations to wage political campaigns. These tax-exempt groups are organized under section 501(c)(4) of the tax code, including prominent issue groups such as the National Rifle Association and the Sierra Club. They are allowed to participate in some political activity, so long as it is not their primary purpose (usually meaning that such political activity constitutes less than half their spending). These groups do not have to report their donors to the IRS or the FEC.

28. We may be among the first to demonstrate this dynamic systematically, but some historical evidence supports our view that campaign finance laws confer advantages on particular factions and party coalitions. At the turn of the 20th century, for example, the national parties began to turn to organized interests when Mugwump reformers created civil service requirements that limited the party organizations' ability to dispense patronage (e.g., La Raja 2008; Mutch 2014). Formal theoretical models in which parties serve as brokers between groups and candidates indicate that moderate candidates should receive more resources when party organizations serve as brokers of campaign funds than when candidates receive money unmediated from interest groups (McCarty 2013). Krimmel (2013) also demonstrates that states with relatively strong party organizations have less polarization today than other states.

29. Boris Shor and Nolan McCarty, "Measuring American State Legislatures," accessed September 13, 2014, at http://americanlegislatures.com/2013/05/21/state-legislatures -and-polarization.

30. We are indebted to Keith Hamm and his team of researchers for allowing us to use their historical data on party finance rules in the states between 1960 to 1996.

31. Milyo has used the data in Adriana Cordis and Jeffrey Milyo, 2013. "Do State Campaign Finance Reforms Reduce Public Corruption?" (working paper, Department of Economics, University of Missouri, 2013).

32. The Ranney Index measure of interparty competition, developed by political scientist Austin Ranney, is a widely used and long-standing indicator of competition for control of government in the American states. The Ranney Index has several components: proportion of success, duration of success, and frequency of divided control in state governments. We are grateful to Thomas Holbrook for providing the most recent data.

Chapter 2

1. See Colorado Secretary of State, "Contribution Limits," accessed July 17, 2014, at http://www.sos.state.co.us/pubs/elections/CampaignFinance/limits/contributions .html#naturalPerson.

2. In support of the unlimited ability to spend money, the leading opinion in *Buckley* included the following: "the concept that the government may restrict the speech of some [in] order to enhance the relative voice of others is wholly foreign to the First Amendment."

3. See *Federal Election Commission v. Wisconsin Right to Life, Inc.*, 551 U.S. 449 (2007); *Citizens United v. Federal Election Commission*, 558 U.S. 310 (2010).

4. See Center for Responsive Politics, "Donor Demographics," accessed September 26, 2014, at http://www.opensecrets.org/overview/donordemographics.php.

5. Comments of Mark Kilmer at Redstate Roundtable #6: Should Conservatives Donate to the RNC, NRSC and NRCC? Viewed January 11, 2015, at http://archive.redstate.com/stories/elections/redstate_roundtable_6_should_conservatives _donate_to_the_rnc_nrsc_and_nrcc.

Chapter 3

1. Arizona, Maine, and Connecticut have "clean elections" financing, which provide a large grant to candidates who choose to forego private financing of their campaigns.

2. The data in our analysis includes all party committees at the state level, which typically means state central committees, legislative campaign committees, and local district committees.

3. David M. Herszenhorn, "A Curious Coalition Opposed Bailout Bill," *New York Times*, October 2, 2008, available at http://www.nytimes.com/2008/10/03/business /03naysayers.html?_r=0.

4. For most groups seeking benefits, it is relatively easy to set up a PAC. At the federal level and in most states, the administrative costs of operating a PAC can be defrayed with revenues of business and professional associations. Not so for advocacy groups, where overhead costs must be paid for with funds raised from individual members (which means there is less money to spend on candidates). Most parties face the same disadvantage, except in states like New York, where parties can raise soft money to pay for administrative overhead.

5. We exclude incumbents who had no opposition.

6. If we estimate the first model without the competitiveness variable, the coefficient for the ideological extremism variable is statistically significant and negative, indicating that parties are a greater source of support for moderate candidates.

Chapter 4

1. The traditional debates about campaign finance reform centered on concerns about corruption, implying the buying of votes by wealthy contributors. While reform advocates continue to cite the problems of corruption, most expert observers agree that influence is not so much about quid pro quo exchanges, but more nuanced and structural forms of power that include the buying of access and effort, as well as gatekeeping roles in helping to choose who runs for and wins office. Some legal scholars have broadened the definition of corruption to include such "economies of influence" (Lessig 2011; Teachout 2014). Underlying these enlarged conceptions of corruption, however, is the notion of unequal influence in the political process (see Hasen 2013).

2. When Shor and McCarty look at individual chambers they find that 59 of the 99 legislative chambers (Nebraska has a unicameral legislature, which Shor and McCarty include as "senate") have seen an increase in polarization, while 24 states have been in a relatively stable relationship to one another over time; 16 chambers experienced a *decline* in polarization during this period.

3. Because we are able to extract the Catalist ideology scores for about half of the state legislators, we can use that subset of legislators to determine the appropriate

model for rescaling the Shor and McCarty ideology scores to be on the same scale as the scores we use for constituents.

4. Models of spatial voting in a two-party system imply that legislators, under electorally competitive conditions, should end up representing the median voter (Downs 1957).

5. Comments of Scott Arceneaux, executive director of the Florida Democratic Party. Phone interview on April 10, 2014.

6. It makes no difference for our findings when we include states with relatively high contribution limits in our category for unlimited. Regarding measures of ideological scores, for an explanation of how they are generated, see Shor and McCarty (2011) and Boris Shor, "Measuring American Legislatures," available at http://american legislatures.com/data/.

7. The states classified as having professional legislatures are AK, AZ, CA, CT, DE, FL, HI, IL, MA, MI, MN, NC, NJ, NY, OH, PA, SC, TX, WA, and WI.

8. A similar effect exists when we estimate a more stringent model controlling for individual and organizational limits and using state fixed effects.

9. This finding about individual limits generating greater polarization suggests an interesting paradox about the use of contribution limits. On the one hand, these limits might thwart corruption, its appearance, or more basically, the unequal influence of large donors. On the other hand, setting contribution limits incentivizes the candidates to find additional individual donors to achieve the same amount of fundraising. We know from chapter 2 that small donors are highly polarized, and so a system that relies on political appeals to small donors may exacerbate the polarizing tendencies of the campaign finance system.

Chapter 5

1. The UCLA school argues, for example, that primary laws aimed at diminishing the power of party bosses (by turning over the selection of party nominees to the electorate) have been ineffective. They argue that the "party is back" because, despite primaries, party elites control nominations through coordinated endorsements and financial support (Cohen et al. 2008). But we would ask: who are these party elites and have they changed over time? The UCLA school appears to see no distinction between the purist and pragmatist factions of the party, lumping them together as if they were not antagonistic in many situations. Our view is that primaries have given greater power to elites in the purist faction relative to the pragmatists because purists can mobilize factions in low-turnout elections in ways that pragmatists cannot. Pragmatists in party organizations are prohibited by law, or local norms, from choosing and supporting favorite candidates in the primary. Others have made a similar point with respect to the impact of reforms on the success of different kinds of candidates. See, for example, Polsby (1983).

2. To be sure, pragmatists also work outside the formal party structure for various "shadow" party organizations and interest groups, especially economically oriented groups. On the Republican side, these include those who work for the Chamber of Commerce; on the Democratic side, they include some mainstream labor unions.

Both sets of groups seek bread-and-butter benefits such as less (or more) regulation and taxes.

3. As we argued in previous chapters, other valuable inputs include policy expertise, access to large membership groups, and leadership in critical geographic locations (e.g., electoral swing states).

4. We want to be clear that we are not saying that limits and bans have no impact on the total amount of campaign money in elections. They do—to some extent because most participants in elections are not inclined to pay the additional costs of getting around the regulations. The wealthiest and most sophisticated political groups can always conceive of alternatives. The alternatives they choose, however, are not perfectly substitutable.

5. For a record of votes on the McCain-Feingold Act, see Govtrack.us at https://www.govtrack.us/congress/votes/107-2002/h34, accessed August 6, 2014.

6. Super PACs may accept unlimited contributions and spend unlimited sums so long as they do so independently of parties and candidates. Super PACs report the names of their donors to the Federal Election Commission, which are then made public. The 501(c)4 organizations derive their names from the IRS tax code and are officially "social welfare" organizations, which may spend money on elections so long as such activities are not their primary activities (in practice, this means they must spend less than half of total expenditures on elections). These organizations may also raise unlimited sums, but the difference is such organizations do not have to disclose their donors publicly.

7. Philip Rucker, "Governors Christie, Walker and Kasich Woo Billionaire Sheldon Adelson at Vegas Event," *Washington Post*, March 29, 2014. Available at http://www.washingtonpost.com/politics/governors-christie-walker-and-kasich-woo-adelson-at-vegas-event/2014/03/29/aa385f34-b779-11e3-b84e-897d3d12b816_story.html.

8. Theodoric Meyer, "How Much Did Sheldon Adelson Really Spend on Campaign 2012?" *ProPublica*, December 20, 2012. Retrieved August 22, 2014 at http://www.propublica.org/article/how-much-did-sheldon-adelson-really-spend-on-campaign-2012.

9. Attentive donors enlarge their influence by investing in races early rather than jumping on the bandwagon toward the end of a race. The inclination to give early, particularly during primaries, helps shape the candidate field and the issue agenda of political campaigns. While the formal party organization coordinates with policy-demanding groups in the early stages of an election, the enthusiasm and financial heft of activists (working through their organizations or directly with candidates) gives them a strong bargaining position vis-à-vis the pragmatists in the party. The pragmatists, who are the ultimate realists, acquiesce to helping to elect ideological candidates whom the purists have settled upon.

10. Some recent research from Dimock et al. (2014) and Ahler and Broockman (2014) suggests that some Americans are not necessarily moderate, but express extreme positions on both sides of the ideological spectrum, depending on the policy. Political scientists use the term "issue constraint" to describe those who are ideologically consistent in their views. We do not doubt that a large portion of the electorate lacks issue constraint, and even embraces extreme positions on the left and right. However, we suspect many of these citizens are not very interested in politics and do not vote with high frequency.

11. This figure is calculated by comparing the share of money donated by individuals in the outer third of the ideological spectrum to that donated by those in the middle third.

12. One recent study indicates that liberal Republican and conservative Democratic state legislators are less likely to run for Congress than those at the ideological poles (especially among Republicans), because these potential candidates do not see themselves as "fitting" ideologically into the national parties (Thomsen 2014). We believe they get this message, in part, from the activists and donors who tend to support candidates in their race for Congress.

13. Paul Blumenthal, "Chris Murphy: 'Soul-Crushing' Fundraising Is Bad for Congress," *Huffington Post*, May 7, 2013. http://www.huffingtonpost.com/2013/05/07/chris-murphy-fundraising_n_3232143.html.

14. In Connecticut, for example, Professor Gary Rose has noted that the legislative leaders in this state, which has long been noted for its moderate politics, have become more ideological (email exchange, August 6–7, 2014). Recent changes to the campaign finance law now give party leaders more control over financing of elections, which some observers fear will give party leaders too much power. Given that the leaders in either party have strong policy preferences, one logical consequence is that this change will make the parties more ideological. We disagree because these party leaders are not extremists and they reflect the mainstream positions of the party caucus. We believe that giving these leaders more power will reduce the possibility that extremist factions in either party will emerge to finance elections in any meaningful way.

15. An earlier decision, *Wisconsin Right to Life v. FEC* (2007), had already opened the door to such spending by narrowly defining electioneering spending. The FEC claimed under the BCRA of 2002 that groups could not air broadcast ads mentioning a federal candidate in the weeks leading up to an election. Chief Justice Roberts, in the majority opinion, argued this restriction was overly broad and set a standard that an ad can be restricted only if it is "susceptible of no reasonable interpretation other than as an appeal to vote for or against a specific candidate."

16. The Taft-Hartley Act of 1947 prohibited corporations and unions from making direct expenditures in connection with an election campaign for federal office.

17. The rise in IEs at both the state and federal levels predated these court decisions. *Citizens United* and *SpeechNow.org* simply made it easier for different groups to embrace IEs.

18. For more background on the data collection go to "Independent Spending's Role in State Elections, 2006–2010," National Institute on Money in State Politics. Accessed September 24, 2014. http://classic.followthemoney.org/press/ReportView.phtml?r=481&ext=1#Methodology.

19. Dan Eggen and T. W. Farnam, "Pair of Conservative Groups Raised $70 Million in Midterm Campaign," *Washington Post*, December 2, 2010. http://www.washingtonpost.com/wp-dyn/content/article/2010/12/02/AR2010120205667.html?wprss=rss_politics.

20. See, for example, the editorial "The Court's Blow to Democracy," *New York Times*, January 21, 2010.

21. The parties have been able to make independent expenditures as a way of avoiding constraints on supporting their candidates through contributions or coordinated

expenditures. In the decision *Republican Federal Campaign Committee v. FEC*, 533 U.S. 431 (2001), the Court held that the First Amendment prohibits the application of the party expenditure provision of the act to "an expenditure that the political party has made independently, without coordination with any candidate." Note, however, that political parties, in contrast to nonparty groups, must raise their funds under contribution limits required by law; nonparty groups face no such limits according to the decision in *SpeechNow.org v. FEC* No. 08-5223, D.C. Cir. March 26, 2010.

22. Byron Tau, "Last Call for State Parties?" *Politico*, February 16, 2014. Available at http://www.politico.com/story/2014/02/last-call-for-state-parties-103559.html.

23. Telephone interview with election law attorney Neil Reiff of Sandler Reiff Lamb Rosenstein & Birkenstock, P.C., in Washington, D.C., June 11, 2014.

24. Byron Tau, "Last Call for State Parties?" *Politico*, February 16, 2014. Available at http://www.politico.com/story/2014/02/last-call-for-state-parties-103559.html.

25. Karen Tumulty, "Super PACs' Spending Isn't Always Welcomed by Candidates They Support," *Washington Post*, August 5, 2014. Available at http://www.washington post.com/politics/super-pacs-spending-isnt-always-welcomed-by-candidates-they -support/2014/08/04/ecc36ed6-18ed-11e4-9349-84d4a85be981_story.html.

26. Greg Sargent, "Breaking: Wisconsin Dems Throw Weight behind Drive to Recall GOP Senators" (The Plum Line), *Washington Post*, March 3, 2011. http://voices .washingtonpost.com/plum-line/2011/03/breaking_wisconsin_dems_throw.html.

27. Paul Bedard, "Democratic Party, GOP Warn They Could Die," *Washington Examiner*, June 5, 2014. http://washingtonexaminer.com/over-political-parties-say -laws-regs-are-putting-them-out-of-business/article/2549322.

Chapter 6

1. Our inclination to believe that the institutional flow of money is exacerbating polarization seems buttressed by findings that the underlying mass donor populations have not changed much in the past 40 years. Donors have always been ideological, but they were no more ideological during the years of increasing polarization than when the party officeholders were much more moderate (La Raja and Wiltse 2012). What has changed is the channels through which campaign dollars flow and the proportion of campaign support coming from different constituencies. Candidates rely more heavily on individual donors and "purist" groups than on benefit-seeking PACs (see Barber 2013). New uses of technology and the prominent role of partisan media in the past two decades may have helped mobilize donors to support like-minded politicians and groups rather than simply supporting party candidates, regardless of ideological positions.

2. See Keenan Steiner, "Progressive Groups Threaten Corporations on Political Giving," March 12, 2012, Sunlight Foundation (blog). Accessed September 30, 2014, at http://sunlightfoundation.com/blog/2012/03/12/progressive-groups-threaten -corporations-political-giving/.

3. The charges of leaders in Tea Party organizations that the IRS harassed them in the lead-up to the 2012 elections is a case in point. Regardless of whether the intent was to focus on conservative groups or not, the IRS did not seem prepared to make

decisions about what constitutes electoral activity, and their ham-handed efforts hurt the legitimacy of the organization. See Gregory Korte, "Tea Party Groups Detail 'Harassment' by IRS," *USA Today*, June 4, 2013, at http://www.usatoday.com/story /news/politics/2013/06/04/irs-tea-party-harassment/2388203/.

4. See New York City Campaign Finance Board, "Public Matching Funds." Accessed September 27, 2014, at http://www.nyccfb.info/candidates/candidates/publicmatching funds.aspx.

5. One study suggests that small donors tend to finance more ideological candidates (Bonica, McCarty, Poole, and Rosenthal 2013). In pursuing the small donor, partisan groups radicalize their messages, highlight their ideological affinity with the small donor, and demonize the other side. See Matt Bai, "The Scourge of Small-Money Politics," *Yahoo News,* August 7, 2014. Available at http://news.yahoo.com/the-scourge-of -small-money-politics-083659479.html.

6. National Conference of State Legislatures (NCSL), "Public Financing of Campaigns: An Overview" (updated January 23, 2013). Accessed March 23, 2013, at http:// www.ncsl.org/research/elections-and-campaigns/public-financing-of-campaigns -overview.aspx#Party_Public_Financing.

7. Jenny Wilson, "New Campaign Finance Rules Meant Rolling Back Some Post-Rowland Reforms," *Hartford Courant*, June 19, 2013, available at http://articles .courant.com/2013-06-19/news/hc-campaign-finance-changes-20130611_1_outside -spending-campaign-spending-much-political-parties.

8. At the federal level, the national committees played a similarly vital role for a short while in presidential contests. From 1992 to 2004, the DNC and RNC gained prominence because their presidential nominees accepted public funds and could not raise and spend private funds. The parties, however, could use their funds (including soft money prior to 2002) to advertise and build coordinated campaigns to mobilize voters.

9. Telephone interview, August 29, 2014, with Ken Martin, chair of the Minnesota Democratic-Farmer-Labor Party.

10. Joint Testimony of Neil Reiff and Donald McGahn before the Senate Committee on Rules and Administration, April 30, 2014. The two lawyers have served as counsel for Democratic and Republican party committees, respectively. McGahn served as a commissioner at the Federal Elections Commission from 2009 to 2013.

11. Quoted in Byron Tau, "Last Call for State Parties," *Politico*, February 16, 2014, available at http://www.politico.com/story/2014/02/last-call-for-state-parties-103559.html.

12. Some argue that the parties are as wealthy now as before the reforms were passed. However, inflation-adjusted figures show that financing for the national committees is flat or declining (La Raja 2013). At the state level, parties are emphatically raising and spending less money, especially in support of federal elections (Reiff 2012). Given the strengthening of the party system, we would argue the parties should be infinitely richer than they were in the 1970s during the candidate-centered era.

13. See Code of Federal Regulations, Title 11–Federal Elections, Section 110.5. Accessed September 30, 2014, at http://www.gpo.gov/fdsys/pkg/CFR-2011-title11-vol1 /xml/CFR-2011-title11-vol1-sec110-5.xml.

14. Data compiled by the National Conference of State Legislatures show that in Connecticut in 2013, the law increased contribution limits to parties. In Nevada in 2013, the parties no longer had to comply with several PAC regulations for committees they

created or sponsored. See 2014 campaign finance database accessed September 27, 2014, at http://www.ncsl.org/research/elections-and-campaigns/campaign-finance-database -2014.aspx.

15. See Luke Wachob, "2013 State Legislative Trends: Campaign Contribution Limits Increase in Nine States" (Alexandria, VA: Center for Competitive Politics, 2014). Accessed September 27, 2014, at http://www.campaignfreedom.org/wp-content /uploads/2014/02/2014-04-25_Legislative-Review_Wachob_2013-State-Legislative -Trends-Increasing-Contribution-Limits.pdf.

16. These states included Alabama, Arizona, Florida, Michigan, Minnesota, North Carolina, and Wyoming.

17. One reform advocate, Josh Silver, director of United Republic, argues that poll-testing of the electorate indicates that voters do not get excited about campaign finance unless the issue is framed in terms of traditional quid pro quo corruption (Silver 2013). Thus, reformers tend to focus on lurid quid pro quo corruption as a way to attract attention for the cause, even if this does not reflect what is going on. For this reason, United Republic has made fictionalized videos of cigar-smoking politicians on the take from money interests or senators behaving like pole-dancing strippers to get cash. See, for example, https://www.youtube.com/watch?v=6VEFXB0uNRI. Silver's organization has sent its staff in the guise of lobbyists to a congressional fundraiser. The phony "lobbyists" then accidentally drop an opened suitcase of cash at the feet of the member of Congress. Of course, this is all caught on video.

18. Nancy L. Rosenblum describes the evangelical resonance of Progressive reformers in her excellent book, *On the Side of Angels*, suggesting that the anticorruption efforts invoked biblical references of chasing the money-lenders from the temple (2008, 171).

19. Hume believed that parties based too strongly on principle were capable of "madness" and "fury," which would pull the political system apart. See David Hume, *Essays, Moral, Political and Literary*, Part I, VIII: Of Parties in General. Available at Library of Economics and Liberty. Accessed September 30, 2014, at http://www.econlib .org/library/LFBooks/Hume/hmMPL.html.

20. Among the pragmatic interests, we emphatically favor the political parties over the business interests in financing campaigns. One reason is that business interests tend to have a bias toward conservative candidates; another is that business interests overwhelming support incumbents, which gives officeholders significant advantages in elections over challengers. See Fouirnaies and Hall (2014).

21. See Bob Bauer's insightful comments on the political craft of balancing multiple constituencies and electoral self-interest in "Politicians: The Good, the Bad, and the Corrupt—and Their Different 'Constituencies'," July 31, 2014, in his blog *More Soft Money Hard Law*. Accessed September 27, 2014, at http://www.moresoftmoneyhard law.com/2014/07/politicians-good-bad-corrupt-different-constituencies/.

22. Nancy Rosenblum makes a similar argument about election reforms, such as direct primaries, that constrained party organizations during the Progressive era. Such reforms, she argues, did not necessarily limit the clout of party elites. but did absolve them from the "obligation of responsibility" (2008, 301).

23. See Eliza Newlin Carney, "Democrats Reintroduce DISCLOSE Act," *Roll Call*, June 24, 2014, at http://blogs.rollcall.com/beltway-insiders/democrats-reintroduce -disclose-act.

24. Phone interview with Jaxon Ravens, chair of Washington State Democrats, on July 17, 2014; phone interview with Matt Fenlon, executive director of Massachusetts Democratic Party, on March 13, 2014.

25. Robert Costa, "Mitch McConnell and Free Speech," *National Review*, June 19, 2012. Accessed September 29, 2014, at http://www.nationalreview.com/articles/303220 /mitch-mcconnell-and-free-speech-robert-costa.

26. Pew Research: Center for the People and the Press, "Public Priorities: Deficit Rising, Terrorism Slipping," January 23, 2012, available at http://www.people-press.org /2012/01/23/public-priorities-deficit-rising-terrorism-slipping/.

27. See, for example, testimony to New York State's Moreland Commission to Investigate Public Corruption Public Hearing (September 24, 2013) from Ian Vanderwalker of the Brennan Center for Justice: "Lowering contribution limits from their current sky-high levels will reduce the disparity between what most can afford to give and the highest contributions, ensuring that the public match acts as a strong incentive for candidates to seek out donations from average New Yorkers. In order to make lower contribution limits meaningful, loopholes must be closed and there must be a strong, independent enforcement agency." Accessed September 30, 2014, at http://www.brennancenter.org /analysis/moreland-commission-public-financing-can-restore-trust-government.

28. Some groups of reformers and newspaper editorial boards have been pushing for a constitutional amendment that would set spending limits on campaigns and establish a standard that corporations are not natural persons and therefore lack the same rights to free speech as individuals. Senate Joint Resolution 19 proposes such an amendment to the constitution. See Editorial Board, "An Amendment to Cut Political Cash," *New York Times*, September 10, 2014. http://www.nytimes.com/2014/09/11 /opinion/an-amendment-to-cut-political-cash.html?emc=edit_tnt_20140911&nlid =2166340&tntemail0=y&_r=0 and https://beta.congress.gov/113/bills/sjres19/BILLS -113sjres19rs.pdf.

29. Thomas B. Edsall, "Who Needs a Smoke-Filled Room?" (Opinion Pages), *New York Times,* September 9, 2014. See http://www.nytimes.com/2014/09/10/opinion/karl -rove-the-koch-brothers-and-the-end-of-political-transparency.html?_r=0.

Bibliography

Abramowitz, Alan I. 1991. "Incumbency, Campaign Spending, and the Decline of Competition in U.S. House Elections." *Journal of Politics* 53 (1): 34–56.

Ackerman, Bruce A., and Ian Ayres. 2002. *Voting with Dollars: A New Paradigm for Campaign Finance*. New Haven: Yale University Press.

Ahler, Douglas J., and David E. Broockman. 2014. "How Ideological Moderation Conceals Support for Immoderate Policies: A New Perspective on the 'Disconnect' in American Politics." Working paper, Institute of Governmental Studies, University of California–Berkeley.

Aldrich, John H. 1995. *Why Parties? The Origin and Transformation of Political Parties in America*. Chicago: University of Chicago Press.

American Political Science Association (APSA). 1950. "Toward a More Responsible Two-Party System." *American Political Science Review* 44 (3): Supplement.

Ansolabehere, Stephen, John M. deFigueiredo, and James M. Snyder. 2003. "Why Is There So Little Money in U.S. Politics?" *Journal of Economic Perspectives* 17 (1): 105–30.

Ansolabehere, Stephen, James Snyder, and Charles Stewart. 2001. "Candidate Positioning in U.S. House Elections." *American Journal of Political Science* 45 (1): 136.

Bafumi, Joseph, and Michael C. Herron. 2010. "Leapfrog Representation and Extremism: A Study of American Voters and Their Members in Congress." *American Political Science Review* 104 (3): 519–42.

Baldassarri, Delia, and Andrew Gelman. 2008. "Partisans without Constraint: Political Polarization and Trends in American Public Opinion." *American Journal of Sociology* 114 (2): 408–46.

Barber, Michael. 2013. "Ideological Donors, Contribution Limits, and the Polarization of State Legislatures." Unpublished manuscript: Available at http://michaeljaybarber.com/new-page-2/.

Bartels, Larry M. 2008. *Unequal Democracy: The Political Economy of the New Gilded Age*. Princeton: Princeton University Press.

Bauer, Robert F. 2013. "Right to Do Politics and Not Just to Speak: Thinking about the Constitutional Protections for Political Action." *Duke Journal of Constitutional Law and Public Policy* 9:67–86.

Baumgartner, Frank R. 2009. *Lobbying and Policy Change: Who Wins, Who Loses, and Why*. Chicago: University of Chicago Press.

Bawn, Kathleen, Martin Cohen, David Karol, Seth Masket, Hans Noel, and John Zaller. 2012. "A Theory of Political Parties: Groups, Policy Demands, and Nominations in American Politics." *Perspectives on Politics* 10 (3): 571–97.

Bernstein, Jonathan. 1999. "The Expanded Party in American Politics." Unpublished doctoral dissertation. University of California: Berkeley.

Bernstein, Jonathan, and Casey B. K. Dominguez. 2003. "Candidates and Candidacies in the Expanded Party." *PS: Political Science and Politics* 36:165–69.

Bianco, William T. 1999. "Party Campaign Committees and the Distribution of Tally Program Funds." *Legislative Studies Quarterly* 24:451–69.

Boatright, Robert G. 2013. *Getting Primaried: The Changing Politics of Congressional Primary Challenges*. Ann Arbor: University of Michigan Press.

Bonica, Adam. 2013. "Mapping the Ideological Marketplace." *American Journal of Political Science*. Forthcoming. Available at SSRN: http://ssrn.com/abstract=2148801.

Bonica, Adam, Nolan McCarty, Keith T. Poole, and Howard Rosenthal. 2013. "Why Hasn't Democracy Slowed Rising Inequality?" *Journal of Economic Perspectives* 27 (3): 103–24.

Bramlett, Brittany, James Gimpel, and Frances Lee. 2010. "The Political Ecology of Opinion in Big-Donor Neighborhoods." *Political Behavior* 33 (4): 1–36.

Broder, David S. 1972. *The Party's Over: The Failure of Politics in America*. New York: Harper & Row.

Brooks, David. 2014. "Party All the Time." *New York Times*, April 3.

Brunell, Thomas L. 2005. "The Relationship Between Political Parties and Interest Groups: Explaining Patterns of PAC Contributions to Candidates for Congress." *Political Research Quarterly* 58 (4): 681–88.

Burden, Barry C. 2004. "Candidate Positioning in US Congressional Elections." *British Journal of Political Science* 34 (2): 211–27.

Cain, Bruce E. 2014. *Democracy More or Less: America's Political Reform Quandary*. Cambridge: Cambridge University Press.

Cain, Bruce E., John A. Ferejohn, and Morris P. Fiorina. 1987. *The Personal Vote: Constituency Service and Electoral Independence*. Cambridge, Mass.: Harvard University Press.

Canes-Wrone, Brandice, David W. Brady, and John F. Cogan. 2002. "Out of Step, Out of Office: Electoral Accountability and House Members' Voting." *American Political Science Review* 96 (1): 127–40.

Cohen, Marty, David Karol, Hans Noel, and John Zaller. 2008. *The Party Decides: Presidential Nominations Before and After Reform*. Chicago: University of Chicago Press.

Conger, Kimberly H. 2010. "A Matter of Context: Christian Right Influence in U.S. State Republican Politics." *State Politics & Policy Quarterly* 10 (3): 248–69.

Cordis, Adriana, and Jeffrey Milyo. 2013. "Do State Campaign Finance Reforms Reduce Public Corruption?" Working Papers, Department of Economics, University of Missouri.

Cotter, Cornelius P. 1989. *Party Organizations in American Politics*. Pittsburgh, Pa.: University of Pittsburgh Press.

Croly, Herbert David. 1963. *The Promise of American life*. Hamden, Conn.: Archon Books.

Damore, David F., and Thomas G. Hansford. 1999. "The Allocation of Party Controlled Campaign Resources in the House of Representatives, 1989–1996." *Political Research Quarterly* 52 (2): 371–85.

Davis, Tom. 2012. "Centrist Republicans, Alive and Well." *Washington Post*, April 20.

Desmarais, Bruce A., Raymond J. La Raja, and Michael S. Kowal. 2014. "The Fates of Challengers in U.S. House Elections: The Role of Extended Party Networks in Supporting Candidates and Shaping Electoral Outcomes." *American Journal of Political Science* 59 (1): 194–211.

Dimock, Michael, Jocelyn Kiley, Scott Keeter, and Carroll Doherty. 2014. "Political Polarization in the American Public." Washington, D.C.: Pew Research Center.

DiSalvo, Daniel. 2012. *Engines of Change: Party Factions in American Politics, 1868–2010*. New York: Oxford University Press.

Downs, Anthony. 1957. *An Economic Theory of Democracy*. New York: Harper.

Ensley, Michael. 2009. "Individual Campaign Contributions and Candidate Ideology." *Public Choice* 138 (1): 221–38.

Feingold, Russell D. 1988. "Representative Democracy versus Corporate Democracy: How Soft Money Erodes the Principle of 'One Person, One Vote.'" *Harvard Journal on Legislation* 35 (2): 377–86.

Fenno, Richard F. 1978. *Home Style: House Members in Their Districts*. Boston: Little, Brown.

Fenton, Jacob. 2014. "Look Who's Benefiting from Citizens United: Unions Wrote More Big Checks Than Corporations in 2013." In sunlightfoundation.com.

Fiorina, Morris P., and Samuel J. Abrams. 2009. *Disconnect: The Breakdown of Representation in American Politics*. Norman: University of Oklahoma Press.

Fiorina, Morris P., Samuel J. Abrams, and Jeremy Pope. 2005. *Culture War?: The Myth of a Polarized America*. New York: Pearson Longman.

Fouirnaies, Alexander, and Andrew B. Hall. 2014. "The Financial Incumbency Advantage: Causes and Consequences." *Journal of Politics* 76 (3): 711–24.

Francia, Peter L., John C. Green, Paul S. Herrnson, Lynda W. Powell, and Clyde Wilcox. 2003. *The Financiers of Congressional Elections: Investors, Ideologues, and Intimates*. New York: Columbia University Press.

Francia, Peter L., and Paul S. Herrnson. 2003. "The Impact of Public Finance Laws on Fundraising in State Legislative Elections." *American Politics Research* 31 (5): 520–39.

Frymer, Paul. 1999. *Uneasy Alliances: Race and Party Competition in America*. Princeton: Princeton University Press.

Gerken, Heather. 2014. "The Real Problem with Citizens United: Campaign Finance, Dark Money, and Shadow Parties." *Marquette Lawyer* (Summer): 11–25.

Gilens, Martin. 2005. "Inequality and Democratic Responsiveness." *Public Opinion Quarterly* 69 (5): 778–96.

Gilens, Martin. 2012. *Affluence and Influence: Economic Inequality and Political Power in America*. Princeton: Princeton University Press.

Gimpel, James G., Frances E. Lee, and Shanna Pearson-Merkowitz. 2008. "The Check Is in the Mail: Interdistrict Funding Flows in Congressional Elections." *American Journal of Political Science* 52 (2): 373–94.

Green, John Clifford, Mark J. Rozell, and Clyde Wilcox. 2003. *The Christian Right in American Politics: Marching to the Millennium*. Washington, D.C.: Georgetown University Press.

Grossmann, Matthew. 2012. *The Not-So-Special Interests: Interest Groups, Public Representation, and American Governance.* Stanford: Stanford University Press.

Grossmann, Matt, and Casey B. K. Dominguez. 2009. "Party Coalitions and Interest Group Networks." *American Politics Research* 37 (5): 767–800.

Hacker, Jacob S., and Paul Pierson. 2010. *Winner-Take-All Politics: How Washington Made the Rich Richer—and Turned Its Back on the Middle Class.* New York: Simon & Schuster.

Hall, Andrew B. 2014. "How the Public Funding of Elections Increases Candidate Polarization." Working paper. Available at https://dl.dropboxusercontent.com/u/11481940/Hall_publicfunding.pdf.

Hall, Richard L., and Frank W. Wayman. 1990. "Buying Time: Moneyed Interests and the Mobilization of Bias in Congressional Committees." *American Political Science Review* 84 (3): 797–820.

Hamm, Keith E., Michael J. Malbin, Jacklyn J. Kettler, and Brendan Glavin. 2014. *Independent Spending in State Elections, 2006–2010: Vertically Networked Political Parties Were the Real Story, Not Business.* Washington, D.C.: Campaign Finance Institute.

Hasen, Richard L. 2013. "Is 'Dependence Corruption' Distinct from a Political Equality Argument for Campaign Finance Laws? A Reply to Professor Lessig." *Election Law Journal* 12:315.

Hasen, Richard L. forthcoming 2016. *Money, Politics, and the Decline of American Democracy.* New Haven: Yale University Press.

Hassell, Hans J. G. 2014. "Party Control of Party Primaries: Nominations for the U.S. Senate 2004–2012." Unpublished manuscript.

Heberlig, Eric S., and Bruce A. Larson. 2012. *Congressional Parties, Institutional Ambition, and the Financing of Majority Control.* Ann Arbor: University of Michigan Press.

Heberlig, Eric, Marc Hetherington, and Bruce Larson. 2006. "The Price of Leadership: Campaign Money and the Polarization of Congressional Parties." *Journal of Politics* 68 (4): 992–1005.

Herrnson, Paul S. 1988. *Party Campaigning in the 1980s.* Cambridge, Mass.: Harvard University Press.

Herrnson, Paul S. 1989. "National Party Decision Making, Strategies, and Resource Distribution in Congressional Elections." *Western Political Quarterly* 42 (3): 301–23.

Herrnson, Paul S. 2009. "The Roles of Party Organizations, Party-Connected Committees, and Party Allies in Elections." *Journal of Politics* 71 (4): 1207–24.

Herrnson, Paul S., Ronald G. Shaiko, and Clyde Wilcox. 2005. *The Interest Group Connection : Electioneering, Lobbying, and Policymaking in Washington.* Washington, D.C.: CQ Press.

Hogan, Robert E. 2000. "The Costs of Representation in State Legislatures: Explaining Variations in Campaign Spending." *Social Science Quarterly (University of Texas Press)* 81 (4): 941–56.

Hubbard, R. Glenn, and Tim Kane. 2013. "In Defense of Citizens United: Why Campaign Finance Reform Threatens American Democracy." *Foreign Affairs* (July/August).

Hunter, James Davison. 1991. *Culture Wars: The Struggle to Define America.* New York: Basic Books.

Issacharoff, Samuel, and Jeremy Peterman. 2013. "Special Interests After Citizens United: Access, Replacement, and Interest Group Response to Legal Change." *Annual Review of Law and Social Science* 9 (1): 185–205.

Jenkins, Shannon. 2006. "The Impact of Party and Ideology on Roll-Call Voting in State Legislatures." *Legislative Studies Quarterly* 31 (2): 235–57.

Johnson, Bertram. 2010. "Individual Contributions: A Fundraising Advantage for the Ideologically Extreme?" *American Politics Research* 38 (5): 890–908.

Katz, Richard S., and Peter Mair. 1995. "Changing Models of Party Organization and Party Democracy: The Emergence of the Cartel Party." *Party Politics* 1 (1): 5–28.

Klarner, Carl, William Berry, Thomas M. Carsey, Malcolm Jewell, Richard Niemi, Lynda Powell, and James Snyder. 2013. "State Legislative Election Returns (1967–2010). ICPSR34297-v1." Ann Arbor, Mich.: Inter-university Consortium for Political and Social Research [distributor], 2013-01-11. doi:10.3886/ICPSR34297.v1.

Kolodny, Robin. 1998. *Pursuing Majorities: Congressional Campaign Committees in American Politics*. Norman: University of Oklahoma Press.

Kolodny, Robin, and Diana Dwyre. 1998. "Party-Orchestrated Activities for Legislative Party Goals: Campaigns for Majorities in the US House of Representatives in the 1990s." *Party Politics* 4 (3): 275–95.

Kolodny, Robin, and Angela Logan. 1998. "Political Consultants and the Extension of Party Goals." *PS: Political Science and Politics* 31 (2): 155–59.

Krasno, Jonathan. 2011. "Political Parties in the Capital Economy of Modern Campaigns." In *Facing the Challenge of Democracy*, edited by Paul M. Sniderman and Benjamin Highton. Princeton: Princeton University Press.

Krimmel, Katherine. 2011. "Special Interest Partisanship: The Transformation of American Political Parties in Government." (PhD Dissertation) Dept. of Political Science. New York: Columbia University.

La Raja, Raymond J. 2008. *Small Change: Money, Political Parties, and Campaign Finance Reform*. Ann Arbor: University of Michigan Press.

La Raja, Raymond, J. 2013. "Why Super PACs: How the American Party System Outgrew the Campaign Finance System." *The Forum* 10 (4): 91.

La Raja, Raymond J., and Brian F. Schaffner. 2014. "The Effects of Campaign Finance Spending Bans on Electoral Outcomes: Evidence from the States about the Potential Impact of Citizens United v. FEC." *Electoral Studies* 33:102–14.

La Raja, Raymond J., and David L. Wiltse. 2012. "Don't Blame Donors for Ideological Polarization of Political Parties." *American Politics Research* 40 (3): 501–30.

Layman, Geoffrey C., Thomas M. Carsey, John C. Green, Richard Herrera, and Rosalyn Cooperman. 2010. "Activists and Conflict Extension in American Party Politics." *American Political Science Review* 104 (2): 324–46.

Layman, Geoffrey C., Thomas M. Carsey, and Juliana Menasce Horowitz. 2006. "Party Polarization in American Politics: Characteristics, Causes, and Consequences." *Annual Review of Political Science* 9 (1): 83–110.

Lessig, Lawrence. 2011. *Republic, Lost: How Money Corrupts Congress—and a Plan to Stop It*. New York: Twelve.

Leyden, Kevin M., and Stephen A. Borrelli. 1990. "Party Contributions and Party Unity: Can Loyalty Be Bought?" *Western Political Quarterly* 43 (2): 343–65.

Lindaman, Kara, and Donald P. Haider-Markel. 2002. "Issue Evolution, Political Parties, and the Culture Wars." *Political Research Quarterly* 55 (1): 91–110.

Malbin, Michael J. 2013. "Small Donors: Incentives, Economies of Scale, and Effects." *The Forum* 11 (3): 385–411.

Mann, Thomas E., and Norman J. Ornstein. 2012. *It's Even Worse Than It Looks: How the American Constitutional System Collided with the New Politics of Extremism.* New York: Basic Books.

Masket, Seth E. 2009. *No Middle Ground: How Informal Party Organizations Control Nominations and Polarize Legislatures.* Ann Arbor: University of Michigan Press.

Masket, Seth E., and Michael G. Miller. 2014. "Does Public Election Funding Create More Extreme Legislators? Evidence from Arizona and Maine." Working paper. Available at https://sites.google.com/site/millerpolsci/research/pubfund.

Mayer, Lloyd Hitoshi. 2014. "Taxing Politics." Working paper, 2014 Annual Meeting of the American Political Science Association, August 28–31.

Mayhew, David R. 1986. *Placing Parties in American Politics: Organization, Electoral Settings, and Government Activity in the Twentieth Century.* Princeton: Princeton University Press.

Mayhew, David R. 2000. *America's Congress: Actions in the Public Sphere, James Madison through Newt Gingrich.* New Haven: Yale University Press.

McCarty, Nolan. 2013. "Reducing Polarization by Making Parties Stronger." Hewlett Foundation Workshop on Solutions to Political Polarization in the United States.

McCarty, Nolan M., Keith T. Poole, and Howard Rosenthal. 2006. *Polarized America: The Dance of Ideology and Unequal Riches.* Cambridge, Mass.: MIT Press.

McGerr, Michael E. 1986. *The Decline of Popular Politics: The American North, 1865–1928.* New York: Oxford University Press.

Michels, Robert. 1949. *Political Parties: A Sociological Study of the Oligarchical Tendencies of Modern Democracy.* Glencoe, Ill.: Free Press.

Migally, Angela, and Susan Liss. 2010. *Small Donor Matching Funds: The NYC Election Experience.* New York: Brennan Center for Justice at New York University School of Law.

Milkis, Sidney M. 2009. *Theodore Roosevelt, the Progressive Party, and the Transformation of American Democracy.* Lawrence: University Press of Kansas.

Milkis, Sidney M., and Jerome M. Mileur. 1999. *Progressivism and the New Democracy.* Amherst: University of Massachusetts Press.

Moon, Woojin. 2004. "Party Activists, Campaign Resources and Candidate Position Taking: Theory, Tests and Applications." *British Journal of Political Science* 34 (4): 611–33.

Mullins, Brody, and Ann Zimmerman. 2010. "Target Discovers Downside to Political Contributions." *Wall Street Journal,* August 7.

Mutch, Robert E. 2014. *Buying the Vote: A History of Campaign Finance Reform.* New York: Oxford University Press.

Nokken, Timothy P. 2003. "Ideological Congruence Versus Electoral Success: Distribution of Party Organization Contributions in Senate Elections, 1990–2000." *American Politics Research* 31 (1): 3–26.

Odegard, Peter H. 1928. *Pressure Politics: The Story of the Anti-Saloon League.* New York: Columbia University Press.

Ostrogorski, M., and Fredrich Clarke. 1902. *Democracy and the Organization of Political Parties, by M. Ostrogorski, translated from the French by Frederick Clarke, with a preface by the Right Hon. James Bryce.* New York: Macmillan.

Overby, Peter. 2014. "Outside Group Mirrors Successful Strategies of Political Parties." *National Public Radio,* August 22.

Panebianco, Angelo. 1988. *Political Parties: Organization and Power.* New York: Cambridge University Press.

Persily, Nathaniel. 2014. "Bringing Big Money out of the Shadows." In *New York Times (Opinion),* April 2.

Persily, Nathaniel, and Kelli Lammie. 2004. "Perceptions of Corruption and Campaign Finance: When Public Opinion Determines Constitutional Law." *University of Pennsylvania Law Review* 153:119–80.

Pfeffer, Jeffrey, and Gerald R. Salancik. 1978. *The External Control of Organizations: A Resource Dependence Perspective.* New York: Harper & Row.

Pildes, Richard H. 2014. "How to Fix Our Polarized Politics? Strengthen Political Parties." In *Washington Post (Monkey Cage* blog), February 6.

Pildes, Richard H. 2015. "Romanticizing Democracy, Political Fragmentation, and the Decline of American Government." *Yale Law Journal* 124:804–52.

Polsby, Nelson W. 1983. *Consequences of Party Reform.* Oxford; New York: Oxford University Press.

Primo, David M., and Jeffrey Milyo. 2006. "Campaign Finance Laws and Political Efficacy: Evidence from the States." *Election Law Journal: Rules, Politics, and Policy* 5 (1): 23–39.

Rauch, Jonathan. 2014. "The Case for Corruption." *The Atlantic,* February 19.

Reiff, Neil. 2012. "The Weakening of State and Local Parties." In *Campaign & Elections,* July 16.

Richert, Catherine. 2012. "Stealth Donor Gives Millions to GOP Candidates, Causes." *Minnesota Public Radio (MPR),* February 1.

Rigby, Elizabeth, and Gerald C. Wright. 2013. "Political Parties and Representation of the Poor in the American States." *American Journal of Political Science* 57 (3): 552–65.

Rogowski, Jon C. 2014. "Electoral Choice, Ideological Conflict, and Political Participation." *American Journal of Political Science* 58 (2): 479–94.

Rohde, David W. 1991. *Parties and Leaders in the Postreform House.* Chicago: University of Chicago Press.

Rosenblum, Nancy L. 2008. *On the Side of the Angels: An Appreciation of Parties and Partisanship.* Princeton: Princeton University Press.

Rosenthal, Cindy S. 1995. "New Party or Campaign Bank Account? Explaining the Rise of State Legislative Campaign Committees." *Legislative Studies Quarterly* 20 (2): 249–68.

Samples, John Curtis. 2006. *The Fallacy of Campaign Finance Reform.* Chicago: University of Chicago Press.

Schattschneider, E. E. 1942. *Party Government.* New York: Farrar and Rinehart.

Shaw, Charles. 2012. "Minnesota Republican Party Units Losing Cash Race So Far This Year." *Capitol Report,* August 1.

Shea, Daniel M. 1995. *Transforming Democracy: Legislative Campaign Committees and Political Parties.* Albany: State University of New York Press in cooperation with the Center for Party Development, Washington, D.C.

Shor, Boris, and Nolan McCarty. 2011. "The Ideological Mapping of American Legislatures." *American Political Science Review* 105 (3): 530–51.

Shor, Boris, Christopher Berry, and Nolan McCarty. 2011. "Replication Data for: A Bridge to Somewhere: Mapping State and Congressional Ideology on a Cross-Institutional Common Space." http://hdl.handle.net/1902.1/15682 UNF:5:KXwF /TPc7wZDZEznc9dxQw== V2 [Version].

Silver, Josh. 2013. "How One State Senate Just Screwed the Whole Nation." *Huffington Post,* June 24.

Skinner, Richard M. 2007. *More Than Money: Interest Group Action in Congressional Elections.* Lanham, Md.: Rowman & Littlefield.

Skinner, Richard M., Seth E. Masket, and David A. Dulio. 2012. "527 Committees and the Political Party Network." *American Politics Research* 40 (1): 60–84.

Snyder, James M., Jr. 1990. "Campaign Contributions as Investments: The U.S. House of Representatives, 1980–1986." *Journal of Political Economy* 98 (6): 1195–227.

Snyder, James M., and Michael M. Ting. 2002. "An Informational Rationale for Political Parties." *American Journal of Political Science* 46 (1): 90.

Sorauf, Frank J. 1992. *Inside Campaign Finance: Myths and Realities.* New Haven: Yale University Press.

Squire, Peverill. 2007. "Measuring State Legislative Professionalism: The Squire Index Revisited." *State Politics & Policy Quarterly* 7 (2): 211–27.

Stephanopoulos, Nicholas O. 2015. "Aligning Campaign Finance Law." *Virginia Law Review* 100.

Stone, Walter J., and Elizabeth N. Simas. 2010. "Candidate Valence and Ideological Positions in U.S. House Elections." *American Journal of Political Science* 54 (2): 371–88.

Teachout, Zephyr. 2014. *Corruption in America: From Benjamin Franklin's Snuff Box to Citizens United.* Cambridge: Harvard University Press.

Thomsen, Danielle M. 2014. "Ideological Moderates Won't Run: How Party Fit Matters for Partisan Polarization in Congress." *Journal of Politics* 76 (3): 786–97.

Tokaji, Daniel P., and Renata E. B. Strause. 2014. "The New Soft Money: Outside Spending in Congressional Elections." A Project of Election Law at the Ohio State University Moritz College of Law.

Trubowitz, Peter, and Nicole Mellow. 2005. "'Going Bipartisan': Politics by Other Means." *Political Science Quarterly* 120 (3): 433–53.

Underkuffler, Laura S. 2013. "Captured by Evil: The Idea of Corruption in Law." Online resource, p. 1. New Haven: Yale University Press.

Verba, Sidney, Kay Lehman Schlozman, and Henry E. Brady. 1995. *Voice and Equality: Civic Voluntarism in American Politics.* Cambridge, Mass.: Harvard University Press.

Wallison, Peter J., and Joel M. Gora. 2009. *Better Parties, Better Government: A Realistic Program for Campaign Finance Reform.* Washington, D.C.: AEI Press.

Wattenberg, Martin P. 1984. *The Decline of American Political Parties, 1952–1980.* Cambridge, Mass.: Harvard University Press.

Wildavsky, Aaron. 1965. "The Goldwater Phenomenon: Purists, Politicians and the Two-Party System." *Review of Politics* 27:386–413.

Wilson, James Q. 1962. *The Amateur Democrat: Club Politics in Three Cities.* Chicago: University of Chicago Press.

Index